THE PENN STATE SERIES
IN GERMAN LITERATURE

*German Baroque Poetry 1618–1723*, by Robert M. Browning

*War, Weimar, and Literature: The Story of the Neue Merkur, 1914–1926*, by Guy Stern

GERMAN BAROQUE POETRY

ROBERT M. BROWNING

# GERMAN BAROQUE POETRY

## 1618–1723

THE PENNSYLVANIA
STATE UNIVERSITY PRESS
University Park and London

ISBN: 0–271–01146–7
Library of Congress Catalog Card No. 77–136959
Printed in the United States of America
Designed by Marilyn E. Shobaken

# CONTENTS

## PREFACE

The present volume on German poetry of the seventeenth century is the first in a projected series of three, which are to trace the development of the German lyric from circa 1620 to 1890. My purpose in this volume has been to treat the poetry of the Baroque in broad outline and mainly from the standpoint of characteristic poets, whom I have tried to show in their singular as well as generic nature. In other words, this is not a book on the theory of baroque poetry and its use of rhetorical devices so much as a book on specific poets and their themes.

Anyone who tries to work in the field of seventeenth-century German literature soon discovers dismaying lacks. For many poets there are still no reliable editions of their works, monographs exploring the various figures in depth are in most cases still to be written, even the general developmental lines of the century are to a considerable degree uncertain and the subject of speculation. This leaves the historian of literature, whose primary task is rather to summarize accepted opinion than to attempt original evaluations, in a most uncomfortable and sometimes hardly tenable position. I have tried to come to terms with this situation by concentrating on characterizations of the poets themselves, gained, insofar as possible, from perusal of their works. Besides imparting purely historical information I have tried to arouse in the present day reader, especially in the younger reader, who may be approaching the German Baroque for the first time, a sense of involvement and, I hope, moderate enthusiasm.

The reader should note that biographical and bibliographical information is introduced in the notes following the first main introduction of the poet under discussion. The only exception is the biographical information on Günther.

My debt to my predecessors is as large as I could make it, given my abilities and the time at my disposal. I am only too aware that it is not large enough. For encouragement and criticism while working on these chapters I am indebted to a number of colleagues, especially Edson M. Chick, Dartmouth College, Lore B. Foltin, University of Pittsburgh, Hubert Heinen, University of Texas (Austin), and Otto K. Liedke, Hamilton College. My debt to Hamilton College for released time and financial assistance and to the Hamilton College Library for help in procuring books and microfilms is particularly great. I should like to mention specifically my gratitude to Richard W. Couper, former Acting President of Hamilton College (now President of the New York Public Library), to John W. Chandler, President, Hamilton College, to Winton Tolles, Dean, and to Mrs. Eugenia W. King, Interlibrary Loan Librarian. My wife I would like to thank for her patience and unfailing understanding.

The book itself I dedicate to my students.

 GERMAN BAROQUE POETRY

CHAPTER ONE

## OPITZ AND RENAISSANCE POETRY

One of the striking features of German literature, which from a general European standpoint is deviant in a number of respects in any case, is its curious belatedness. In the choir of nations its voice is almost the last to enter. Even with the seventeenth century it cannot be said to have achieved European stature, except in its own estimation. A glance at the situation in neighboring lands quickly reveals the eccentric position of Germany.

After the recession of the spring tide of song in the late Middle Ages, there followed in the German lands a long period of drought, a stark contrast to the exuberant flowering in other nations. The Renaissance hardly fructified German vernacular poetry in the fifteenth and sixteenth centuries. It has been suggested that Germany had a Reformation instead of a Renaissance, and that the energies that might have gone into the making of poetry went into the making of polemics. The devisive effect of the Reformation also weakened any incipient sense of national unity. The national spirit in France, England, Spain, Portugal, and Holland awoke with national expansion, centralized government, world ex-

3

ploration and trade. It awoke with the sense of a national mission, and with it awoke the new national literatures. Germany was a house divided against itself, strongly decentralized and without the impetus that created the Holy Roman Empire, weak because it had too many centers of gravity rather than because it had none; thus it remained outside the mainstream. So one can argue. The trouble with such arguments is the trouble with all arguments ex post facto. Had there actually been a flowering of Geman poetry in the fifteenth and sixteenth centuries despite these conditions, we may be sure that the historians of ideas would have been just as fertile in adducing reasons to account for it. They would have only needed to give their indications a positive instead of a negative sign. The spirit bloweth where it listeth. Perhaps this is the true "reason." Besides, when Germany did begin to bring forth a national literature in the European vein, it was still a nation divided against itself and even more divided than ever: the beginnings of this literature coincide with the Thirty Years War.

The case of Italy, torn by internal strife, overrun by foreign invaders, weak, decentralized, with no more sense of national mission than Germany, could serve as another counter-example. For it was in Italy that modern European literature came into being. By the seventeenth century, Italy had given the Western world some of its most precious and most seminal poetry and had established conventions which were to prevail, at least in the lyric, throughout Europe until the eighteenth century. One need but recall the names of such poets as Dante, Petrarch, Ariosto, Tasso, Michelangelo, Sannazzaro, and Guarini. In the theory of literature (Dante, Boccaccio, Cinthio, Minturno, Castelvetro) Italy also leads the chorus.

The flowering of a national literature in Spain in the *siglo de oro* is hardly less impressive. By the seventeenth century or during it, Jorge de Montemayor, Garcilaso de la

4

Vega, St. John of the Cross, Cervantes, Lope, Góngora, Quevedo, and Calderón have appeared on the scene, all names of European stature. The performance of France is less striking but still impressive enough. Having received again from Italy, transformed by Neoplatonism and developed by great poets, impulses that had originated in France itself in Provençal poetry, the French were not long in establishing a "modern" and pronouncedly national literature. The key names here are Ronsard and Du Bellay, the central group the Pléiade, whose revolutionary pretensions, though exaggerated, were still not wholly unfounded when taken within the French context. French literature as a national movement may with some justice be said to have received its charter in Du Bellay's manifesto, *Deffense et Illustration de la Langue Françoyse* (1549).

England's "nest of singing birds" had long since greeted the dawn by the seventeenth century, and that century itself was destined to produce in John Milton the second greatest poet of the English tongue. Even Dutch literature, soon to serve as one of the chief stimuli for the German Baroque, had caught fire from Italy in the sixteenth century and produced by the middle of the next most of its classic works. The accident of fate that caused the poems and plays of Hooft, Bredero, Vondel, and Huygens to be written in one of the "minor" European languages is the main reason most of us know so little about them.

In this incredible florescence of the European spirit—and we have barely glanced at the performance in literature and said nothing of painting, music, architecture, science or philosophy—Germany had taken but little part (painting is the main exception). Its contribution was the Reformation and the Reformation looked back toward the Middle Ages as much as it looked forward toward the New Learning and the New Poetry.[1]

Not that this should be construed to mean *Germania*

5

*non cantabat.* There was, as a matter of fact, much song; the fifteenth and sixteenth centuries are even the golden age of the Volkslied; it only means that Germany had not yet made connection with the mainstream of European literature. Neither had it, except in a kind of half-conscious and degraded fashion, retained any connection with the indigenous German poetry of the Middle Ages. Not even scholars had more than a faint inkling, if they had that, of who Walther von der Vogelweide, Wolfram von Eschenbach, and Gottfried von Strassburg were. The manuscripts of their works were destined to gather dust for yet many years to come. It was hardly thought possible to write anything but hymns, ballads, and polemic-didactic pieces in German. Poetry that made pretensions to cultivation was written in Latin. There were, to be sure, neo-Latin poets of the first rank in Germany. The most celebrated was Jakob Balde (1603–68). It is not our intention to disparage them, they simply do not belong to our story except in a peripheral way.

The influence of neo-Latin poetry on seventeenth-century German literature is not easy to assess. In a sense it might be said to be all-pervasive. It was the medium through which the classical tradition was transmitted and kept alive, and most of the poets of the age wrote Latin as well as German verse. Yet in another sense one could consider it of secondary importance for the very reason that it was *too* classical in cast and to a large degree free of the influences that shaped European literatures in the vernacular. Certainly, in the development of that type of poetry which we regard as peculiarly "baroque" its influence was not decisive, if for no other reason than that it held to the "middle level" of speech and in general eschewed the florid style.[2] Nevertheless much of the poetry written in German in the seventeenth century is neo-Latin in spirit. As humanists, the poets were at home in both Latin and German, the great neo-Latinists much more so in the former than in the latter. They usually found it impossible to write poetry in the new style in German. Apparently the stylistic-sociological levels were for them too disparate. They could conceive of German, it seems, only as a popular medium for communication with the uneducated and thus inevitably fell back into the old-fashioned patterns of folk verse when they tried to express themselves in German.

As for the Volkslied, it too is a separate chapter and belongs in another book. Suffice it to say at this point that its influence on "standard" seventeenth-century German poetry was very slight. Besides the Volkslied, there had flourished from the fourteenth century a more sophisticated song form known as the "Gesellschaftslied" or bourgeois song, a distant relative of Minnesang and a closer, but sociologically distinct, relative of the Volkslied. Toward the end of the sixteenth and the beginning of the seventeenth century this form, in the hands of two of its chief exponents, the poet-musicians Jakob Regnart (1540–99) and Johann Hermann Schein (1586–1630), grew even more sophisticated as it became strongly Italianate both in text and music. It was once thought to have marked the beginnings of seventeenth-century German lyric in the new vein, but this thesis has been disproved.[3] It was a musically but not a poetically significant phenomenon, despite the very respectable quality of a number of the texts. The poets looked elsewhere for their models.

In Georg Rodolf Weckherlin (1584–1653), on the other hand, we find a true, if lonely, precursor of the new manner.[4] Weckherlin was a Swabian and for a time court-poet to the Duke of Württemberg. Later he entered the service of the English crown and rose under James I and his successor Charles to the position of "Latin Secretary," thus becoming Milton's immediate predecessor in this office. His *Oden und Gesänge* (1618–19), though strongly influenced by Ronsard and Du Bellay, betray an original and vital talent that still charms us by its freshness. Had he, rather than Martin Opitz,

7

whose rise came a few years later, been the one to succeed in furnishing the model for the revival of German poetry, something approaching an organic development of the new out of the old might have taken place. For Weckherlin, despite his affinity for the sophisticated Renaissance lyric of France, has not completely lost touch with the simpler and earthier folk tradition—a union of the two might have been accomplished. As it happened, Opitz brought about their almost complete divorce.

What Weckherlin was trying to do, though in a much less methodical and conscious manner, was essentially what Opitz and his school were actually to accomplish: introduce into German the New Poetry. His limited success was due mainly to two factors. The first: Opitz' phenomenal rise put Weckherlin in the shade, made him seem outmoded, and nipped in the bud any influence he might have exercised upon other poets. The second factor was directly related to the first: Weckherlin sought to transfer to German verse Romanic principles of prosody, according to which each verse has a prescribed number of syllables but unlimited possibilities of variation in accent. The reform introduced by Opitz made this kind of treatment seem eccentric indeed, though it must be admitted that it is a plausible way of handling German verse.

> *Dein leben / dessen end uns plaget /*
> *War wie ein tag schön und nit lang /*
> *Ein stern vor des morgens aufgang . . .*

Lines with feminine ending here have nine syllables, those with masculine ending have eight. They cannot be scanned according to any set pattern. Here is another example from a sonnet written in alexandrines (twelve syllables in masculine lines, thirteen in feminine):

> *Ihr augen / die ihr mich mit einem blick und plitz*
> *Scharpf oder süss nach lust könt strafen und belohnen;*

8

*O liebliches gestirn / Stern / deren liecht und hitz*
*Kan / züchtigend den stolz / der züchtigen*
   *verschonen...*

Very possibly no one would have ever objected to this; in
fact, it might in time have come to be regarded as a peculiar
beauty of German prosody had not Opitz later branded it
as a glaring fault when metrical stress and word accent do
not coincide. Weckherlin was overruled and himself shows
signs of trying to hew to the Opitzian line in later revisions.

In certain respects, however, Weckherlin is more suggestive of future developments than Opitz and his school;
for one thing, he is much more "baroque." His official occasional poetry, written to add glamor to a ducal festival, to
commemorate the death of a high personage, celebrate a
wedding etc., is naturally strongly oriented toward its courtly audience and itself strives to be as courtly as possible.
Grandiose, pompously encomiastic, addicted to rhetorical
devices, it displays the grand manner in full panoply, though
the folds of its voluminous robes may sometimes still fall
rather awkwardly.

In much of his amatory verse Weckherlin follows the
reigning Petrarchan convention, sometimes succumbing to
every excess this convention had fallen heir to in the course
of centuries. He then composes his pieces in a highly intellectual fashion, incorporating every possible rhetorical figure
and constructing, like the English "Metaphysicals," a problem
to be solved rather than a poem to be read for pleasure. But
in other instances his love poems have a simplicity and inwardness almost reminiscent of the Volkslied. A good example of this aspect of his talent is the song "Waiss ich nicht";
an example of his "metaphysical" mode is the sonnet "Von
ihren überschönen Augen," the first quartet of which is quoted above.[5]

Sincere manliness and patriotic fervor are also well within
Weckherlin's register, as is immediately apparent from the

9

sonnet "An das Teutschland." He was the first German poet
to use the sonnet form successfully as well as one of the first
to write in alexandrines, the characteristic line of the age.
"An das Teutschland" illustrates his mastery of both:

> *Zerbrich das schwere Joch / darunder du gebunden /*
> *O Teutschland / wach doch auff / fass wider einen*
> *muth /*
> *Gebrauch dein altes hertz / und widersteh der wuht /*
> *Die dich / und die freyheit durch dich selbs überwunden.*
>
> *Straf nu die Tryanney / die dich schier gar*
> *geschunden /*
> *Und lösch doch endlich auss die (dich verzöhrend) glut /*
> *Nicht mit dein eignem schwaiss / sondern dem bösen blut*
> *Fliessend auss deiner feind und falschen brüdern wunden.*
>
> *Verlassend dich auf Got / folg denen Fürsten nach /*
> *Die sein gerechte hand will (so du wilt) bewahren /*
> *Zu der Getrewen trost / zu der trewlosen raach:*
>
> *So lass nu alle forcht / und nicht die zeit hinfahren /*
> *Und Got wirt aller welt / dass nichts dan schand und*
> *schmach*
> *Des feinds meynayd und stoltz gezeuget / offenbahren.*

[*Gott wird offenbaren, dass des Feinds Meineid und Stolz*
*nichts als Schande und Schmach gezeugt hat.*]

Then there is the Weckherlin of the Rabelaisian vein,
as in the "ode" "Drunkenheit," an infectious and amusing
re-creation of a bacchanalian revel among comrades of the
Thirty Years War and their women. Here we see them at-
tacking, instead of Tilly's forces, a roast suckling pig and a
calf's head:

> *Sih / wie mit brechen / schneiden / beissen /*
> *Dem lieben feind wir machen grauss!*
> *Lass mich das Spanfärlein zerreissen /*

*Stich dem Kalbskopf die augen auss:*
  *So / so / wirf damit an die Frawen /*
*Die / wenn sie schon so süss und milt /*
*Doch könden hawen und auch klawen:*
  *Es gilt / Es gilt.*

In the following passage the merry company is already seeing pink elephants:

*Ha! duck den kopff / scheiss / heiss / Meerwunder.*
*Nu brauset / sauset laut das Meer;*
*Ein regen / hagel / blitz und dunder /*
*Hey / von Heyschrecken ein Kriegsheer.*
  *Ho! schlag den Elefanten nider /*
*Es ist ein storck / ha nein / ein lauss /*
*Glick zu / gut nacht / kom küss mich wider /*
  *Das liecht ist auss.*

Weckherlin loves life. This is the source of his freshness and charm. There are passages of almost Keatsian voluptuousness, swooning with fullness of the senses, in such a poem as "Die vierte Eclog von der Herbst zeit." Here the varieties of wine grapes are offering themselves to the harvesters with the magic of their names, colors, and qualities:

*Die Glefener schwartz braun / und die Gutedle weiss /*
*Die Muscateller gelb / Gänssüsser und*
  *Treutschtrauben /*
*Und die Traminer roht / mit schmollend-süssem fleiss*
*Den Lesern gleichsam sich auf opfern abzuklauben.*

And here "Florido" hints in broad libidinal images to his "Marina" that her charms are like the peach he holds:

*Ach! widerholet er / wie schön ist dise Frucht /*
*Ist der Herbst-Pfersich nicht dick / rohtlecht /*
  *halb-gespalten?*

11

*Dass schawend ihn nur an empfind ich die Liebsucht /
Und wünsch alsbald von dir / du weist was / zuerhalten.*

The latitude of Weckherlin's register and the manifold-ness of his forms is impressive, especially when one remembers that he stands at the beginning of an era without name-worthy predecessors in his own tongue. One cannot suppress a sense of regret that the beginnings he made were destined to be abortive. For it was a poet of a quite different stamp who was to set the tone of the age.

Martin Opitz (1597–1639)[6] must by any European standards be accounted a minor poet, but he plays a major role in the history of German literature. It would not be an exaggeration to call the seventeenth century "the age of Opitz." His influence, however, is due not so much to the quality of his verse as to the paradigmatic nature of his example and the geniality of his central idea, which was none other than to reform German literature in accordance with the prevailing trends in other nations, especially France and Holland. Like Columbus, Opitz was not able to make his egg stand on end without first cracking the shell; he was able to carry out his reform only at the expense of a clean break with national tradition. This tradition, it is true, must seem in our eyes very backward, indeed medieval, for it had not yet made any effective connection with the new Renaissance poetry. Still, as the example of Weckherlin seems to indicate, it might have been possible, given a reformer with a less ironclad mind than that of Opitz, to bring about some kind of union between the two and thus create a truly *German* poetry instead of the derivative variations *in* German on European Renaissance poetry which were the actual fruit of Opitz' reform.

Opitz was by temperament a scholar and a pedagogue rather than a poet. He was a typical humanist, learned and

12

proud of his learning, with a flair for verse. His appeal was likewise to the scholar and he stood godfather to a whole generation of scholar poets. His godchildren were typically learned young men like himself who had composed Latin verses, carefully modelled on the ancients, since grammar school. All writers of cultivated verse (*Kunstpoesie* as opposed to *Volkspoesie*) in this age were learned; the poet was by definition *doctus*. There was no question of some child of nature "whistling his woodnotes wild" and getting away with it. These humanists looked down upon the common herd and popular literature in the native tradition. Their minds were a perfect fit with that of Opitz, he was their born *praeceptor poeticae*.

Opitz' reform came in the shape of a slim volume (the modern reprint has sixty pages) entitled *Buch von der Deutschen Poeterey* (Breslau, 1624), which can be read in an evening and absorbed in a week. It is nothing but an abridgement or *Reader's Digest* version of a long line of classical and/or Renaissance poetics from Horace to Scaliger to Ronsard-Du Bellay. Its novelty lies solely in its being tailored to the specific demands of German. It soon fathered a whole progeny of similar handbooks, some of them quite elaborate, none of them essentially different.[7] The last of this line was Gottsched's *Critische Dichtkunst*, which appeared just over a hundred years later, in 1730.

The "reform" instituted by Opitz comes down to this: he showed his countrymen that they too, by observing a few fairly simple rules and by keeping a close watch on their language and grammar, could produce very respectable verse in German in the Renaissance manner. He of course did not promise to make silk purses out of sows' ears. Native talent was assumed, as was humanistic learning, the *sine qua non* of every poet of the age, but given these, one should be able, by following Opitz' recipe, to write a poem that would pass muster, even in the estimation of the Dutch. Opitz does

13

not pretend to provide anything but technical know-how. But this was just what was needed. Content in our sense of the term is hardly discussed in the *Poeterey* and this for the very good reason that for the age content and subject matter were still essentially one—to treat of kings, for example, meant ipso facto to write in the grand manner and on a high theme. Nor is there anything approaching what we think of as aesthetic criticism. The ethos is humanistic-patriotic. That is, it is assumed that humanistic ideals, deeply tinged by Christianity to be sure, are the only ones that can come into serious consideration, and the Germans are exhorted in the name of their national pride to glorify the mother tongue by German song, as, according to the testimony of Tacitus and Strabo, they once did in ancient times, and, as Opitz knows more or less vaguely, they also did in the Middle Ages (he cites the example of Walther von der Vogelweide). German verse of his own day and the century and half preceding Opitz ignores as unworthy of serious comment, and, from the standpoint of the New Poetry, not without a semblance of justice.

Opitz' overriding poetic ideal and basically that of the whole age is "elegance" (*Zier, Zierlichkeit*), by which is meant "decorum" or "fittingness" as well as "gracefulness."[8] One can get a fair idea of what Opitz means by "elegance" from the chief rules that he lays down to achieve it. One must:

Use language that is pure, i.e., High German untinged by dialect.

Have careful regard for clear sentence structure and correct grammar.

Be able to create new words by compounding, so as to increase the number and heighten the effectiveness of one's epithets.

Take cognizance of sound values and the significance of tropes.

14

Be aware of levels of speech.

Have regard above all for the "dignity" ("das ansehen und die dignitet") of poetic speech, which consists principally in the metaphoric use of language ("in den *tropis* und *schematibus*"). To achieve this goal it is permissible to ransack the ancients.

Keep one's rhymes pure.

Avoid hiatus, etc.

It is not hard to see that all this indicates a drastic break with ordinary speech, that its main striving, in fact, is to create a separate realm where poetry may lead its existence in "dignity" and "elegance." Opitz would have been the last to follow Luther's advice in his "Sendbrief vom Dolmetschen":

> Denn man muss nicht die Buchstaben in der lateinischen Sprache fragen, wie man soll Deutsch reden . . . sondern man muss die Mutter im Hause, die Kinder auf der Gassen, den gemeinen Mann auf dem Markt drum fragen, und denselbigen auf das Maul sehen, wie sie reden und darnach dolmetschen; da verstehen sie es denn und merken, dass man deutsch mit ihnen redet.

From the standpoint of the history of German verse, however, Opitz' most important piece of advice is undoubtedly that concerning meter. In order to judge its importance, one must have some notion of the metrical situation in the popular tradition.

The Meistersinger of the 15th and 16th centuries, such as Hans Rosenplüt and Hans Sachs, and those who emulated them, such as Martin Luther in his hymns, had already established alternation as a norm for verse, but they had not demanded that metrical stress coincide with natural word accent. Thus Luther feels no compunction about writing (in "Ein feste Burg"):

*dér alt böse feínd*
*mít ernst érs itzt meínt*

15

or: "láss fahrén dahín." Accommodations were of course made in singing. Opitz' contribution was to retain alternation but to require at the same time that metrical stress and linguistic accent coincide. As obvious as this may seem to us, it was for seventeenth-century German poetry a far-reaching innovation. The authority of Opitz raised it to the level of a "law."

Opitz was of the opinion that only two meters were possible in German, the iambic ($\cup-$) and the trochaic ($-\cup$), which meant, in effect, that he thought German verse must have a strictly alternating beat. Later theorists and experimentors were however not long in introducing the dactyl ($-\cup\cup$).

As to forms, Opitz discusses primarily the sonnet, quatrains (or epigrams) and the "ode," which is for him a song form. Rhyme is regarded as essential to verse in the vernacular, which was the universal view. The alexandrine is for him, as for the age in general, the heroic verse par excellence, but it is also suitable for reflective poetry.

Opitz' success was phenomenal and immediate. He was not merely followed, he was adulated. To us it must seem a bit strange that a whole nation should allow one man to dictate taste in this fashion. The reason has rather more to do with the history of education than with national psychology, though patriotic pride undoubtedly also played a considerable part. To gain a better idea of why the Opitzian reform was so eminently successful it may help to glance briefly at the rhetorical tradition and its role in humanistic education.

Though German humanism was, so far as its view of ultimate truths was concerned, deeply rooted in the Christian tradition, it was at the same time, so far as its way of presenting these truths was concerned, just as firmly rooted in the traditions of ancient rhetoric. Rhetoric of a Ciceronian-Quintilianian cast remained a living force until far into the eighteenth century and profoundly influenced literary theory and practice.[9] One subscribed without reservation to the doctrine *rhetorica nutrix omnium artium*, rhetoric the nurse of all the arts, and of course above all the arts of speech. Today we are inclined to regard poetical and oratorical discourse as distinct ways of speaking, the first being "intransitive," an end in itself, "pure" speech, the second transitive, i.e. aimed at influencing action. This distinction is modern. Certainly it was not the view of sixteenth- and seventeenth-century humanists. Of them it would be nearer the truth to say that they regarded poetry more as rhymed rhetoric or versified oratory. Poetry too was thought of as a way of influencing action, though that action might be largely inward, i.e. emotional. The aim of poetry, like that of oratory, was *persuasion*, the winning over of the heart and mind.

This pathetic-ethical aspect of seventeenth-century German poetry becomes more pronounced as the century advances and is indeed its characteristically "baroque" feature. It evinces itself in manneristic excess. As it grows clearer and clearer to the poets themselves what they are actually doing, namely, applying the devices of (classical) rhetoric to German verse, there is a noticeable striving for ever more elaborate ornament, expansion, bizarre metaphor, piling up of noun on noun and phrase on phrase, in short, the whole spectrum of rhetorical devices in exuberant excess, what is known derogatorily as "Schwulst" or bombast (the "swollen" style). It is as though they asked themselves: if some is good, why shouldn't more be better? Another root of such extravagance, however, undoubtedly lies in the fact that the themes treated by the poets of the period are traditional and fairly limited in number—the world's transitoriness, stoic heroism, longing for peace, both temporal and eternal, carpe diem, praise of one's mistress, these are among the most frequent. The striving to present these traditional themes in an ever new and more striking manner inevitably led to excess. For a single idea

17

more and more forceful expression was sought. Exactitude was not the goal but impressiveness. The reader was to be *overwhelmed*. From the standpoint of the ethos of this tradition the manneristic use of rhetorical devices can be explained as a way of influencing action, or in this case, of influencing emotion.

What Opitz did, then, was simply this: He showed his countrymen how to apply the rhetorical tradition, with which every schoolboy was already thoroughly familiar, to *German* verse. He was therefore not dictating taste, he was following it. He showed his compatriots what they really meant. This was his revelation and this the reason why he immediately found numerous adherents.

This pervasive attitude helps to account for a number of things in German seventeenth-century poetry. For one, since the rhetorical method could to a large degree be applied more or less mechanically, it accounts for the tremendous number of poetasters, eager pupils anxious to prove that they too had got their lesson. For another, it accounts for the rejection of the much more simple and direct (and to us much more heartfelt) popular tradition. It helps to account, as we have implied, for the typically baroque excesses, which were in part at least only the result of thinking through to its logical conclusion the basic premise, and finally, it accounts, paradoxically enough when one remembers that the aim was *persuasio*, in a large measure for the "aloofness" of so much baroque verse, what Günther Müller denominated its "Distanzhaltung."[10] The reason probably lies primarily in the reduction of personal experience to general terms in order to make it rhetorically viable, something approximating the opposite pole of the later treatment of personal experience symbolically.

Opitz' own verse, as is widely recognized today, is not yet "baroque." Rather it maintains the "middle level" of discourse typical of the classical tradition from Horace to Ronsard;

in other words, it is what is called Renaissance lyric. That it lacks fire is not in itself characteristic of the Renaissance lyric, but rather of Opitz' own temperament. Attempts to show that Opitz is a poet of subtlety and depth have not been very convincing.[11] What one must allow him is accomplished form—there are few signs of the rank beginner in a new medium.

Günther Müller and Friedrich Gundolf have characterized his verse very accurately.[12] Both stress its coldness and intellectuality. All of Opitz' poems, Gundolf points out, are at bottom didactic, whatever the overt theme. Tone and method of penetrating his material remain substantially the same, whether he is writing an elegy, a sonnet, or a song. Typically, he takes an idea, illustrates it by examples and ornaments it by images, then draws the conclusion. Nothing could be less passionate than his love poetry, though he assiduously imitates (translates and adapts) Petrarch and the Petrarchans (e.g. Gambara). He admits himself in the first poem of the *Teutsche Poemata* that his interests lie elsewhere:

> *Diss Buch ist mein beginn in lieb und auch das ende:*
> *Ein ander besser Werck zu dem ich jetzt mich wende,*
> *Das soll vor diesem Buch so vielmahl besser sein,*
> *Je besser Weisheit ist als Venus süsse Pein.*

As a theme for his "book" philosophy is superior to love. In fact, according to the "Dedicatio," the right sort of amatory poetry, namely that in a Platonic vein, is itself but disguised ethics: "dass also der Jugent die Lehre der Tugenden durch diese verblümbte weiss eingepflanzt wird, und sie fast unwissend darzu gelangen."[13] There is no reason for us not to think that this was Opitz' honest opinion. It is a doctrine that goes back at least as far as Dante, or even the troubadours. The rhetorical tradition demanded poetry with a purpose, *prodesse* must not be forgotten at the expense of *delectare*. This is the reason we constantly find disquisitions on the

19

"uses" of poetry in this tradition. As for the "use" of his book as a whole, Opitz is perfectly clear. German is as good a language for poetry as any, one can by no means admit

> es sey unser Teutsches dermassen grob und harte, dass es in diese gebundene Art zu schreiben [i.e. in regular meters and with rhyme] nit könne füglich gebracht werden: weil noch biss auff diese Stundt im Helden-buche und sonsten dergleichen Gedicht und Reimen zu finden sein, die auch viel andere Sprachen beschemen solten. *Ihm sey aber doch wie ihm wolle, bin ich die Bahn zu brechen, und durch diesen anfang unserer Sprache Glückseeligkeit zu erweisen bedacht gewesen.*[14]

If "Weisheit" is indeed Opitz' burning interest, then one would expect to find the heart of his production and the key to his sensibility in such longish, moralistic, reflective poems in alexandrines as "Trostgedichte in Widerwertigkeit Dess Krieges," "Vielguet" (a place name) and "*Zlatna*, Oder von der ruhe dess gemüthes." In these he is concerned with finding peace of mind in the midst of a troubled world and the specious temptations of "success." The ethos is almost monastic, which is not unusual with scholars. And yet, having said this, one must admit to a certain doubt. This is his theme certainly, but is it really the key to his sensibility? It is very hard to know to what degree the monastic ethos in such poems stems from a sense of "decorum," i.e. from a sense of what is fitting for the particular genre of the longish reflec-tive poem on the state of the world and man's place in it, and to what degree it stems from the poet's own feeling. This is a problem that constantly arises in the interpretation of all baroque poetry and it is basically insoluble. Try as we may, we cannot enter wholly into the mentality of the age and see it from within. From this standpoint the Baroque must, it seems, remain, if not a closed book, then one open only wide enough for us to be able to read the ends of the lines. We know, for example, that as much as Opitz praises the idyllic simplicity of Transylvania in "Zlatna," he could hardly wait to get back to more civilized surroundings. And he earned his livelihood as a court official and lived as a man of the world, not as a retiring schoolmaster or modest gentleman farmer buried in his books in some remote corner of the world, which would appear to be his ideal. If one is inclined to say with Nietzsche: "Ich mache mir aus einem Philosophen gerade so viel, als er imstande ist ein Beispiel zu geben," then one will not think much of Opitz as a "philosopher." Nonetheless, perhaps we can say with Gundolf that the conflict between "Sinnenglück und Seelenfrieden" was his "problem." Opitz' "personality," like that of so many seventeenth-century poets, will no doubt always remain for us a mystery.

Many of the poems in *Teutsche Poemata* are translations or adaptations from Greek, Latin, Italian, French, and Dutch sources. Opitz' striving is to set an example, "die bahn zu brechen," not to display originality in our sense of the word. Besides, originality was not yet regarded as a particular virtue in poets. This is but another aspect of the rhetorical tradition and its emphasis on technique. The poet did not so much attempt to express *his* feeling as what "one" should feel about a given theme or situation. Thus in a sense Opitz' first collection of verse is a kind of anthology illustrating modish themes and their treatment in the New Poetry. Go ye and do likewise, he says by implication to his compatriots, as he had said explicitly in the *Poeterey*. They did.

One of the most widely imitated pieces in the 1625 edition of the *Poemata* was "Ihr schwartzen Augen / ihr," which I quote as an example of Opitz at the height of his form. Though it contains one very inept line (verse 14), it well illustrates the suppleness his verse could sometimes achieve and shows at the same time how thoroughly at home he was in the conventions of the Renaissance lyric. Though a Lied,

21

its effectiveness is not diminished for lack of a tune. Only since the Baroque do we find German lyrics meant to live by the word alone, independently of music.

> *Ihr schwartzen Augen | ihr | unnd du | auch schwartzes*
>   *Haar |*
> *Der frischen Flavien | die vor mein Hertze war |*
>     *Auff die ich pflag zu richten |*
>     *Mehr als ein weiser soll |*
>     *Mein Schreiben | Thun und Tichten |*
>     *Gehabt euch jetzund wol.*
>
> *Nicht gerne sprech' ich so | ruff' auch zu Zeugen an*
> *Dich | Venus | und dein Kind | dass ich gewiss hieran*
>     *Die minste Schuld nicht trage |*
>     *Ja alles Kummers voll*
>     *Mich stündlich kränck' und plage |*
>     *Dass ich sie lassen soll.*
>
> *Ihr Parcen | die ihr uns das Thun des Lebens spinnt*
> *Gebt mir und ihr das was ich ihr | und sie mir gönnt |*
>     *Weil ich's ja soll erfüllen |*
>     *Soll zähmen meinen Fuss |*
>     *Und wieder Lust und Willen*
>     *Auch nachmals sagen muss:*
>
> *Ihr schwartzen Augen | ihr | unnd du auch schwartzes*
>   *Haar |*
> *Der frischen Flavien | die vor mein Hertze war |*
>     *Auff die ich pflag zu richten |*
>     *Mehr als ein weiser soll |*
>     *Mein Schreiben | Thun und Tichten |*
>     *Gehabt euch jetzund wol.*

Paul Fleming (1609–40)[15] is the most highly gifted of the poets who followed immediately in the wake of Martin Opitz.

In their view of the nature of poetry, as also in their Stoic-Christian view of life, the two men reveal great similarities, but Fleming possesses an inner fervency which is quite foreign to Opitz. Some of Fleming's verse can still move us, while that of Opitz has now only historical importance. Even so, Fleming must be accounted a fairly minor poet by European standards. This becomes all too apparent when we examine the whole corpus of his work rather than confining ourselves to the selections that appear in the anthologies. These are his lucky hits, the performance as a whole is by no means so impressive.

This is the picture one gets: Fleming is an eager imitator of Opitz both in themes and forms; furthermore he is an ardent Petrarchan, which is to say that he especially develops one aspect of the Renaissance lyric introduced into German by Opitz, one of whose aims was to show his countrymen how to "Petrarchize." In addition, one finds poems in which Fleming seems peculiarly himself: poems of manly directness, gay songs, lyrics of great tenderness on the themes of longing and constancy. To us, it seems undeniable that Fleming has his own tone, the thing that seems questionable is whether he was aware of it. It seems to appear by accident, not design. Those poems in which it strikes us are intermingled with others of an almost unbelievably inferior quality and strongly derivative nature.

In his collected works we find an unconscionably large number of purely occasional pieces, the bane of baroque poetry in any case: Hochzeitsgedichte, Leichengedichte, Glückwünschungen—these make up at least two-thirds of his production. Not all are bad of course, but not many are better than mediocre, and most are hardly more than made-to-order platitudes decked out in rhetorical figures and manufactured according to the universally accepted maxim: *bene dicere hoc est ornate dicere*. Not that one should blame Fleming for this—he is only following the taste of his time; the most one

23

can blame him and his fellow versifiers for is publishing as serious poetry private condolences and congratulations. To us, lack of self-criticism seems a striking feature of the Baroque. Our impatience is due to our different view of the nature of poetry. In the seventeenth century, if the rhetorical demands of a theme had been met, if it had been shown what "one" should feel about a given theme according to the rules of "decorum," then one had composed a perfectly respectable and publishable poem. Baroque lyric is, in Heideggerian terms, almost exclusively a poetry of "das Man" (was *man* fühlen, sagen, glauben, denken soll), not of the individual as a value in himself, and certainly not of sudden revelation of hidden meaning (Lichtung des Verborgenen). It could be, indeed it could not help being, this kind of poetry, because the age found its governing norms in the social order, not in the individual, and its ultimate truths in revealed religion, not in private theories. For this reason, too, it could subscribe so unreservedly to the doctrine of "decorum" and the normative poetics derived from this doctrine. The attitude toward the individual and the attitude toward poetry are merely two aspects of the same basic Weltanschauung. The concept of a given order transcending the individual but also encompassing him and giving him meaning through *place* or *role* are fundamental to both. The poet did not regard himself as an exception to this order, rather he saw it as his glory to exemplify it as fully as possible by playing *his* role to the extent of his abilities.

An excellent illustration of this attitude may be found in the sonnet which Fleming, according to tradition, composed three days before his death as his own epitaph:

*Ich war an Kunst und Gut und Stande gross und reich,*
*des Glückes lieber Sohn, von Eltern guter Ehren,*
*frei, meine, kunte mich aus meinen Mitteln nähren,*
*mein Schall floh überweit, kein Landsmann sang mir*
    *gleich,*

24

*von Reisen hochgepreist, für keiner Mühe bleich,*
*jung, wachsam, unbesorgt. Man wird mich nennen hören,*
*bis dass die letzte Glut diss Alles wird verstören.*
*Diss, deutsche Klarien, diss Ganze dank' ich euch.*

*Verzeiht mir, bin ichs wert, Gott, Vater, Liebste,*
    *Freunde,*
*ich sag' euch gute Nacht und trete willig ab.*
*Sonst alles ist getan bis an das schwarze Grab.*

*Was frei dem Tode steht, das tu er seinem Feinde.*
*Was bin ich viel besorgt, den Othem aufzugeben?*
*An mir ist minder Nichts, das lebet, als mein Leben.*[16]

At first blush it may look as though this poem refutes
what we have just said about baroque poetry and its attitude
toward the individual: "*Ich* war . . ." / "*mein* Schall . . ." /
"Was bin *ich* viel besorgt . . ." Isn't all this ego-centered? It
soon becomes evident, however, that the ego is here primarily the representative of a class, not of an individual. The
individual is remarkable not for his own sake but for the
exemplary way in which he has played the role assigned to
him. The role was that of a poet, above all, a German poet:
"Mein Schall floh überweit, *kein Landsmann* sang mir gleich
. . ." That is, his fame was bounded only by the boundaries
of the German language itself—he was the supreme German poet of his day. And this fame, the second quartet
assures us, will last until the end of time: "Man wird mich
nennen hören, / bis dass die letzte Glut diss Alles wird verstören." But this immortality he owes not to himself but to
the German Muses ("Klarien"), whose faithful servant he
has been: "Diss, deutsche Klarien, diss Ganze dank'ich euch."

Especially revealing from the standpoint of our argument
is the sestet. Here the persona of the sonnet, like an actor at
the end of an Elizabethan play, steps forward and addresses
the audience, begging their indulgence if his acting has been
bad (he is of course convinced it wasn't!). The metaphor is

25

that of life as a stage: ". . . und trete willig ab," and gladly make my exit. God was the prime spectator of this drama, then society as represented by family, beloved, friends. Death holds no terrors because the actor has played his role well and with all the energy at his command: "für keiner Mühe bleich" (line 5)—he paled at no effort. Now let Death play *his* role: "Was frei dem Tode steht, das tu er seinem Feinde." We are here in the atmosphere of a medieval morality. The last line brings the paradoxical climax: "An mir ist minder Nichts, das lebet, als mein Leben." My life, Fleming says (or the persona of his sonnet says), is in my art and it is immortal. This body may fall prey to sickness and death, but through my art I live on. The medieval atmosphere has suddenly disappeared; the ethos is again classical-Renaissance: fame as immortality, life "on the lips of other men."

The "I" of this poem sees itself only as a member of a social order with a certain role to play. This is the idea on which the whole poem rests—what looks like self-glorification is actually a kind of modesty few of us would be capable of. It is a modesty that takes pride in representing a degree, a step, in an order that extends from the lowest creature to the divine. The octet defines the particular degree to which the "I" has been assigned and tells how the "I" has represented it. The sestet draws the conclusion by bringing the "I" face to face with death. It shows what results from playing one's part in an exemplary manner. The final boast is not so much personal as societal—this "I" will live on because it has fulfilled the role assigned to it, that of a poet. The poet has a special place only in so far as he can create that which is "immortal." He does so, however, not by expressing *himself*, but by expressing the beliefs and ideals to which the social order is committed.

The clarity of line that Opitz gave the German sonnet is well illustrated by this example from Fleming. The sonnet was a favorite form of the age partly because of its intellectual structure, the way it could be used almost as a versified syllogism, with the conclusion in the form of a *pointe* in the last line. Petrarch, the great master of this form and the father of the sonneteering mode, had used the sonnet above all as an instrument of self-confrontation, a way of presenting the conflict within himself. The poets of the Baroque tend to use it as an instrument of persuasion or as a peculiarly apt vehicle for the display of ingenuity.

Fleming's Petrarchistic verse, i.e., the verse in which he is consciously Petrarchizing in the manner of Opitz and the poets of the Pléiade, is on the whole weak and frigid. He seems obsessed with giving currency in German to a mania that had already passed its peak in other European literatures.[17] It lacks all sense of inner necessity and thus leaves one cold. We must remember of course that when we speak of Petrarchism and Petrarchizing, we are not so much speaking of Petrarch as of his second- and third-rate imitators, who had reduced his incomparable poetic abundance to schematic formulas and clichés and his exquisite insights into the workings of the soul almost to the level of behavioristic psychology. A large percentage of the verse in this manner (not only Fleming's naturally) is about objects associated with the beloved—her ring, umbrella, looking glass, gloves, etc., or about particular parts of her person—hair, mouth, eyes, hands, breasts, even eyebrows. The idea was to see how much poetic mileage one could get out of such subjects and above all to see how ingenious one could be in one's praise. Such productions are highly typical of the age. When Fleming caters to this mode, we have the feeling that he is being untrue to himself, though it is very doubtful that his contemporaries did. For us, his most convincing tones are heard in those songs that center about the motifs of constancy and longing, most of which he composed toward the end of his short life, when he had, if not cast aside Petrarchism, at least learned to move within its conventions with greater ease and

27

naturalness. It is not for nothing that "Ein getreues Herze wissen" is the only secular song by Fleming that is still sung today. Of his pieces in this later and more harmonious, "truer" manner, perhaps the best is "An Anemonen, die Liebste." The note of tenderness without sentimentality (which was not in any case a vice of the age) that we hear in these songs, together with their sure rhythms and elegant form, make them the gems of Fleming's love lyrics. They rank with such unquestionable successes as his spring song in buoyant trochees "Lass uns tanzen, lass uns springen" or the wooing song in gay dactyls "O liebliche Wangen."

Fleming's religious poetry carries force and conviction, the only question is whether it is not more Stoic-humanistic in spirit than Christian. Certainly the ethic of such a sonnet as "An Sich" ("Sey dennoch unversagt. Gieb dennoch unverloren"), which seems so central to Fleming's fundamental sensibility, is pronouncedly Stoic. This is of course a secular rather than a sacred poem, but even the well known hymn "In allen meinen Taten" is hardly more than Stoicism in Christian guise. The most powerful of his religious poems (one hesitates to say sacred) is undoubtedly "Lass dich nur nichts tauren" (*tauren* equals *dauern*, *entmutigen*). It too is in the same Stoic vein:

> *Lass dich nur nichts tauren*
> *mit trauren /*
> *Sey stille /*
> *Wie Gott es fügt /*
> *So sey vergnügt /*
> *Mein Wille.*

Perhaps the most impressive thing about Fleming's verse as verse is his masterly use of rhythms to convey not only mood but ethical stance. Firmness of faith, staunchness of character, unflinching resoluteness—these he knows especially well how to convey through his rhythms. One might well call him a lyricist of the will. One of the best of these poems of the will is "Lob eines Soldaten zu Fusse," a "Rollengedicht" or poem impersonating a character. It begins:

*Ich bin ein Mann ins Feld: mein kühner Muth ist grooss.*
*Ist grösser als ich selbst / ich fürchte keinen stooss.*
*Ich scheue keinen Schuss. Die Liebe so zu leben*
*Hat mir in meinen Sinn von Jugend an gegeben /*
*Dass ich mich was versuch'. Es wird nicht jedermann*
*Zum Kriege ausserkohren. Wer Pulver riechen kann /*
*Auff balg und stoos besteht / nicht die Karthaunen*
    *scheuet /*
*Der ist ein Mann / wie ich....*

Since Fleming spent almost six poetically productive years in exotic lands, we naturally find echoes of this experience in his work, though these are not as numerous as one might expect nor are they really central to his production. It is seldom that he lets us *see* the foreign lands he was so proud to have visited ("von Reisen hochgepreist"). In "Liefländische Schneegräfin," a longish epithalamium in narrative style, there are gay, exuberant descriptions of Baltic customs (including "bundling"); in a poem called "In Gross-Neugart der Reussen, M. DcXXXIV," which has a strongly autobiographical note, one may actually get a glimpse through sophisticated Western eyes of rural seventeenth-century Russia, which is held up as a model of the simple life, much as Opitz praises rural Transylvania in "Zlatna" for similar reasons. But on the whole there is hardly any attempt to fathom the foreign as such. The exotic as a theme for poetry was not discovered until more than a hundred years later. In the seventeenth century one's own norms were still regarded as regulative for all men. A sonnet with the intriguing title "Er redet die Stadt Moskaw an, als er ihre vergüldeten Türme von Fernen sahe. 1636 März" turns out to be a piece of ordinary Petrarchizing in which the golden domes of Russia's sacred

29

city are compared with Basilene's golden hair, which of course surpasses them in beauty. If the rhetorical tradition could not turn something to its own use, it ignored its existence.

The treatment of nature in poetry belonging to this tradition is of the same order. Nature is not seen as a life in itself, an independent *bios*: either it is a mere backdrop for human action or it is anthropomorphized and thus taken into the general micro-macrocosmic scheme, made an actor itself. If man is "die kleine Welt" and contains within himself the design of "die grosse Welt," then it follows that "die grosse Welt" is man and can be so treated. We find examples everywhere. The reader is referred to Fleming's "Lass uns tanzen, lass uns springen" for an especially charming one.

Hans Pyritz has pointed out that if one thinks of "baroque" in the sense of a highly antithetical hyperbolic style, then Fleming's work can hardly be considered baroque, especially not his later and better pieces.[18] I should be inclined to go even farther and say that one cannot really consider him baroque at all, not even when he is Petrarchizing in the most elaborate and derivative fashion. Here too he remains essentially within the stylistic range of the Renaissance lyric. His work as a whole, like that of Opitz, reflects the efforts of Germany to catch up with its neighbors. Its poets are tardy pupils who have to stay in after school to make up their lesson in European literature.

Much less baroque even than Fleming is the gentle Königsberger Simon Dach (1605–59), the author of "Der Mensch hat nichts so eigen."[19] Dach was the most gifted of a group of versifying friends who lived in the East Prussian capital around the middle of the seventeenth century. One member of the circle was the well known composer Heinrich Albert, in whose *Arien* a considerable part of the poetic output of the Königsbergers was first published. Dach's verse is preponderantly strictly occasional in nature: Grablieder,

Hochzeitsgedichte, Trostgedichte, many, perhaps most, written by special request. We also find of course the usual "weltliche" and "geistliche Lieder," the latter being practically versified sermons. In short, it is almost exclusively poetry for a specific purpose, "Gebrauchslyrik." Much of Dach's enormous production, as he himself was aware, is ephemeral and second-rate, having been ground out to order. But there are charming exceptions. We value him today for his simplicity and touching sincerity in the midst of a pompous age sworn to artifice. In so doing, however, it is not unlikely that we misread him, seeing him with eyes beclouded by a sentimentality foreign to his own time. He was by no means in revolt against current conventions, rather he was merely following another less obviously rhetorical one, the convention of the song directed to a burgher audience and written to comfort, inspire, confirm faith, celebrate friendship and marriage. That is to say, he cultivates the *genus humile*, or "lowly style," which a rhetorician of the day defines in these terms:

> Die gemeine / geringe und niederträchtige [i.e. niedrige] / milde Schreibart / so auch die bürgerliche / häusliche / lieblende / scheinende / stille / lindfliessende und fallende genennet werden könte / bestehet in gemeinen / schlechten [schlichten] / einfältigen [einfachen] / geringen / doch eigenen [i.e. not figurative] / deut-und verständlichen Worten.[20]

These adjectives: bürgerlich, häuslich, lieblend [lieblich], still, lindfliessend, schlicht, are precisely those that critics and literary historians have always hit upon to describe Dach's style. It is about the opposite of what we have come to think of as "baroque." But though a person of simple heart to whom the lowly style was psychologically suited, Dach was not, humanistically speaking, a simple man. In the latter years of his life he was professor of poetry at the University of

31

Königsberg (Latin poetry of course) and he was by education and inclination an accomplished classicist, who would have preferred to compose his poetry in Latin and on more Renaissance-like themes, as these lines attest:

*Phöbus [Apoll] ist mir ungewogen,*
*Amor zürnet als sonst nie*
*Wie auch Venus, dass ich sie*
*Durch Betrug hab aufgezogen*
*Und gesagt, ich wollt hinfort*
*Mich der deutschen Reim enthalten*
*Und, o Rom, mich nach den Alten*
*Brauchen deiner Red und Wort.*

But he was the victim of his own success—people kept demanding funeral odes and wedding songs and Dach did not have the heart to refuse (besides, he badly needed the honorarium):

*Auch ich sing in die Welt hinein,*
*Man will es bei den Leichen haben,*
*dass für dem Deutschen mein Latein*
*Wird leider endlich mit begraben.*

Nonetheless, he was by no means insensible to his fame as a German poet and took special pride in having been the first to introduce into Prussia "the art of German rhyme." In this he was a true son of Martin Opitz, whom he revered with the same uncritical enthusiasm as his more wordly brothers in Apollo. Like Opitz, his stylistic ideal is elegance, "Zier":

*Phöbus ist bey mir daheime,*
*Diese Kunst der Deutschen Reime*
*Lernet Preussen erst von mir,*
*Meine sind die ersten Saiten,*
*Zwar man sang vor meinen Zeiten,*
*Aber ohn Geschick und Zier.*

32

One of Dach's most appealing and interesting poems is his "Klage über den endlichen Untergang und ruinirung der Musicalischen Kürbs-Hütte und Gärtchens. 13. Jan. 1641." The "Kürbs-Hütte" or "Pumpkin-Hut" was, as the poem itself tells us, a small garden with a shelter-house beside the Pregel on the outskirts of Königsberg. Here the circle of friends was wont to meet and talk, make music, write, cultivate their flowers, in the world but not of it. In these verses Dach offers his not too profound reflections on life and time, on friendship, fame and the rise and decline of nations, but by always joining his generalizations to direct personal experience he achieves a vividness unfortunately all too rare in seventeenth-century German poetry. This is mainly the result of his cultivation of the *genus humile*, which not only permits but actually requires the direct, homely touch. Many of his poems are so effective because it is also Dach's natural register. At the end of his "lament," Dach reflects on his own fame and states his artistic credo (my emphasis):

> *Mein Lied sol mit der Zunft der Götter mich vermengen,*
> *Darauss mich weder Fall noch Zeit noch Tod soll*
> *drengen.*
> *Es ist kein Reim, wofern ihn Geist und Leben schreibt,*
> *Der uns der Ewigkeit nicht eilends einverleibt.*

Dach's authorship of the famous Low German wedding song "Anke van Tharaw" (Ännchen von Tharau) was disputed for a number of years, but recent research has shown that it is after all by Dach, just as the tradition had always maintained.[21] Thus the world can continue to sing this touching glorification of the bonds of marriage to Silcher's ingratiatingly sentimental melody in the comforting knowledge that it is at the same time honoring the memory of the good poet of Königsberg.

The boundless production of Johann Rist (1607–67),[22] for many years Lutheran pastor in Wedel near Hamburg, is

33

formally dependent on Opitz for its facile smoothness but reflects Rist's own shallow practicality in tone and theme. It is nonpoetry by a nonpoet: utilitarian, stolidly bourgeois, soporifically long-winded. Rist could turn a rhyme and construct a well-made stanza as easily as eating pudding, and the wide popularity he achieved shows that he struck a common chord, but today his work is only of historical interest. It was Rist's declared intention to render "die ganze Theologie" in edifying verse and this ambition he very nearly achieved in his *Himmlische Lieder* (1642) and their sequel *Sonderbare Lieder* (1651). Best known to fame is the hymn "O Ewigkeit, du Donnerwort" ("Ernstliche Betrachtungen der unendlichen Ewigkeit") in sixteen eight-line stanzas. The third, in its involuntary comicality, is irresistibly reminiscent of a parody by Wilhelm Busch:

> *O Ewigkeit du machst mir bang' /*
> *O Ewig / Ewig ist zu lang' /*
> *Hie gilt fürwar kein Schertzen:*
> *Drumb / wenn ich diese lange Nacht*
> *Zusampt der grossen Pein betracht' /*
> *Erschreck' ich recht von Hertzen /*
> *Nichts ist zu finden weit und breit*
> *So schrecklich als die Ewigkeit.*

Besides the hymn and sacred meditation, Rist also cultivated the pastoral and the "historisches Lied" or reflective-descriptive poem in which events of the day are examined for their moral significance. One might call them homiletic ballads or balladesque homilies. His supreme hero is Gustavus Adolphus. These were collected in his first book of verse, *Musa teutonica* (1634). The pastorals, which are adapted from the French, display his not unimpressive formal facility to advantage.

Rist's verse shows in an exemplary fashion the spiritual

neutrality of the Opitzian reform. It was a method and a method only—anything was grist for its mill.

Though both are outright moralists, the Silesian nobleman, Friedrich von Logau (1604–55),[23] is as much to the point as Rist is beside it, and this not only because Logau cultivated the pithy epigram in the manner of Martial rather than the windy homily but also because Logau has a timeless quality that makes him the contemporary of every age. Lessing, who was the first to rescue him from undeserved obscurity by publishing a selection from his work in 1759, honored him not only because he felt a spiritual kinship with Logau's relentless honesty and hatred of sham but also because Logau possesses a strong vein of human warmth and kindness very similar to that of Lessing's own Nathan. For though he can be cutting, Logau is never cynical. In the words of Lessing himself: "So witzig Logau ist, so zärtlich, so fein, so naif, so galant kann er auch sein!" (34th Literaturbrief).

The main body of Logau's verse appeared in 1654 under the title of *Salomons von Golaw* [Logaw] *Deutscher Sinn-Getichte Drey Tausend*. He is a consummate master of his chosen genre, whether he formulates his insights as popular proverbs or whether he phrases them in carefully balanced and wittily pointed alexandrines. But though a conscious formalist, Logau is stylistically as unbaroque as Simon Dach, if by "baroque" one means manneristic excess. His plain, supple verse never calls attention to itself but only to its subject:

*Wenn nur der Sinn recht fällt, wo nur die Meinung recht,*
*So sei der Sinn der Herr, so sei der Reim der Knecht.*

35

In matters of form, Opitz is his acknowledged master, though Opitz was by no means the epigrammatist Logau was:

> *Im Latein sind viel Poeten, immer aber ein Virgil.*
> *Deutsche haben einen Opitz, Tichter sonsten eben viel.*

Logau's message is contained in the ageless admonition "Know thyself! Become what thou art!"

### LEBENSREGEL
*Bis [sei], wer du bist; lass jeden auch für dir sein, wer*
*er ist.*
*Nicht, was du nicht kanst, was du kanst, sei dir zu sein*
*erkiest [erwählt].*

This admonition he especially addresses to his own fatherland, sometimes as scathing scorn at German adulation of all things foreign, particularly all things French, as in the couplet "Franzosenfolge" (Imitation of the French):

> *Narrenkappen samt den Schellen, wenn ich ein Franzose*
> *wär,*
> *Wollt' ich tragen; denn die Deutschen gingen stracks wie*
> *ich so her.*

Since his rediscovery in the eighteenth century Logau's fame has never dimmed, rather it has grown ever brighter. Who touches his book, touches a man.

CHAPTER TWO

## HYMNISTS, MYSTICS, AND THE POETRY OF MEDITATION

Of all Western literatures, German is richest in hymns.[1] This of course came about through the Reformation. The classic German hymnist is indeed Luther himself, though he did not consider himself a poet (in which he was mistaken) and though he wrote only thirty-seven hymns.

The Catholic Church did not reject the hymn on principle—and there are of course magnificent Catholic hymns—but it allowed it only extra-liturgically, not as an integral part of the mass, which is a sacred rite performed by the priest and not dependent upon congregational participation. Thus the hymn plays a somewhat peripheral role in Catholicism. The Lutheran idea is radically different. Since every believer is ipso facto also a priest (see Luther's "open letter" to Pope Leo X, "Von der Freiheit eines Christenmenschen"), the congregation has both the right and the duty to participate in the divine service. The minister brings the word of God in his sermon and by reading from the Scripture. The congregation participates by praying together and, above all, by singing together. "For out of the abundance of the heart the mouth speaketh." He who truly believes cannot help singing. This was Luther's stand.

The Protestant hymn came to be more and more an ideal reflection of the life of the "free Christian" (free because relieved of the burden of sin through his belief in Christ's sacrifice) in all its aspects, even in the ordinary tasks of daily life. In his hymns the Protestant saw a transfiguration of his own life as a believer. No wonder then that the hymn is the most important poetic expression of the sixteenth century, when there was no way of life that excluded religiosity and when most of the literature was produced by Protestants.

The hymn is a severely limited form. Being poetry with a purpose, it must put the message first, rhetoric second. Because it must be understood by everyone, its language must be fairly clear and simple. For these reasons it resists "baroquization." Since it brings a traditional message, its phraseology is likewise prescribed by tradition, especially by the Bible and older hymns. Because it speaks for the whole body of believers rather than for the individual (or if for the latter, then in his character as a member of that body), its stance must be fundamentally objective, oriented on dogma rather than private feeling. And yet, though oriented on dogma, the hymn, to be successful, must express dogma in terms of feeling. If it fails to do this, we are left with the bare bones of doctrine and deprived of one of the main functions of the hymn: to cheer, comfort, and inspire confidence.

When one considers these severe limitations it is not surprising to find that great hymnists are as rare as great poets in any other genre. For the Protestant hymn the danger of failure lay in two opposing directions: in its role as purposive poetry it was easy for it to become merely polemical or shallowly utilitarian, for example, a singable catechism. This was a danger the sixteenth century did not always succeed in avoiding. As doctrinal poetry that must yet express

38

its ideas in terms of feeling, it ran the double risk of becoming, on the one hand, too abstract or, on the other, too subjectively emotional. It was the latter danger to which it was later destined to succumb most frequently, as many an eighteenth-century pietistic hymn and many a nineteenth-century one in all branches of Protestantism bear ample witness. There is in the Protestant hymn a creeping tendency toward subjectivity, which in its more extreme manifestations becomes sickly sentimentality.

In spite of all these limitations and inherent dangers, the Lutheran hymn is an outstanding achievement of the age of the Reformation and of the Baroque. At its best it has warmth and inwardness *and* objectivity. It was the main vehicle by means of which the deepest emotional values were transferred from the late Middle Ages to the eighteenth century. In the course of the eighteenth century a profound change occurred, one that will occupy us again later. To anticipate and somewhat over-simplify: the fervency that had been turned toward the Beyond, toward the Divine, came to be turned, as faith weakened but the need to worship remained, toward the Here and Now, toward the creation rather than the Creator. The beginnings of this process of secularization can be observed even in the Baroque.

The most important sixteenth-century hymnists after Luther are perhaps Nicolaus Selnecker (1530–93) and Philipp Nicolai (1556–1608). Selnecker already feels the burden of trying to follow in the footsteps of the master:

> *Lutherus singt uns allen vor,*
> *Nach Gottes Wort führt den Tenor;*
> *Wir singen nach und zwitschern mit,*
> *Gott will solch Stimm' verachten nit.*

Nicolai is the author of two classic hymns that show distinct traces of medieval mysticism: "Wie schön leuchtet der Morgenstern," which he himself called "a spiritual bridal song sung by the soul to its heavenly bridegroom, Jesus Christ," and the even more successful hymn of the heavenly Jerusalem, "Wachet auf, ruft uns die Stimme." The strophic form, as is the case with many older German hymns, is modeled on the highly artificial Meistergesang, a debased descendant of the medieval Minnesang. The first stanza of "Wachet auf":

> *Wachet auff, rufft uns die Stimme*
> *der Wächter sehr hoch auff der Zinnen,*
> *wach auff, du Statt Jerusalem!*
> *Mitternacht heisst diese Stunde,*
> *sie ruffen uns mit hellem Munde:*
> *wo seydt ihr klugen Jungfrawen?*
> *Wolauff! der Bräutgam kömpt,*
> *steht auff, die Lampen nempt.*
> *Halleluia!*
> *Macht euch bereit zu der Hochzeit,*
> *ihr müsset ihm entgegen gehn.*

With the Silesian pastor Johannes Heermann (1585–1647) we again enter the age of the Baroque. Opitz's all-pervasive influence immediately makes itself felt. Heermann was in fact a personal friend of Opitz and the first of the Lutheran hymnists to write in accordance with the rules of the Opitzian reform. With Heermann the epoch of the liturgical hymn, which dominated the sixteenth century, comes to an end. His *Devota musica cordis, Hauss- und Herz-Musica* (1630) contains songs intended more for private than for public worship. The epoch of the "edifying" hymn, or "Erbauungslied," has begun. Heermann's hymns can be read purely as lyrics, with no thought of singing. The question is then of course whether they are still truly hymns.

In keeping with his striving for elegance is Heermann's introduction of the alexandrine into the hymn, as in his moving and dramatic "In Krieges- und Verfolgungsgefahr," which is cast in the form of a prayer. His most famous hymn, and one which truly deserves that name, "Herzlieber Jesu, was hast du verbrochen," is even written in a loose imitation of the Sapphic strophe, a classical ode form with a long history in German, but hardly a form that we can conceive of Luther using. Its sixth stanza runs (Christ in the hands of His captors is addressed):

*O grosse Lieb, o Lieb ohn alle Masse,*
*Die dich gebracht auf diese Marterstrasse!*
*Ich lebte mit der Welt in Lust und Freuden,*
   *Und du musst leiden!*

Characteristic of Heermann's poetry is a strong sense of that bitter "Angst" that we especially associate with Andreas Gryphius, and Heermann was, as a matter of fact, Gryphius' favorite contemporary German poet. Though it is undoubtedly a very personal fear, it is also a typically Lutheran one, the fear, namely, that faith may fail at the crucial moment and the soul be delivered forever into the toils of Satan, the classical Lutheran "Anfechtung." Luther himself expressed it unforgettably, though preteritively and as belonging to the history of man before Christ's coming, in the second and third strophes of "Nu freut euch, lieben Christen, gmein":

*Dem teuffel ich gefangen lag,*
*Im tod war ich verloren,*
*Meyn sund [Sünd'] mich quelet nacht und tag,*
*Darynn ich war geporen.*
. . . . . . . . . . . .
*Die angst mich zu verzweyffeln treyb [trieb],*
*Das nichts den sterben bey mir bleyb [blieb],*
*Zur hellen must ich sincken.*

41

The same fear and the same Lutheran soul-struggle underlie Heermann's prayer "In grosser Not." Here, however, the figurative death of which Luther speaks (life in sin equals death), has become literal, taking much of the edge off the liturgical-dogmatic value and reducing the general application to a much more personal one. Luther speaks of *man's* situation (though he uses the first person singular), Heermann, in the following lines, speaks of *his*. (The baroque manner is evident not only in the use of the alexandrine but also in the swiftly changing metaphors, which are not developed organically but merely applied outwardly in a decorative-illustrative fashion.)

> *Hier lieg ich armer Wurm / der fast kein Glied mehr*
> *regt:*
> *Auf den sich alle Noht mit Hauffen hat gelegt.*
> *Das Hertze wil für Angst im Leibe mir zerspringen:*
> *Mein Leben kämpfft / und muss jetzt mit dem Tode*
> *ringen.*
> *. . . Drum komm Herr Christ und eyl:*
> *Vertreib des Teuffels List / zerbrich des Todes Pfeil.*
> *Er brüllet wie ein Löw': er kömbt in vollen Springen /*
> *Und wil mich schwaches Schaff / als einen Raub*
> *verschlingen.*
> *In mir ist keine Krafft. Du aber bist der Mann:*
> *Der ihn auch durch ein Wort und Wincken schlagen*
> *kan.*
> *Sey du mein Schirm und Schild: lass mich kein Angst*
> *und Leiden /*
> *Auch kein Anfechtungsqual von deiner Liebe scheiden.*

Paul Gerhardt (1607–76)[2] is by far the most famous German hymnist after Luther and the classic hymn writer of the

Baroque, to which, however, he belongs more because of his formal elegance than his innate temper. Gerhardt is too balanced and temperate to strike one as truly baroque. Utter trust in divine Providence is the ground chord of his work, a trust so firm that it brings secure inward peace. The temptation to doubt, which represented a true soul-struggle for Luther and Heermann, is resolved by Gerhardt with almost too great ease in one of his "morning songs":

> *Wach auf, mein Herz, und singe*
> *Dem Schöpfer aller Dinge,*
> *Dem Geber aller Güter,*
> *Dem frommen Menschenhüter.*
>
> *Heint [heute nacht], als die tunkle Schatten*
> *Mich ganz ümgeben hatten,*
> *Hat Satan mein begehret,*
> *Gott aber hats gewehret.*
>
> *Ja, Vater, als er suchte,*
> *Dass er mich fressen möchte,*
> *War ich in deinem Schosse,*
> *Dein Flügel mich beschlosse.*
>
> *Du sprachst: Mein Kind nun liege,*
> *Trotz dem, der dich betriege! [betrügen möchte]*
> *Schlaf wohl, lass dir nicht grauen,*
> *Du solt die Sonne schauen.*

Though thoroughly Lutheran in doctrine, spirit and morality, Gerhardt is not really "ein zum zweitenmal dichtender Luther," as one historian of literature has called him.[3] He is quite lacking in the defiant bellicosity and tragic depth of the great reformer. In Gerhardt's work, as Paul Hankamer has pointed out,[4] another side of Luther and Lutheranism dominates, the tendency of the movement toward "das Volkhafte," nearness to the people. (Not for nothing is Luther

the man of popular legend who threw his inkhorn at the
Devil, the inspired translator of the Scriptures into language
all can understand, the writer of Christmas songs for children
and the earthy conversationalist of the "Table Talks.") This
aspect of Lutheranism Gerhardt embodies in what one might
call a reduced baroque style. The rhetorical mode of the
age—to which all hymn writers bowed after Heermann—is
transformed in his songs into popular simplicity, approaching
that of the Volkslied.

The lack of tension beween this world and that of the
spirit makes Gerhardt seem to be already dwelling in Beulah-
land and gives his poetry an other-worldly sweetness and
innocence that can hardly fail to touch us, though we may
smile at its artlessness. The sweet purity so characteristic of
Gerhardt arises from his conviction that this world, though
imperfect, is *God's* world, a world in which, as we have just
seen in this "morning song," the Devil, who for Luther is still
"der Herr *dieser* Welt," is as good as powerless. No imagery
is more typical of Gerhardt than that of God's protective
care, an image expressive of our filial relation to the godhead.
We find examples everywhere (see stanzas quoted!).

Gerhardt's poetry is remarkable for its feeling for nature,
though neither he nor any other poet of the age can of course
be called a nature poet in the modern, i.e. romantic, sense.
His attitude is thoroughly characteristic of his century: great
as his joy in nature may be, he still sees it fundamentally as
an emblem, a sign unto man of the divine, and at bottom not
truly real. In his well known "Summer Song" he may join
in nature's general rejoicing, but there is no trace of a *merging*
with nature, which is in effect reduced to a sign of the promise
of much greater and more genuine joys beyond:

> *Geh aus, mein Herz, und suche Freud*
> *In dieser lieben Sommerzeit*
> *An deines Vaters Gaben;*
> *Schau an der schönen Gärten Zier*

44

*Und siehe, wie sie mir und dir*
*Sich ausgeschmücket haben.*

*Die Bäume stehen voller Laub,*
*Das Erdreich decket seinen Staub*
*Mit einem grünen Kleide;*
*Narcissus und die Tulipan,*
*Die ziehen sich viel schöner an*
*Als Salomonis Seide.*

*Die Lerche schwingt sich in die Luft,*
*Das Täublein fleugt aus seiner Kluft*
*Und macht sich in die Wälder;*
*Die hochbegabte Nachtigall*
*Ergetzt und füllt mit ihrem Schall*
*Berg, Hügel, Thal und Felder.*

*Die Glucke führt ihr Völklein aus,*
*Der Storch baut und bewohnt sein Haus,*
*Das Schwälblein speist die Jungen;*
*Der schnelle Hirsch, das leichte Reh*
*Ist froh und kömmt aus seiner Höh*
*Ins tiefe Gras gesprungen.*

. . . . . . . . . . . . .

*Ich selbsten kann und mag nicht ruhn;*
*Des grossen Gottes grosses Thun*
*Erweckt mir alle Sinnen;*
*Ich singe mit, wenn alles singt,*
*Und lasse, was dem Höchsten klingt,*
*Aus meinem Herzen rinnen.*

*Ach, denk ich, bist du hier so schön*
*Und lässt du uns so lieblich gehn*
*Auf dieser armen Erden,*
*Was will doch wohl nach dieser Welt*
*Dort in dem reichen Himmelszelt*
*Und güldnem Schlosse werden!*

45

In spite of the childlike joy that streams through this verse, it is not true nature poetry. Basically it is no different, though it is certainly more lovely, than one of those enigmatic drawings with an interpretive motto—an "emblem" in the technical sense—so beloved of the age. And this is the way Gerhardt expects us to read it. His time was utterly given to a dualistic, moralizing-theologizing vision—these were the spectacles through which it viewed the world.

Among Gerhardt's most important hymns (only 134 are preserved) are the song for Advent, "Wie soll ich dich empfangen," certainly one of his most beautiful productions and perhaps the most perfect artistically; "Nun lasst uns gehen und treten," a moving prayer of thanksgiving reflecting the experience of war; "O Häupt voll Blut und Wunden," inspired by a Latin hymn and mystical in tone (though Gerhardt was no mystic); "Befiehl du deine Wege," probably the best known of his twenty-nine songs of "Cross and Consolation"; "Nun ruhen alle Wälder," one of the most familiar songs in the German language and, indeed, practically a "folksong"; and "Ein Lämmlein geht und trägt die Schuld," a hymn for Passion Week remarkable for its depth of feeling. Our enumeration might go on at considerable length; it would only prove how much alive Gerhardt has remained. Of no other poet of the Baroque, not even of the greatest, Andreas Gryphius, can this be said.

Insofar as it is in the vernacular, the poetry of the German Baroque was produced almost exclusively by Protestants, while the art and architecture of the period is almost wholly Catholic. Lutheranism is a religion of the Word and the Book, of the inner rather than the outer senses. Johann Sebastian Bach, the Milton of music, was also of course a Lutheran. The Jesuit priest Friedrich Spee (1591–1635)[5] is the exception that proves the rule. His work, though not polemical, unmistakably bears the stamp of the Counter-Reformation, so vigorously promulgated by the order to which he belonged. His cycle of religious verse, *Trutznachtigall*, was first published in 1649, fourteen years after his death. It is a remarkable collection in more ways than one.

First of all in regard to metrics: though Spee's relation to Opitz is not completely clear, most of the evidence seems to indicate that Spee arrived at the principle of coincidence of metrical and natural word accent independently of Opitz and his *Poeterey*. It would otherwise be hard to understand why he makes such a point of this discovery in the "Vorred dess Authoris" preceding the cycle, in which Opitz is not mentioned. Furthemore, if he had been following the famous Silesian, it is strange that he did not follow him more closely, both in the formulation of his metrical principles and in such respects as the use of dialect and contractions, which Opitz taboos but Spee allows. Like Opitz, Spee is very proud of his poetical accomplishments in his native tongue, though his very insistence upon this point and its uniqueness would again indicate that he must have been unaware of his predecessor. "This book," he states in his preface, "is called *Trutz Nachtigal* [i.e. Excelling the Nightingale, or As Good as the Nightingale], because it sings as sweet and lovely as any nightingale [trutz allen Nachtigalen], and in fact downright poetically, so that it may well raise its voice in the company of very good Latin poets and others too. For that one can very well speak and compose poetically not only in Latin but also in German will immediately become apparent from this book." At fault is not the language, but those without the courage to use it.

Spee writes, however, not primarily for his own glory but *ad majorem Dei gloriam*, that God may have poets in German too. To this end, his book is based to a large degree on the principle of parody or "contrafacture" of wordly

47

themes, motifs and concepts, translating them into religious terms. It is also very probable that he set a number of his poems, each of which was provided with a tune, to secular melodies. The tradition is an old one. Thus one of the basic themes of the first part of the cycle, that of the Bride, or Sponsa (Anima/Psyche, the Church) seeking the Bridegroom (Christ-Cupido), who has wounded her with the arrow of (divine) love, is at once a parody of the Petrarchan mode in amatory poetry and a continuation of the traditional ecclesiastical interpretation of the Song of Songs, going back to Bernard de Clairvaux (died 1153) and his *Sermones de cantico canticorum*. Another extensively used mask is that of the Vergilian or Theocritan eclogue, in which shepherds vie with each other in the praise of God in His works, in worshiping the Christ Child, in interpreting the meaning of the Saviour's death, etc. In other words, the pagan pastoral is parodied in Christian terms.

It is common to deprecate Spee as sentimental, but this is to miss the point of his art and above all to approach it with a modern Protestant mentality. It is no more sentimental than a heavily ornamented Jesuit church. Joseph von Eichendorff, the great Catholic poet of German Romanticism, defends *Trutznachtigall* against this modern charge very well: "Es sind religiöse Minnelieder; und gleichwie man dem weltlichen Minnegesang, als das demselben zugrunde liegende edle und schöne Zartgefühl nicht mehr empfunden und verstanden ward, den Vorwurf spielender Tändelei zu machen begann, so hört man wohl auch jetzt, nachdem der alte Glaube ausgegangen, denselben Tadel gegen die Speeschen Dichtungen erheben."[6] The whole point of Catholicism's outward splendor lies in the striving to make the supernatural available to the senses, i.e., it is emblematic. Through it earth-bound man is to be given a way of identifying with the means of eternal salvation. The Counter-Reformation went farther in this direction than the Church had ever gone before or has gone since. Spee's work is a typical expression of this striving. The element in his work that is most likely to offend the modern sensibility is precisely that in which he is most typical of his time and most consistently applies the basic principle of sensualizing the supersensual.

We see the method perhaps most clearly in those poems which are written on the model of a Jesuit "composition" in the manner of Loyola's famous "spiritual exercises." A "composition" in this sense means first of all "seeing the place." It is an effort of the imagination to clothe the idea with visible form. Thus the person taking the exercises may be asked to imagine Christ on the cross, then to converse with Him, asking Him "about His becoming a man and dying for my sins." Then the penitent is to ask himself what he has done for Christ and what he ought to do for Him. The whole colloquy is in the tone of a friend speaking to a friend.[7] The forty-sixth poem in *Trutznachtigall*, "Eine Christliche Seel redet von dem Creutz, und wunden Christi," is a fine example of this method of inward realization through outward projection. The Protestant (especially the Calvinist!) mind, it is true, may well find such verses as these, with their overabundant rhyme, their tone of agitated fervency, their punning, a bit too much of a good thing:

> *Manche stunden* JESU *wunden*
> *Ich mir setz ob augen mein.*
> *Thu mich wenden zu den händen*
> *Zu der seit- und füssen sein.*
> *O du bester / Creutz baläster!* [*Armbruster*]
> *Ich dan ruff in aller eyl.*
> *O zur stunde mich verwunde /*
> *Schiess herab die nägel-keyl.*

Spee is drawn much nearer to the brink of questionable taste in his attempt to sensualize, "zierlich reissen dar / Und mahlens nach dem leben," the oneness of Father, Son, and

49

Holy Ghost in a poem on "The Most Holy Trinity, considered theologically as well as poetically" (*TN* no. 29). He realizes that he is treading on dangerous ground. Who, he asks, can depict such a thing "without offense"? But his basic drive to phenomenalize—which is essentially what he means by treating "poetically"—seems to know no bounds. A modern poet, were he to tackle such a theme, would treat it symbolically; Spee treats it literally, and this is the source of his failure:

> *Der Vatter seufftzet ohne ruh*
> *Zu seinem Sohn verliebet:*
> *Der Sohn ihm wider seuffzet zu /*
> *Sich gleichem fewr ergibet*

> *Zu gleich dan er / zu gleich dan der*
> *Mit gleichem brand befangen /*
> *Mit seufftzen hin / mit seufftzen her*
> *Bezeugens ihr verlangen.*

> *Ahà der Vatter seufftzen thut*
> *Zu seinem Sohn geschwinde;*
> *Ahà der Sohn auch seufftzet gut*
> *Mit eben selbem winde.*

But such failures, which certainly prove that Spee is no Dante, are after all a condition of his strength. His strongly visual bent, his urge to phenomenalize, is the source of his best, as well as his worst, poetry. He has the talent of the truly "naive" poet for myth-making, quite a different thing from decking out concepts in swiftly changing inorganic metaphors drawn from every source under the sun so characteristic of the run-of-the-mill baroque poet. When he does not seize upon the wrong object, Spee's literalizations, so embarrassing in the example just cited, can become miniature nature myths of irresistible charm. The only other poet of the age who can equal him in this is Catharina Regina von Greiffenberg (see pp. 68–77), though Weckherlin and Gerhardt may come close. The rest are too firmly rooted in the rhetorical tradition with its emphasis on the purely figurative to be capable of myth-making. Perhaps, too, they lack Spee's child-like love of God's creation? At any event, we will look in vain for anything resembling such verses as these in the other poets of the century (*TN* no. 9):

> *Heint spät auff braunen Rappen*
> *Der Mon in starkem lauff /*
> *Gundt mitternacht erdappen /*
> *Mit ernsten triebe drauff:*
> *Nit mangelts an Trabanten /*
> *An Sternen klar / und hell /*
> *An gleichen Liechts-verwanten /*
> *Welch ihn begleiten schnell.*

Or these, on the creation of the stars, here seen as the sheep of the moon, the celestial shepherd (no. 30):

> *Er [Gott] spritzet ab ein kräfftigs wort*
> *Von lind gerührter zungen /*
> *Gleich deine Schäfflein mancher sort*
> *In blawen felden sprungen . . .*

Brentano, a great admirer of Spee, has hardly anything more magical and at the same time more amusing. And the following verses (no. 32), describing sheep in the fold at night, are nearly worthy of a Mörike:

> *Wan friedlich unser Herd / und schaff*
> *Nach späthem widerkawen /*
> *Bereuschelt [leicht berauscht] mit gelindem schlaff /*
> *Die süsse Weid verdawen.*

For their suggestive force the following lines from *TN* no. 22, "Lob Gottes auss beschreibung der fröhlichen Sommerzeit," equal anything in Weckherlin or (later) in Brockes and for

51

their tender empathy surpass anything written before Matthias Claudius:

> *Bald auch die zahm / und fruchtbar bäum*
> *Sich frewdig werden zieren /*
> *Mit weichem obs / mit kinder träum /*
> *Nuss / äpffel / kirsch- und biren [Birnen].*
> *Die biren gelb / die äpffel roth /*
> *Wie purpur die Granaten /*
> *Die pfersich bleich wie falber todt /*
> *Die kirschen schwartz gerathen.*

Though not so pronouncedly emblematic, Spee's attitude toward nature, in spite of his closeness to it and his keen, ever delightful descriptions of brooks, mountains, field, forest, insects, and animals, is not fundamentally different from Gerhardt's: nature is a sign unto man of God's love. Like the psalmist's, Spee's nature poetry is praise of God in His works, nature as an independent *bios* would be unthinkable for him (no. 23):

> *Von deiner lieb umgeben /*
> *O schöpfer aller ding /*
> *Im trawren muss ich leben /*
> *Wan ich von dir nicht sing.*

But passages such as those just quoted, though not infrequent, are more like the raisins in the cake than the cake itself. The total impression is different. Spee's paucity of strophic forms (typically: an eight-line stanza of four stresses per line—either iambic or trochaic—alternating rhyme, each stanza divided syntactically into two distinct parts: four plus four) combined with extreme regularity of meter, concentration on one theme—God's love of man—the inordinate length of many poems, the tone of constant fervency, which one critic has excellently characterized as "agitato, ma non troppo,"[8] all this gives the cycle as a whole a monotonous, litany-like air.

Nonetheless, it is only by studying the work as an entity that one discovers one of its most interesting features, namely, its sacramental structure.[9] *Trutznachtigall* contains fifty-one poems.[10] These are arranged thematically, albeit in an irregular, "baroque" fashion, in groups of seven, plus the interpretive opening and closing poems: i.e., one plus seven times seven plus one. Seven is used as the basic number not so much because there are seven sacraments as because seven is the number symbolic of perfect order and completion, being composed of three, the number associated with heaven, spiritual order, the Trinity, and four, the number symbolic of the earth, terrestrial space, the human situation, the cross. The union of heaven and earth, of the godhead with creation, is the basic message of Spee's work, just as it is the central mystery of the Christian religion: the Incarnation. In the rites of the Church, this union is of course symbolized above all in its central sacrament, the Eucharist, in which the believers partake of the divine body in the guise of the earthly "accident" of the bread. The final, i.e. fifty-first poem of *Trutznachtigall* is a poem on the meaning of the Eucharist: "Am heiligen Fronleichnam Fest [Corpus Christi], von dem Hochwürdigen Sacrament dess Altars" and is in effect the key to the interpretation of the whole cycle. (With equal justice one might say that the whole cycle is an interpretation of the meaning of the Eucharist.)

The union of the divine and the earthly was and is effectuated through love, and it is of love and love only—or the deeds of love—that Spee sings, though of two kinds of love, the first, which fills the Sponsa-Lieder, being "die Liebe der Begierlichkeit," or passion for a certain object, and the second, which forms the main theme of the eclogues and of the other poems in the latter part of the cycle, being "die Liebe der Gutwilligkeit" or benevolence, i.e. love of one's neighbor, which for Spee includes all creation and is the religious basis of his love of nature.[11] The great example of love is of course the Father's love for us in sending the Son to die for our sins, and it is the birth of Christ that forms the "off-center center" of Spee's cycle. This central event is framed by poems on the Passion and the Resurrection, though it is immediately preceded by poems reminiscent of the Psalms praising God in His creation, i.e. reflecting the religious state of the world before the Saviour's birth. The shepherds' longing to *see* God (no. 32) is then fulfilled in the Christmas poems. This "eccentric center" is balanced by a second "center," the poem on the great Jesuit missionary St. Francis Xavier (no. 19). That is to say it is balanced by a poem on a man who through his own deeds fulfilled the teaching of love and gave us a glorious example of imitatio Christi. (Xavier is the only person in the cycle belonging to "our" world.) Thus *Trutznachtigall* really has two "centers," one human and one divine, closely interrelated. This is only another exemplification of the fundamental message of the whole cycle. With great subtlety Spee uses the irregular, off-center forms of baroque art to express his central idea.

One should not leave Spee without saying a word about his supposed "mysticism." Whether we consider him to be a mystic or not will naturally depend upon our view of mysticism itself. If we regard "Gelassenheit," or self-abnegation, ridding oneself of the earthly to the point of perfect nonchalance toward all that affects us in this sphere, as the fundamental step on the way to attainment of the unio mystica, it would seem that Spee is a poor candidate for the honor. This is not his great striving. Though his striving is indeed to become aware of God on *this* plane and to unite with Him *here*, this must take place in the way the Church provides, namely, through the Sacraments. The final, and decisive, poem shows how *all* believers can unite with the divine and offer themselves with the Son:

*Der lebend Leichnam unzertrennt /*
*Zugleich im himmel droben /*
*Zugleich ist aller ort und end /*
*Wo jenes brodt erhoben.*

If this be mysticism, then all who believe in the doctrine of the Church are mystics. Furthermore, Spee is a poet, and in his view the making of poetry consists on the one hand in the phenomenalization, the making present to the senses, of the noumenal, and on the other in the noumenalization (in practice, the emblematization) of the phenomenal. It is in this latter aspect above all that he belongs to his age. But he never throws the emphasis so strongly on the immanental as to forget the transcendental, nor on the transcendental so strongly as to forget the immanental. In short, he truly believes in the Incarnation. He never says God *is* His creation, but he says again and again that creation is godly. Much more than most poets of his time, Spee takes the world of the senses seriously and finds a beauty in it that he delights to convey. He takes it seriously because he loves it, and he loves it because it is godly, though not because it is God.

In the work of Johann Scheffler (1624–77),[12] known to the world by his pseudonym "Angelus Silesius," we meet a true mystic. The *Cherubinischer Wandersmann* (1657) is one of the most famous documents of Western mysticism, though it is questionable whether "Western" has much meaning in this context, since all kinds of mysticism, wherever and whenever found, bear a strong family resemblance. *Cherubinischer Wandersmann* contains 1,676 poems divided into six books. There are ten sonnets and a few poems of four lines or more, the rest are rhymed alexandrine couplets. The title—which was not applied to the collection until the second edition in

55

1675, when the sixth book was also added—refers to the "cherubinic" way of attaining union with the godhead, namely, through knowledge (the attribute of the cherubim). It stands in implicit contrast to the "seraphic" way to such union, i.e. through love (the attribute of the seraphim). The second way is pursued by Scheffler in *Heilige Seelenlust*, which appeared in the same year.

A work which even the deepest minds of German Romanticism found hard to fathom we cannot expect to explicate in any detail in a few pages. "Manche von diesen Sprüchen," wrote Friedrich Schlegel, "sind mir nach dem ganzen Inhalte ihres tiefen Sinnes erst nach mehreren Jahren völlig klar geworden, so leicht fasslich sie Anfangs lauten." And Schopenhauer speaks of the "bewunderungswürdigen und unabsehbar tiefen Angelus Silesius." From the standpoint of the history of literature, Scheffler's formal accomplishments are more important than his philosophical position, though we must immediately add the caveat that one cannot be fully appreciated without the other.

As a mystic seeker ("Wandersmann") Scheffler is not and can not be original so far as content is concerned. It is therefore no blame to call him derivative. He does and must derive from the mystical tradition from Plotinus to Jakob Böhme; he is especially indebted to the prince of German mystics, Meister Eckhart (c. 1260–c. 1327). To this tradition Scheffler lends typical baroque form. And even in this he is not original but rather the fulfiller of an already extant genre: the epigram in alexandrines (also in alexandrine couplets). This form he develops to the point of virtuosity. His main predecessor, at least in so far as this form was used as a vehicle for mystical thought, was Daniel Czepko (died 1660), whose *Sexcenta monodisticha sapientium* had circulated in manuscript among members of the Frankenberg circle since around 1650. (They were not published in full until 1930.) At first sight, many of Czepko's aphorisms seem almost in-

distinguishable from Scheffler's, but if we compare them, it
soon becomes apparent that Scheffler is the far better poet.

*Der Weise, wo er steht, weiss nichts von Ort und Zeit:*
*Er lebt zwar hier, und ist doch in der Ewigkeit.*

[*Czepko*]

*Mensch, wo du deinen Geist schwingst über Ort und*
*Zeit,*
*So kannst du jeden Blick [Augenblick] sein in der*
*Ewigkeit.*

[*Scheffler*]

Scheffler's couplet expresses the same basic idea as Czepko's:
time and space are not real, they can be overcome in the
mystic experience. But what has happened poetically? Scheffler has dynamized Czepko. The latter talks *about* the wise
man, the former addresses us directly ("Mensch"!); Czepko's
sage is passive ("steht" "weiss"), Scheffler urges activity
("schwingst über"), a dynamic process. Besides being metrically awkward, Czepko's second line is also broken down
into a prosaic argument with *zwar* and *doch*, whereas Scheffler's shows forth in a long sweeping rhythm the moment of
fulfillment: the rhythm reflects with beautiful precision the
overt statement. One talks *of* transcending time and space,
the other *does* it, rhythmically.

Another example:

*Die Seel und Gott die stehn in unzertrennter Pflicht;*
*Ging Eines hin, ich weiss das Andre stünde nicht.*

[*Czepko*]

*Ich weiss, dass ohne mich Gott nicht ein Nu kann leben;*
*Werd ich zunicht, er muss von Not den Geist aufgeben.*

[*Scheffler*]

Again dynamism and personalization: Czepko's "ich weiss"
stands in an unemphatic position in the middle of the second

57

line; Scheffler places it at the head of his startling statement:
*I know* that God cannot live an instant without me. The pale
abstraction "Ging *Eines* hin" becomes "Werd *ich* zunicht";
the metaphorically colorless "stünde nicht" in Czepko becomes in Scheffler the shocking and meaningfully ambiguous
"den Geist aufgeben."

A final example:

*Wer nicht kann selig sein, läg er gleich in der Höllen,*
*Gehört nicht oben auf, wie fromm er sich kann stellen.*
[*Czepko*]

*Wer in der Hölle nicht kann ohne Hölle leben,*
*Der hat sich noch nicht ganz dem Höchsten übergeben.*
[*Scheffler*]

The thought is again strikingly the same, the superiority of
Scheffler's formulation again strikingly evident. Both distichs
say: inward peace is not dependent upon outward circumstances, but "in der Hölle ohne Hölle leben" *shows* us what
this means, while "selig sein, obgleich in der Hölle" merely
*tells* us. Compared to Scheffler's way of expressing the equivalent idea, Czepko's phrase "gehört nicht oben auf" has a
primitive air. His poetical poverty is especially apparent in
the meaningless rhyme *Höllen—stellen*, a far cry from *leben—
geben*. The first couplet has the ring of advertising doggerel,
the second of gnomic wisdom.

Much of the fascination of this kind of poetry lies in the
tension between form and content. The form is rational, the
content irrational. Every poetaster of the seventeenth century
learned to use the alexandrine couplet; they learned to because it could be taught. Yet its possibilities in the hands of
a master like Scheffler seem almost inexhaustible.[13] This is
largely because Scheffler knows how to play off form against
content. The underlying purpose is to shock the reason into
a sense of its own inadequacy, and this through the exploitation of a highly rational form.

58

One of the basic texts of Christian mysticism is found in John 17, 3: "And this is life eternal, that they might know thee the only true God, and Jesus Christ, whom thou hast sent." To "know God" was interpreted as beholding Him in His essence. Thomas Aquinas discusses three ways of achieving knowledge of the divine: (1) by means of the reason through the creation, which, though not God, has its being from Him—image of the ladder, gradual ascent; (2) through revelation, the way of the prophets and the apostles—descent of the divine; (3) through elevation, the mystic way—man raised to the deity.

Of the third way St. Thomas says that it alone is perfect—only thus can the divine be beheld as it is. (The German term is *Gott schauen*, the Latin *Deum intueri*.) Elevation to (union with) the deity is of course in the final analysis a gift of grace; the mystic is interested above all in establishing the condition propitious to receiving this gift. He is interested in the *way*. It is his experience that direct knowledge of God means perfect peace, that is, utter freedom from all drives of the will. Therefore he bends his will to subjugating his will, to achieving what the German mystics call "Gelassenheit" (*CW* I, 24):

DU MUSST NICHTS SEIN, NICHTS WOLLEN
*Mensch, wo du noch was bist, was weisst, was liebst und hast,*
*So bist du, glaube mir, nicht ledig deiner Last.*

If we can empty ourselves of ourselves, God will flow in; this is His fundamental longing. Christian mystics express this under the image of God's being born in us: man must become "the spiritual Mary" (*CW* I, 23). First of all, for his own salvation (*CW* I, 61):

IN DIR MUSS GOTT GEBOREN WERDEN
*Wird Christus tausendmal zu Bethlehem geboren*
*Und nicht in dir, du bleibst noch ewiglich verloren.*

59

But also, as soon becomes apparent, for God's (*CW* I, 201):

### WARUM WIRD GOTT GEBOREN?
*O Unbegreiflichkeit! Gott hat sich selbst verlorn,*
*Darum will er wiederum in mir sein neugeborn.*

Fundamental to the mystical view is the doctrine of the unreality of time and space. These are purely human categories. In God, the true reality, there is no past, present or future, but only an "ewges Nun" (*CW* I, 133), and in Him, as Scheffler never tires of reiterating through one of his most meaningful rhymes, *Ort* and *Wort* (logos) are also one. Nonetheless, God has need of both time and space: He finds them in man. Creator and creation, God and I, are interdependent, and that above all because: Das Ich ist der *Ort*, wo das *Wort* geboren wird. Thus man is just as much the "saviour" of God as God of man. *CW* I, 205 is to be taken in this sense.

### DER ORT IST DAS WORT
*Der Ort und 's Wort ist eins und wäre nicht der Ort,*
*Bei ewger Ewigkeit! es wäre nicht das Wort.*

It is easy enough to understand why the mystic is always in danger of being accused of heresy. Meister Eckhart was condemned by the Church for pronouncements no bolder than Scheffler's (bull of Pope John XXII, March 27, 1329). The mystic tends to heresy because he tends to become his own redeemer. He has, *qua* mystic, hardly any need of the Church and her sacraments or even of the historical Jesus. He himself is constantly giving birth to the Son and uniting with Him as His bride, Son and Mary in one. Catholic theologians have, to be sure, defended Scheffler's orthodoxy, but outside the Church there seems to be no student of the *Wandersmann* who has been convinced by their arguments. It is mainly in Books I, II, and V that we find the daring mystical speculations for which Scheffler is famous. In Book III he turns to Christ and the saints, sinking himself in contemplation of them, while Book VI (not added until 1675) is as though by another hand, no longer mystically exclusive in tone, but rather homiletically popular: a preacher bent on conversion. This change in tone and attitude is like a preview of the course of Scheffler's life and work as a whole, his way from cherubinic mystic to seraphic preacher and singer to fanatical advocate of the Counter Reformation.

In *Heilige Seelenlust, oder geistliche Hirtenlieder der in ihren Jesum verliebten Psyche*, Scheffler turns from the cherubinic to the seraphic way and from the mystical to the orthodox interpretation of union with the divine. For this reason it has been argued with some cogency that *Heilige Seelenlust* must have been composed after the poet's conversion to Catholicism and later than the pronouncedly mystical sections of the *Wandersmann*.[14] *HS* contains 205 poems divided into five books. The first three, which constitute a closed cycle, appeared in the same year (but not in the same place) as *CW* (1657). Book IV was published separately, but probably in the same year (Ellinger). Book V was not added until 1668.

The cyclic nature of the first three books, which constitute a kind of liturgical year, is readily apparent. Book I (40 poems) sings of the longing of Psyche (the soul), who sometimes appears in the mask of a lovelorn shepherdess, for her beloved, Jesus, the Good Shepherd, the Bridegroom. (The underlying imagery is of course from the Song of Songs.) It closes with songs of rejoicing at his birth. Book II (24 poems) treats the theme of the Passion; Book III (59 poems) the Resurrection and imitatio Christi, closing with a beautiful hymnic poem of longing for union with the godhead. The first three books are dedicated to Jesus Christ, the fourth to Mary. The last two parts are no longer song *cycles* but song *books*.

The dedications to Christ and Mary at once strike the note that pervades *HS*, the note of sacred parody, an un-

61

usually fruitful source of artistic tension throughout the Baroque. These dedications are precisely in the manner of a subject addressing his sovereign in a typically servile seventeenth-century *dedicatio*. The songs—original editions contained the melodies—are likewise to a considerable extent parodies ("Kontrafakturen") of secular amatory verse; others are recast hymns, both of Catholic and Protestant provenience. Scheffler himself calls attention to this aspect of his work in his preface and urges his fellow poets to follow his example:

> O ihr Poëten wie seyd ihr solche Thoren, dass ihr eure Hertzen und Sinne euren Dorinden, Flavien, Purpurillen, und wie sie weiter heissen, ergebet . . . Wendet hier eure Erfindungen und Federn an; hier hier in dem unvergleichlichen Angesichte Jesu Christi, ist die allerfreundlichste Anmuttigkeit, die allermuttigste Liebligkeit, die allerlieblichste Huldseligkeit, und allerhuldseligste Schönheit.

How skillfully he parodies a secular love song may be seen from the recasting of Opitz's widely imitated "Ihr schwartzen Augen ihr" (see p. 22), entitled "Sie beklaget die verfallen Augen Jesu Christi" (*HS* II, 49). The first stanza:

> *Ihr keuschen Augen ihr, mein allerliebstes Licht,*
> *Das meinem Bräutigam und Heiland itzo bricht,*
> *Ihr Augen voller Huld,*
> *Voll himmelischer Lust,*
> *Was habt dann ihr verschuldt,*
> *Dass ihr verbleichen must?*

Not infrequently Scheffler out-sings the poets of Eros at their own game.

As a technical performance *HS* is a source of astonishment. Metrically and rhythmically perfectly controlled, it contains almost no dead spots. There are an almost unending number of metrical variations and verse combinations, subtly reflecting variations in mood and attitude from the playful to deepest seriousness. The prevailing mood, however, especially in the first three books, is that of longing. Of all the poems in this vein the crown jewel is undoubtedly I, 39, "Sie begehret verwundet zu seyn von ihrem Geliebten":

1

*Jesu du mächtiger Liebes-Gott*
  *Nah dich zu mir:*
*Denn ich verschmachte fast bis in Tod*
  *Für Liebs-Begiehr:*
*Ergreiff die Waffen, und in Eil*
*Durchstich mein Hertz mit deinem Pfeil,*
  *Verwunde mich :/:*

2

*Komm meine Sonne, mein Lebens-Licht,*
  *Mein Auffenthalt;*
*Komm und erwärme mich dass ich nicht*
  *Bleib ewig kalt:*
*Wirff deine Flammen in den Schrein*
*Meins halbgefrohrnen Hertzens ein,*
  *Entzünde mich :/:*

3

*O allersüsseste Seelen-Brunst*
  *Durchglüh mich gantz:*
*Und überform mich auss Gnad und Gunst*
  *In deinen Glantz:*
*Blass an das Feuer ohn Verdruss,*
*Dass dir mein Hertz mit schnellem Fluss*
  *Vereinigt sey :/:*

4

*Dann wil ich sagen dass du mich hast*
  *Erlöst vom Tod*

> *Und als ein lieblicher Seelen-Gast*
> *Besucht in Noth:*
> *Dann wil ich rühmen dass du bist*
> *Mein Bräutigam, der mich liebt und küst,*
> *Und nicht verläst :/:*

We will not be far wrong if we call this one of the supreme lyrics of the German Baroque, a production fully on the level of the best poems of Herbert, Crashaw, and Vaughan. It has been compared to Bernini's famous figure of St. Teresa receiving the dart of the god of divine love, and, in so far as two such distinct modes of artistic expression may be compared at all, with justice. We should note the way in which the alternation of long and short lines reflects the systole and diastole of longing—like great heaving sighs; the use of imperatives hovering between entreaty and command; the wonderfully expressive rhyme, especially in the use of the final unrhymed line ("Waise" or "orphan") that begs for fulfillment. And so on. Scheffler wrote no more perfect poem.

Our Freudian age is bound to regard this kind of poetry as sublimated eroticism and indeed why not? The erotic urge is the most powerful we know; it can be turned to any end, just as a dynamo can power any tool to which it can be connected. More important is another consideration, namely, whether eroticization tends to trivialize the divine theme. In this regard there is considerable difference between seventeenth- and twentieth-century taste as well as between Catholic and Protestant notions of propriety. What one regards as art the other may scorn as *Kitsch*. Being surrounded as we are by so many commercial products (including "art objects") in execrable taste, intellectuals are perhaps oversensitized to this question. Yet it must be admitted that for our sensibility at least Scheffler sometimes dangerously approaches the boundaries of high-class *Kitsch*, especially if we take a

64

poem out of context. *HS* III, 86 is an embarrassing example.
I quote the first stanza:

> *Jesu wie süss' ist deine Liebe!*
> *Wie Honig-flüssend ist dein Kuss!*
> *Der hätte gnug und Überfluss,*
> *Wer nur in deiner Liebe bliebe!*
> *Wie süss' ist es bey dir zu seyn,*
> *Und kosten deiner Brüste Wein!*

This is the tone of the sickeningly sweet pietistic "Seelenlied"
of the latter part of the century and the first half of the next.
It is all too apparent why almost anything singable by Scheffler was incorporated into the hymnals of the Pietists.

The question of mysticism and orthodoxy does not arise
with *HS*. We find here an exoteric, not esoteric, doctrine, and
one wholly in line with the position of the Church. *HS* can
at the most be termed pseudo-mystical. The human situation,
the limitations of time and space, are accepted and the mono-
psychical position abandoned for a dualistic one, which is of
course the sine qua non of the theme of longing and the basis
of all erotic dialectic. Scheffler, like Spee, now regards the
unio mystica as possible (on this plane) only through the
Eucharist. Some of the most fervent poems toward the end
of the cycle (III, 91–98) are devoted to this mystery, but it
is nowhere implied that man can unite with the godhead
other than symbolically, through the consecrated bread.
Significant in the following passage is especially the image
of the *descent* of the divine (rather than of the elevation of
the individual) (II, 97):

> *Allerhöchste Majestät*
> *Wie neigst du dich so tieff!*
> *Dass du kommst vons Himmels Städt*
> *In meines Munds Begrieff!*
> *Dass du dir, O Gottes Sohn,*

*In mir suchst einen Thron!*
*Dass du solche Gnad' und Gütte*
*Anthust dieser irrdnen Hütte!*

III, 98 has a very Spee-like ring and is perhaps the best of the poems on this important theme. The first strophe:

*Du Wunder-Brodt, du wahrer Gott*
*Wer kan die Lieb ermessen,*
*Dass du dich hier, selbst gibest mir*
*Mit Leib und Seel zu essen!*

The closing poem of Book III, among the most successful in the whole cycle, conjures up the true mystic vision of union with the godhead, but only *after* this life:

2

*Du wahres Paradeiss, du ewger Frühlings-Garten,*
*Du breites Blumen-Feld von unerhörten Arten;*
*Wann werd' ich von der wüsten Erden*
*In deine Lustbarkeit versetzt?*
*Wann werd' ich deiner würdig werden,*
*Und ewig seyn von dir ergötzt?*

3

*Du freudenreicher Strahl, wann wirst du mich*
*    verzukken,*
*Und gantz und gar in dich, und deinen Blitz*
*    einschlukken?*
*Wann fällt das Fünklein, meine Seele,*
*Ins Feuer deiner Gottheit ein?*
*Wann soll's sambt ihrer Leibes-Höle*
*Mit dir ein einge Flamme seyn?*

The theme of *contemptus mundi* is much more marked in Scheffler than Spee, indeed so strongly marked that one is sometimes inclined to doubt whether he can truly love, despite all his protestations. Certainly, he cannot love in the

same measure as Spee, as his life itself all too clearly proves.
A phrase like "diese wüste Erde" would be impossible for
Spee. Nature is for Scheffler completely emblematic, of no
value whatsoever in itself. In abandoning the mystical position, he does not, it seems, abandon its system of values: the
earthly is only something to rid oneself of. The body is constantly referred to as a dark cavern in which the soul is im-
prisoned: *Höhle-Seele* is one of the most frequent rhymes
in *HS*. One of the lamentations following the poems on Cruci-
fixion, II, 56 reflects this basic attitude in a gripping way:

> *Ich habe keine Lust an den geschaffnen Dingen,*
> *Mir kan was zeitlich ist nicht eine Freude bringen;*
> *Dess Fleisches Schönheit und ihr Ruhm*
> *Scheint mir wie eine blasse Blum;*
> *Weil meine Lieb gekreutzigt ist.*

And in I, 12, after Psyche has asked the meads and the
meadows, the flowers, brooks, woods, birds, mountains and
valleys where her beloved may be found, she is forced to
answer herself:

> *Er ist bey keiner Creatur.*
> Wer führt mich über die Natur?
>
> . . . . . . . . . .
>
> *Ich muss mich über alles schwingen,*
> *Muss mich erheben über mich . . .*

When Scheffler does turn to nature themes, it is the
sort of nature one might find in a baroque theatrical setting,
purely decorative and purely emblematic, though certainly
not without charm (IV, 20):

> *Der Frühling kommt heran,*
> *Der hulde Blumen-Mann,*
> *Es geht schon Feld und Anger*
> *Mit seiner Schönheit schwanger:*

67

*Der Blüte-Feind, der Nord,*
*Steht auff und macht sich fort;*
*Das Turtel-Täubelein*
*Läst hörn die Seuffzerlein.*

The influence of *HS* on succeeding generations of versifiers was very considerable, especially, as we have indicated,
on those with pietistic leanings, who imitated him ad infinitum
et ad nauseam. His songs furnished out their hymnals. But
even the Lutheran hymnals contain to this very day songs by
Scheffler, though hardly his most characteristic productions
("Mir nach, spricht Christus unser Held" and "Auf, auf, O
Seel, auf, auf zum Streit!" from Book V). A paradox of this
lover of paradox seems to be that he had greater influence on
Protestants than on his co-religionists. But perhaps, as a
counter-reformer, this is exactly what he would have desired.


The significance and quality of the work of the greatest female lyricist of seventeenth-century German literature has
only lately begun to be realized. Even as late as 1967, H.-J.
Frank, to whom we owe most of our knowledge of her life,
if not her art, could write that Catharina Regina von Greiffenberg (1633–94) "doubtless does *not* belong to the few great
poets of her day."[15] It is my conviction that this is a very
wrong estimate and that, on the contrary, Catharina Regina,
along with a scant handful of males, represents the very peak
of German baroque poetry, perhaps indeed of European
meditative poetry of the age. Her reputation in her own
day cannot, it is true, have been very great or at least not
very wide. Her *Geistliche Sonette, Lieder und Gedichte*, on
which her poetic fame must largely rest, were published in
only one edition (in 1662) and even this the bookseller had a
hard time disposing of. But because her contemporaries ne-

68

glected her is no reason why posterity should do so. And, as a matter of fact, her contemporary fame may not have been so slight as the sale of her poetry would indicate. Some of the shining lights of literature of her own time, S. von Birken, Joh. Klaj, Philipp von Zesen, and Duke Anton-Ulrich of Braunschweig-Wolfenbüttel (who dedicated part of his five-volume novel *Aramena* to her) admired her greatly.

Catharina's forte is poetry of meditation of intense incandescence and great daring. Among the 250 sonnets in her cycle of 1662 there is hardly a failure, though there are a number that do not quite come up to the standards she herself sets. It must be remembered, however, that the poetess is thinking in terms of a *cycle*, rather than of individual poems, and that within the framework of the whole each unit fulfills a function. The first 100 sonnets are organized as follows:

1–9: *prologus ante rem*: on the nature of the present undertaking.

10–18: God's wondrous ways (Providence).

19–27: Examples (Biblical, hagiographical, personal) of the wonder of God's ways.

28–37: On the power of Faith.

38–48: God's goodness and mercy (especially the mercy of misfortune).

49–57: De profundis (but with the conviction that the final end will be well).

58–67: On Constancy (for Catharina the virtue par excellence).

68–74: On Faith (its strange nature).

75–81: On her delayed undertaking (i.e. her poetry)—theology and art.

82–93: Why suffering is good ("Des Kreutzes Nutzbarkeit").

94–100: The triumph of constancy and faith—rejoicing in the victorious outcome.

69

The development of the thought in this part of the cycle is on the whole from the general to the particular and from the historical to the personal and immediate, from God's providential mercy toward Biblical heroes of faith to His mercy toward Catharina Regina, who in her faith is like a second Abraham whose Isaac is her life's work, her book.[16] The view of the divine presented here is thoroughly Biblical and therefore thoroughly non-Newtonian. Her God is no absentee manager of a perfectly automated factory but a God who knows the number of every hair on our heads, a God without whose will not a sparrow can fall. He is an utterly personal and therefore completely incomprehensible, inconceivable being. Our attitude toward such a God can only be faith, fullest trust. For that reason Catharina's "Gedenkspruch" is "W. G. W." (Wie Gott Will).

When a person with this concept of the supreme being looks about him, he sees marvels on every hand—nothing but miracles. There is for him no difference (as Hamann says) between the natural and supernatural, for there is *only* the supernatural. Catharina's fundamental reaction to the world—not to some mystic "insight" into the "beyond" but to *this* world—is therefore wonder (*G.S., L.u.G*, p. 360):

> *Nur von Gottes Gnad sing ich*
> *weil ich mich*
> *ganz in sie* verwundert.

Her striving is to inspire us, her readers, with this same sense of wonder. It is the ancient poetic task. The extent to which she succeeds is the measure of her poetry, and she often succeeds marvelously well. For the willfully blind and mentally lazy there may be no hope; they have already condemned themselves to the limbo of the indifferent on the outskirts of Hell; but for those who can pull aside the "curtain of indolence" (no. 227),

*Göttliche Wunder in allem man siehet /*
*Wann man den Vorhang der Faulheit aufziehet.*

For Catharina, as later for Browning, there is hardly a sin that can equal "the unlit lamp, the ungirt loin." Her ethic is a strenuous one; to trust in God does not mean that one should not keep one's powder dry.

Catharina conceives of her work as praise, as returning thanks to the Creator for His infinite goodness and mercy. She prays for nothing, except that her praise (which is by definition impossible!) may in some way be adequate to the gifts received. Her song, like that of Rilke's Orpheus, is basically pure celebration, "ein Hauch um nichts," a breath that sues for nothing.

*Ach lobe / lobe / lob ohn unterlass und ziel /*
*den / den zu loben du / O meine Seel / gebohren!*
. . . . . . . . . . . . . . . . . . . . .
*Rühm / weil du Othem hast: dieweil du ihn entfangen /*
*allein zu diesem ziel / . . . [no. 6]*

Again like Rilke—the parallels with the latter's artistic ethos are as obvious as they are startling—Catharina is intent upon making man's "oldest sorrows more fruitful." This is the argument of her numerous poems on "Des Kreutzes Nutzbarkeit": "Nie versagt ihr die Stimme am Staube."

Related to this ethos, the joyous reverse of the medal so to speak, is the concept of the world as God's body and man as His organs of sense, whose office it is to see, hear, smell, taste, and feel the divine for the divine: "Sein' [Gottes] Süssheit sich zu Mund will aus den Früchten schwingen," she says in one of her sonnets on the joys of spring (no. 224). For a Christian poet with such a view of the physical nature of the divine and the divine nature of the physical the revelation of revelations is of course the Incarnation and the wonder of wonders the Eucharist: "Ach aller Wunder Haupt!

der Mensch den Schöpffer *isst*" (no. 180). Catharina's is a strongly sensual, especially a strongly oral, nature; her poems on the Eucharist throb with a passion that would be shocking were it not for her perfect purity of heart.[17] The same is true of her poems on the wounds of the Saviour, a variation of this motif. Gersch's selection contains the following baroquely beautiful, for us surely startling example (p. 70):

> *Ich will ein Bienlein sein, dem Jesus-Klee zufliegen.*
> *Auror' und Tithon*[18] *ich lass ruhig schlafen liegen;*
> *Das selbste Feder-Volk noch schlummert auf dem Ast,*
> *Da ich zu schiffen schon durch Lüfte bin gefasst*
> *Nach meinem Blumen-Port. Die Purpur-Perlen*[19]
>  *scheinen*
> *Den Sternen selber vor mit ihren Himmels-Feinen.*
> *Sie machen seel-gesund, doch tödlich lieb-erkrankt.*
> *Sie löschen Höllen-Glut, entzünden, dass es fankt*
>  *[funkt],*
> *Das Feur der Dankbarkeit. Ich setze ganz mit Zittern*
> *Die Zunge gierig an, besorge, anzubittern*
> *Den schon erz-grossen Schmerz; saug also fein gemach*
> *Das Mark des Himmels ein. O angenehme Sach!*
> *Ich saug der Gottheit Saft. Ich trink den Bronn der*
>  *Sonnen.*
> *Der Geist der selbsten Stärk kommt her in mich*
>  *geronnen.*
> *Der Drei- und Einheit-Klee gibt hier sein Honig her.*
> *Wenn man die Allheit hat, was will und wünscht man*
>  *mehr?*

The startling thing here is not the figure of the bee sipping at the wounds of Christ. We find this often enough in the religious verse of the period. It is the intense identification of the "I" with the bee. The poetess *becomes* a bee, a bee raised, to be sure, to a highly sophisticated religious consciousness, who knows that in sucking the nectar of the "Jesus-clover" it sucks "the source of the sun," since Christ is the creator of that heavenly body and at the same time our own sun, the sun of life. The image is at once wholly physical *and* wholly spiritual. Note especially how in lines 11–13 the rhythm reflects the gentle expansion and contraction of the apian abdomen! Orality and theology. One has become the other. Such identification of the "I" with its analogue is very rare in the Baroque. It almost seems an example of the "Du in mir, ich in dir" that we associate with romanticism. Nonetheless, the poem is thoroughly baroque and by no means in revolt against the conventions of the period, and this not merely because it is composed in alexandrines. First of all, by overtly stating that the analogue *is* an analogue ("Ich" equals "Bienlein") it proceeds in a completely nonromantic manner. Further: it sets the time of day not by evocation of the magic of pre-dawn but by a dryly humorous mythological reference to the dawn goddess and her lover, who are left soundly sleeping. It delights in typical seventeenth-century paraphrase: "Feder-Volk," "Blumen-Port," etc. Above all, it preserves, for all the intensity of emotion so vividly conveyed, an air of rhetorical distance that permits the emphasizing of doctrine. It is completely unsentimental because completely controlled, and it is controlled by the rhetorical mode. This mode it fulfills in an exemplary fashion, proving, if proof were needed, that it is possible to write great lyrical poetry in other than the romantic convention.

Central to Catharina's concept of the relationship between God and man is the idea of "Spiel." Her God, as we emphasized before, is a God of mystery, whose ways toward man are unfathomable. We can only trust that in His "seltsame Geist-Regierung" He knows best. Without faith we are lost, given over to meaninglessness. Therefore the supreme virtue of the Christian is constancy. This is the only rule he has to go by in the strange game God plays with us (no. 66):

> *Es wird der Göttlich Rat durch keine Sach verletzt:*
> *das ganze Welt-Rad Er auf seine Strassen drehet.*
> *Mein Gott! ich lass ihn dir / spiel du mit meinem Sinn*
> *nach deiner dunklen Art. Verbirg / und zeig dich wieder.*
> *Wirff / wie den Ballen / ihn bald Wolken an / bald*
> *nieder.*
> *Dein Hand-anlegen ist gewissester Gewinn.*
> *Dein Schwingen ist mir sanft / dein Fangen mein*
> *Verlangen.*
> *Das was aus deiner Hand / ist allzeit zielwärts gangen.*

Catharina's art is, as Birken put it, "Himmel-abstammend und Himmel-aufflammend." What comes from above, man, if he fulfills his duty, reflects, like a looking glass, back to the source in the form of gratitude and praise. (The poetess's chief metaphor for the divine is light.) In this process, the poet is bound to play a key role. His function is a double one: to open the eyes of his fellow men to the glory of creation and, joining in the divine game, through his poetry to return the ball (reflect the ray) God throws to us (no. 250):

> *Du ungeendter Gott / doch einigs End und Ziel*
> *des Wunder-bunten Runds! das ganze Wesen gehet*
> *aus dir! und auch in dich: in dir sein Ziel bestehet /*
> *der du / unzielbar selbst / hast doch damit dein Spiel.*
> *Weil auch in mich ein Strahl zu schiessen dir gefiel*
> *von deinem Unursprung / den Geist mir eingewehet:*
> *so gib / dass er sich stäts zu seinem Ziel erhöhet.*

In this connection we must say a word about Catharina's "mysticism." R. Newald, the author of a widely used and highly regarded literary history of the period from 1570 to 1750, maintains: "Es ist echte Mystik, die in ihren Versen spricht."[20] But I think one may question this judgment. Newald confuses deep religious feeling with mysticism—a common error. Daly discusses the problem in his Zürich dissertation in some detail (158 ff.) and comes to a conclusion with which I think most thoughtful students of Greiffenberg will agree, namely, that though her work is shot through with mystical ideas, it is not the work of a true mystic. So far as I can determine from a careful perusal of the *Geistliche Sonette, Lieder und Gedichte*, there is only one poem (sonnet no. 191, certainly one of the most astounding poems in the Baroque) that could perhaps be called "mystic," and it will be noted that even here the mystic experience is seen not in terms of elevation but rather as the descent of the spirit:

### ÜBER DAS UNAUSSPRECHLICHE HEILIGE GEISTES-EINGEBEN!

*Du ungesehner Blitz / du dunkel-helles Liecht /*
*du Herzerfüllte Krafft / doch unbegreifflichs Wesen*
*Es ist was Göttliches in meinem Geist gewesen /*
*das mich bewegt und regt: Ich spür ein seltnes Liecht.*

*Die Seel ist von sich selbst nicht also löblich liecht.*
*Es ist ein Wunder-Wind / ein Geist / ein webend*
*    Wesen /*
*die ewig' Athem-Krafft / das Erz-seyn selbst gewesen /*
*das ihm [sich] in mir entzünd diss Himmel-flammend*
*    Liecht.*

*Du Farben-Spiegel-Blick / du wunderbuntes Glänzen!*
*du schimmerest hin und her / bist unbegreiflich klar*
*die Geistes Taubenflüg' in Wahrheits-Sonne glänzen.*

*Der Gott-bewegte Teich / ist auch getrübet klar!*
*es will erst gegen ihr [sich] die Geistes-Sonn beglänzen*
*den Mond / dann dreht er sich / wird Erden-ab\* auch*
*    klar.*

[\*I.e., from the point of view of the earth.]

The identical rhymes of the octet say of course that the essential being ("Wesen") of the Holy Ghost is light ("Liecht"), perfect unto itself and hence unrhymed with anything else. This essential light has, nonetheless, touched, shone upon, the soul of the speaker, imparting to the soul some of its own divine luminosity. An ineffable ("unaussprechlich") grace has been granted. The identical rhymes of the sestet ("glänzen," "klar") show once more the incomparable nature of the divine light, but the metaphorical material strives to describe the indescribable. Only a great poet could find a line like "die Geistes Taubenflüg' in Wahrheits-Sonne glänzen," with its brilliant fusing of the abstract into a vividly plastic, perfectly seeable image. The last two lines contain one of Catharina's favorite metaphors, that of the moon receiving its light from the sun, the receptive soul being the moon. Here it stands parallel to the image of the Pool of Bethesda (John 5, 7), whose waters were troubled by the "angel," the soul being the pool (line 11).

Stylistically, Catharina's poetry ranges from a childlike simplicity of expression to a manneristic compression of multiple meanings and an involved syntax that is almost Gongoristic. Her trademark is the metaphorical composite substantive (again inevitably reminiscent of Rilke for the modern reader!). One finds compounds like these on almost every page of her work: "Stern-Geweb," "Erz-Herz-Herzog," "Erlaubnis-Oel-Laub," "Freuden-Hungers-Not," "Unurgrund," "Leidens-Blei," "Herz-Bereiter" (the Holy Ghost), etc., etc. She can be manneristic to a degree, and there is no German poet more typical of the so-called "High Baroque," yet she is never bombastic. There are no *meaningless* rhetorical tricks and flourishes in her poetry. One is inclined to interpret this as a sign of her deep seriousness (no. 116):

> *Es ist mein ganzes Thun zu deiner Ehr gericht /*
> *und ist mir äusserst Ernst / nicht ein erdichts Gedicht.*

Catharina's poetry is so rich that we can touch only on a few salient features. It is still largely buried treasure.[21] Here is a final example (no. 241), a sonnet in her "simple" style:

## AUF DIE LIEBLICHE SOMMER-UND ERNTE-ZEIT

Du tägliches Wunder und Gnaden-Beginnen /
du Erde voll heimlich und Himmlischer Krafft /
voll unseres Lebens und Hortes Wort-Safft!
die Göttlichen Strahlen lieb-wallen darinnen /

biss dass sie gekörnet den Ausgang gewinnen /
mit sättigem Segen und Leben behafft /
den unsere sichere Sichel wegrafft.
Sein Gnaden-Lob lässet sich niemal aussinnen.

Man fühlet / mit Essen / sein' Lieblichkeits-Lust
in jeglichem Bröslein ist Allmacht vorhanden.
Es wär uns kein Segen noch Leben bewusst /

wann jene nicht neben den Speisen gestanden.
Das Sichtbare weiset unsichtbare Ding /
dass jenes aus diesem unmerkbar entspring'.

The inclusion of Quirinus Kuhlmann (1651–89)[22] in a chapter devoted to hymnists, mystics, and the poetry of meditation is admittedly an anomaly. In spite of the title of his central work, the *Kühlpsalter*, he is no hymnist, for the psalms in his psalter are not meant to be sung; he is not a mystic, for he does not strive to escape from time but to fulfill it; and his work is the very antithesis of meditative. It is true that from a stylistic point of view he might be treated in Chapter 4 along with the mannerists, but mannerism characterizes his work only peripherally. The fact is that wherever one places him he remains an anomaly. Though obviously connected with a number of literary and intellectual currents of his time, he is, as a poet, truly *sui generis*. He is discussed here only because he is a religious poet and because to award him

77

a separate chapter might imply an importance his work does not seem to justify.

The *Kühlpsalter*, which appeared in Amsterdam in 1684–86, is one of the most enigmatic works in German literature. Its difficulty, at least for the uninitiated reader, can hardly be exaggerated. To learn to read it in the spirit in which it is meant is almost impossible for us, and its extreme rarity (there was only one edition) indicates that it may not have been much easier for Kuhlmann's contemporaries. Yet the *Kühlpsalter* is not difficult because it does not "make sense"— it is difficult because it makes too much sense. The sense, however, is quite foreign to our habits of thought and its points of reference usually outside the range of common knowledge. Except for those in Book I, there is hardly a poem in the whole work that can be read with immediate comprehension as one can, with some acquaintance with the conventions, learn to read almost any other baroque poem.

With what monomanic rationality the *Kühlpsalter* is constructed is at once evident from its outward form. The author projected ten books of fifteen psalms each (only eight books were published), i.e., 150 in all, the number of psalms in the Bible. In each book, the first seven psalms are supposed to deal with the "external form" (*eussere gestalt*), the last seven with the "internal form" (*innere gestalt*), while the middle or eighth psalm represents "das Centrum zu beiden." Each book, in other words, is a triptych. The whole work is based on the principle of numerical composition, which is carried to lengths that cannot be explained here. The structurally important numbers are three, five, seven, ten. Ten, which contains three plus seven and two times five, is the "Kronzahl." The verses of the *Kühlpsalter* are exactly numbered; there are 20,018 verses. The number and order of the stanzas is also significant and reflects certain stages in the gradual revelation of the divine plan of salvation, in which Kuhlmann himself (under and through Jesus Christ) is the central figure. In short, form in the *Kühlpsalter* is a theological phenomenon. From the standpoint of the author it is only accidentally aesthetic. His work is anything but "drunken" and "aimless"—given the hypotheses upon which it is based, it is order itself. Kuhlmann meant this order to reflect or even to coincide with the order of the cosmos. It is the Word resaid.

The *Kühlpsalter* is intended as a sacred book, a continuation of the Bible, its third part under the Third Covenant or "Kühlbund," which is the church of God in the third period of salvation. According to Kuhlmann's private mythology, all that happens in time stands in the relationship of Sign (*Zeichen*), Figure (*Figur*), and Fulfillment (*Wesen*). The Old Testament corresponds to the Sign, the New Testament to the Figure, the Kühlbund to the Fulfillment. Thus time itself is of the essence, full of meaning gradually revealed by event, if one can only interpret the signs. In order to do this one must be versed in the interpretation of prophecy and one must be divinely inspired. It is not only the prophecies of the Bible that are important but also the prophecies of those living today: 1 Thessalonians 5, 19 ff., is a central text: "Do not quench the Spirit, do not despise prophesying, but test everything; hold fast what is good . . ." With the correct interpretation of prophecy the *Kühlpsalter* is much concerned, "correct" meaning in its application to the central figure of human history, Quirinus Kuhlmann. All that happens to him, the Chosen One, must have significance. In his life there is not and cannot be such a thing as chance. For this reason the *Kühlpsalter* is first of all an extended account of, or commentary on, his own life. Nonetheless, it is only in a very secondary sense *Erlebnisdichtung*. Each Kühlpsalm is introduced by a "Vorspann" in prose, recounting the circumstances that led to its composition. The exact date is given. The emphasis of the poems, however, is not on the experiences themselves but their sacred significance. The "events" treated in the poems are so transformed as to be

79

almost or even completely unrecognizable. The *Kühlpsalter* has no realistic plasticity, no vividness. If we sometimes think it does, we are probably misreading it.

Though Kuhlmann knows that his life is completely guided by the hand of God, he is not infrequently at a loss, at least temporarily, to understand the divine ways. He does not pretend to be able to read the mind of God directly, he only hopes to be able to interpret the signs. And in the end he never fails to interpret them to his own satisfaction. This process gives rise to the basic figure in the *Kühlpsalter*, which is repeated again and again: deep depression and darkness or only the faintest light, gradual comprehension of meaning with concomitant rejoicing and light, and ending in the ecstatic jubilation of visionary fulfillment. In other words, the thematic outline of many psalms repeats the basic figure of Kuhlmann's whole system: Sign, Figure, Fulfillment.

The basic difficulty in reading the *Kühlpsalter* lies in Kuhlmann's use of names. We expect poetry to be metaphorical and baroque poetry to be hyperbolical. Kuhlmann's is neither. It is utterly nonfigurative, at least in intention.[23] His terms are "ontologically correct" (Erk), that is, they have (as Kuhlmann sees it) an essential connection with the object they designate, they are not merely sounds which happen to be associated with certain objects but belong to them by nature. They do not merely designate things, they truly "say" them. A striking example is Kuhlmann's interpretation of his own name, which plays a large role in his work. It was only gradually, in the course of time and in accordance with deepening insight into the divine plan, that Kuhlmann himself became aware of all the implications, only some of which we can mention here.

In the Vulgate, Acts 3, 19 f., we read: "Poenitimini igitur, et convertimini, ut deleantur peccata vestra; ut venerint *tempora refrigerii* a conspectu Domini, et miserit eum qui praedicatus est vobis, Jesum Christum . . ." (Repent therefore, and turn again, that your sins may be blotted out, that *times of refreshing* may come from the presence of the Lord, and that he may send the Christ appointed to you, Jesus...) Kuhlmann, already convinced that he was the "youth" mentioned by Böhme who should save the world, was not long in interpreting himself as the bringer of *tempora refrigerii*, the cooler. He calls to God (K. psalm 30):

> *Dreieinger Vater, hilf! dein Kühler Ostau kühle!*
> *Sei Kühlmann Sudscher hitz, das Ost Nord kühlung*
> *fühle!*
> *Sei Kühlmann mir in mir, ein Kühlmann meinem*
> *Haus...*

His name is a "signature" (in Böhme's sense)—it connotes the mission of the bearer, who is destined to cool the fires of wrath Satan has kindled in the world. If two things have the same name, there is some significant parallel between them, they are ontologically connected. Later he was to discover that his name stood in opposition to "Kohlmann" (man of coals), associated with the pope and papistry through the accident (not an accident for Kuhlmann of course!) that Edward Coleman was involved in the "Popish Plot" disclosed by Titus Oates: "Wi herrlich bildet der nahme Kohlmann das Paebstische Werk ab, der aus seinen heiligen Steinfelsen [seat of Peter, "stone" on which the anti-church is founded] Feuerflammen auswürfet; und der nahme Kühlmann das goettliche Werk, der mit seiner Kühlzeit die Roemische Kohlzeit gaenzlich kuehlet in aller Welt." It appears that the poet had once been mistaken for this same Edward Coleman who was executed in 1678. Kuhlmann was quick to see the divine irony: "Kohlmann gehet unter, weil Kühlmann aufgehet: doch mus der Satan Kühlmann mit Kohlmann vermengen in manchem Lande, weil er es gerne so haette haben wollen, dass ich stat des Kohlmanns gevirtheilet his [hiess], als das Werk Gottes durch alle vir theile der Welt sich virtheilte." (Quoted after Dietze, p. 24¹.) And further (IV, 7, as quoted by Dietze, p. 241):

> *Satan gibt dem Kohlmann kohlen,*
> *Di Gott durch den Kühlmann kühlt:*
> *Rom wird selber weggespühlt,*
> *Wann es London wird wegholen.*
>
> . . . . . . . . . . . . . .
> *Rom kohlt durch Kohlmann Wiclef an:*
> *Den Gott durch Kühlmann kühlen kan.*
> *So ists! so gehts! Gott hats gethan!*

Once on this track there was no stopping. Cabalistic etymological relationships appear everywhere. Claiming that "kuhl" means "blue" in the Silesian dialect (modern dictionaries do not confirm this), and blue being the color of innocence and of heaven as well as (along with white or silver) one of the colors of the city of Breslau ("Blaueres" equals "Breslauers"), Khulmann made his official dress blue and white, and blue his most sacred color. But "Kuhl," so he claimed, is also a dialect word for "Kohl" equals "Senf" (mustard), which of course leads directly to the sphere of the parable of the grain of mustard seed which is "like the kingdom of heaven" and from which springs a plant so large that "birds of the air come and make nests in its branches" (Matth. 13, 31 f.). For Kuhlmann this was a parable or prophecy of the church of the Third Covenant and he the seed from which it should grow.

His given name was naturally also highly significant or "ontologically correct." I will mention two aspects. Quirinus, a local Sabine deity, was identified with Romulus, the legendary founder of Rome. The second Quirinus, i.e. Kuhlmann, is destined to "bury" the city the first Quirinus founded, because it is now the seat of the Anti-Christ and of the humanists, "Quiriten" (*quirites*), whose learning is of Satan. Rome is Babel (III, 4, as quoted by Erk, p. 287):

*Quiriten, hoehrt! Euch hat Quirin gebohren:*
*Quirin, den ihr in Romulus erwürgt.*
*Quiriten, thraent! Euch hat Quirin verloren,*
*Quirin, vor den selbst Jesus Christus bürgt [...]*
*Quirinus hat Quirinusstadt begraben,*
*Weil vom Quirin si solt ihr ende haben.*

In addition, Quirinus equals Quinarius (i.e. Quirinus *A*doles-cens), which of course has an obvious connection with the whole doctrine of the Quintomonarchia or Fifth Kingdom, which shall come at the end of time and last forever, as fore-told in Daniel 7. This kingdom Kuhlmann is destined to usher in.[24]

This is perhaps enough to exemplify Kuhlmann's turn of mind and method of regarding names, the "razón de su sinrazón." The key to this attitude is the conviction that nothing can be due to chance—everything is meaningful, especially all linguistic phenomena, which for Kuhlmann con-sist principally in *names*. Underlying this conviction and ex-plaining it quite logically is the theory of the Adamic lan-guage, dear to the hearts of many in the seventeenth century.

Adam, before the Fall, was in possession of the divine language, in which sound and meaning were one. This lan-guage was the repetition of the creation in the word, its per-fect image. But with the Fall this language was lost, albeit not totally; man still retains its "shadow." With the coming of the Millennium the Adamic language will be restored to man, along with his "paradisiacal form," for he now has animal form, "thirische glider." With the Millennium all cre-ation will again become Paradise. This restoration to the primal state Kuhlmann does not see as a sudden change but as a gradual process, a progress from Sign to Figure to Fulfillment.

Traces of the holy language are still present and may be found in the Scriptures and other inspired prophecies.

Though of course uttered in fallen form (that they may be comprehensible to man in his fallen state), such words still have divine legitimacy. Erk (p. 281) characterizes this sacred tongue as taking an intermediate place between the general fallen language of man and the Adamic language. In comparison to the former it is not accidental, in comparison to the latter it is not sensualistic, i.e. does not possess complete congruence with that which it designates (which makes it translatable). What Kuhlmann attempts in the *Kühlpsalter* is to create—or more accurately: to restore—the divine language as fully as possible. Erk (p. 284) summarizes his aim in these words: "Im Kühlpsalter wird der Versuch unternommen, aus dem Wortschatz der offenbarten Schriften [not limited to the Bible!] eine heilige Sprache zu schaffen, die der Adamischen Sprache verwandt ist und als ihre Vorstufe gelten soll. Darin liegt der Schlüssel zum Sprachgebrauch des Kühlpsalters."

Such language will not strive to be metaphorical—that would vitiate the whole idea. Within the limits imposed by man's fallen state it strives to be *the* word, completely nonfigurative. What figurative usage we do find derives principally from the (sacred) sources rather than from the poet. The question is then whether the *Kühlpsalter* is (1) poetry and (2) whether it is comprehensible. (That it might be poetry without being comprehensible may be conceded.) Clear-cut answers are perhaps hardly possible, but one thing seems fairly certain: it is not truly comprehensible *as* poetry. For Kuhlmann it was prophecy and the interpretation of prophecy, not poetry.[25] Typically, in the saying itself the prophecy is fulfilled, at least "in the spirit." As for its comprehensibility per se, we may say that it is comprehensible to the degree that it falls short of its true aim, which is to suggest the Adamic language or, as one might also say, to the degree that it is after all metaphorical. For in the last analysis, we can understand *only* that which is metaphorical. "Am farbigen

84

Abglanz haben wir das Leben." Metaphorical vividness and revelation stand in opposition. Thus it is hardly surprising that the later psalms in the *Kühlpsalter* are the baldest and least "poetic," hardly more than the bare bones of dogma. The content, at first metaphorically (or poetically) concealed, gradually emerges in its nakedness. The poem discloses its true identity as a treatise on revealed religion, ecstatically as it may demean itself. It is also logical that toward the end of the work Kuhlmann should begin to abandon rhyme, which he in any event seldom succeeds in making ontologically significant.

Erk (p. 345) would appear to be right when he says that Kuhlmann attempts to erase the boundary between language and reality. His whole theory rests on the principle that one shall be the other. But if communication is to take place the subject must have an object.

In the Kühlpsalm 63, Kuhlmann himself points out the ultimate failure of all attempts to "say" the world for God, to return to the spirit that which was created by the spirit, which would be the ultimate praise. Until the earth again becomes Paradise, our speech must remain "a childish babbling" (quoted after Vordtriede, p. 48 f.):

*Brodme durch der Winde Flügel*
*Gottes Gnaden als im Spiegel!*
*Adme [atme] hoch mit Adams Licht!*
*Adme aus dem Gottesbrodem*
*Aus dem krafterfüllten Odem,*
*Voll Jehovas Angesicht,*
*Voll Jehovahs Kraftgericht!*
*Sei des heilgen Brodems Zunder!*
*Brodme lobvoll Gott dem Herrn,*
*Oben, unten nah und fern!*

. . . . . . . . . . . . .
*Zwar Gott loben, wie Gott würdig,*

> *Ist Geschöpfen ewig bürdig,*
> *Weil dies bleibet Gottes Merk.*
> *Doch lässt Gott ein kindlich Lallen*
> *Väterlich ihm wohlgefallen:*
> *Unsre Schwachheit heisst er Stärk,*
> *Weil wir seiner Hände Werk.*

It is only to be expected that, given Kuhlmann's theory of language, the most striking stylistic feature of the *Kühlpsalter* is its tautology and its most typical figure the polyptoton or repetition of the same word in a different inflectional form ("Beerd di Erd als Paradies!", "Recht dunkelt mich das Dunkel," "Wi hellet ihr so hell?", "Kühlt Kühl mit zwölf"). We find this figure everywhere. I quote an extravagant example (IV, 8; Erk, p. 322):

> *Klahr werde von dem klahrsten klahren,*
> *Des klaehrstenklaehrsten klahrauffahren,*
> *Das klaehrer seine klahrheit klaehrt,*
> *I klaehrer klahr sein klahr gebaehrt.*
> *Schoepff ewigst klahr vom klahrtriangel,*
> *Da klahr in klahr waechst ohne mangel,*
> *Im klahrstenklahrstenklahrsten meer*
> *Der klaehrstenklaehrstenklaehrsten klaehr,*
> *Di ewigewigewigst klaehrer*
> *Wird ihrer klahrheit selbstgebaehrer.*

Kuhlmann's use of the polyptoton may be interpreted as a way of stressing the significance of names. "Beerd di Erd als Paradies" says that the true nature of the earth is to be Paradise, to make the earth earthy is to restore it to its primal state. Actually, the words "als Paradies" are not necessary, if we understand the doctrine. "Beerd di Erd" expresses fully what is meant. The verb in such a figure is only the noun in different inflectional form. Its purpose is to bring out the true significance of the noun. Very similar is such usage as: "JehovahJhesusJah *istwarkommt* AllesAllesAlles" (VIII, 10).

Here the verb is meant to show forth the absolute temporal priority of the divine. But as a verb it is actually without function; basically it is a name. The verse consists really of three names expressing the same thing. Kuhlman attempts to construct sentences that are themselves ontologically significant, that "say" the thing itself, that are not symbols but reality. The result, however, is that they are often not sentences.

The epithet, the glory of the ornate manner, hardly occurs in the *Kühlpsalter*. Ornament and periphrasis are suppressed. There is even a tendency to avoid subordinate clauses or to keep them very short. Kuhlmann likes to construct a series of parallel sentences, structures of equal value. (This naturally allows for antithesis, which occurs frequently, especially in passages dealing with the struggle between Good and Evil and those commenting on the difference between appearance and reality.) Highly typical passages consist of nothing but a parallel series of exclamations (Vordtriede, p. 47):

> *O Reich von allen Reichen!*
> *Des Davids Reis! Des Constantinus Blum!*
> *Der Engelswelt zu gleichen!*
> *Des ersten Adams erster Ruhm!*
> *Des Jesuels gesegnet Herrschaftstum!*

Though Kuhlmann's work may attempt to combine the thing referred to and the agent of referral in one, it is a measure of its lack of success that one cannot approach it without taking cognizance of the doctrine on which it rests. Though it may present itself as prophecy and visionary fulfillment of prophecy, it is anything but self-contained. The reason may be that it is basically anti-poetry, because, in the last analysis, it is anti-linguistic: it demands that language be something that it cannot: nonsymbolic. Language has the final word. It takes revenge on the poet by remaining itself— an agent of reference, not the reference itself.

87

CHAPTER THREE

# ANDREAS GRYPHIUS

When one thinks of the German Baroque, the first name that comes to mind is that of Andreas Gryphius (1616–64).[1] And it is true that if we have grasped his message, entered into the world of his forms and imagery, become capable of following his habit of mind, we have indeed seized upon a fundamental aspect of this enigmatic and, beneath it rhetorically uniform surface, puzzlingly manifold, epoch. But Gryphius, though a central figure of the age, is not its summation. His range is too narrow, his message too simplistic, his rejection of so much that delights the human heart too severe for us to rank his work as the classic expression of the Baroque. Two great lyric themes, love and nature, interest him hardly at all. He is, in fact, fundamentally a poet of one theme and that theme is man's fallen state. It is a great one, to be sure, and Gryphius presents it with unequaled, if monotonous, passion. The diapason of his baroque instrument, the rolling drums and shrilling trumpets of his rhetoric can move us still.

Though staunchly Lutheran, Gryphius' deep religiosity has an undogmatic cast. His stance is ontological rather than theological. What is man's condition? This is the great ques-

89

tion of his poetry. The answer is not encouraging. Man is in imminent danger. The world is a theater of war between the forces of evil, represented by all the things man normally prizes: fame, wealth, power, women, and the forces of good, which reside solely in steadfast belief in God's promise. The problem is to keep one's faith in the midst of this world of specious appearances. It is not easy.

A modern poet, and indeed some baroque poets, might present this problem from the standpoint of the temptation of evil and final insight into its true nature. This is not Gryphius' method, at least not in his lyric (in his drama the case is somewhat different). In his lyric the insight into the nothingness of worldly pomp and circumstance is the starting point and the tremendous pathos that informs his work is directed toward the conversion of the reader: we are to be made aware of our true state. *Persuasio* is the guiding principle. In short, Gryphius is above all a preacher.

He early recognized the subject of his sermon. In a poem first published in 1638 (Gryphius was twenty-two) to his admired and beloved half-brother Paul Gryphius, a Lutheran pastor, he states the enduring theme of his work with all clarity (*Werke*, III, 167 ff.):

> *Herr Bruder! O umsonst. Gedenck ich gleich zu zwingen*
> *Die Sinnen himmelan / und von der Lust zu singen*
> *Die dem / was irrdisch ist / und doch nicht irrdisch lebt*[2]
> *Von Ewigkeit bestimmt / wenn gleich der Geist sich*
>   *hebt /*
> *Und segelt durch die Luft . . .*
> *Sinckt doch mein schweres Fleisch! So schweigt die*
>   *Nachtigall /*
> *Wenn nun die heisse Zeit den wunder-süssen Schall*
> *Dem kühlen Wald abschlägt. . . .*
> *Wenn David Lob will singen /*
> *Wenn er die Harffen will mit süssen Händen zwingen /*

*Zuckt Saul den schnellen Spiess. . . .*
*Diss / mein ich / ist die Nacht / in der das Heulen*
   *wehret /*
*Hört an wie Zion klagt: . . .*
*Calliope bind' hier statt meiner Lorbeer-Cron*
*Cypressen um diss Haupt; Ich will den Klage-Ton*
*Mit Seufftzern stimmen an: Ich will die Saiten rühren /*
*Und Augen-klar die Angst der herben Welt ausführen.*
*Mehr schlägt mir Phoebus ab. . . .*

In commenting on this passage we need only add that "Geist"
and "Fleisch" are more evenly balanced in Gryphius' work
as a whole than these lines would lead one to believe. The
total impression gained from his work, despite its sombre
tones and the vision of life as a *danse macabre* (this being of
course the "Fleisch" aspect), is not so much pessimistic as
*heroic*. That life can or at least should be happy does not
even occur to Gryphius. He rejects out of hand all eudae-
monistic philosophies. But we can become heroes of faith,
i.e. the spirit. With Schopenhauer, he might well have said,
"Ein *glückliches Leben* ist unmöglich: das höchste, was der
Mensch erlangen kann, ist ein *heroischer Lebenslauf.*" These
are the two givens: on the one hand our fallen state, on the
other God's promise. The latter makes the former meaningful, but only on the condition that we realize that our state *is*
fallen and that its only true meaning is that of a trial, a test
of faith. It is meaningful only if we reject its own satanic
premises. Gryphius' poetry is concerned with showing us
the one, our fallen state, while reminding us of the other,
God's promise.

One largish group of poems, the thirty-six odes written
between 1640 and 1650, furnishes an unusually clear dem-
onstration of the basic pattern of Gryphius' thought and
feeling.

The term "ode," it should be pointed out, was loosely

91

used in the seventeenth century. Sometimes it means no more than "song," sometimes it seems to indicate a longer lyrical form of a pathetic rather than a meditative nature. Gryphius even includes his sometimes balladesque, sometimes hymnic group of nineteen poems entitled "Thränen über das Leiden JESU CHRISTI" among his odes (as the fourth book). The so-called "Pindaric" ode (which the Germans derived from Ronsard rather than Pindar!) is characterized by strophe and antistrophe of the same length and metrical scheme, followed by an epode of different length and with a different metrical scheme. Gryphius has twelve such "Pindaric" odes among his first three books. The metrical structure can be quite complicated and the highflown tone—all belong to the *genus grande*—invites elaborate *ornatus*.

The first thirty-six odes are divided into three books of twelve poems each, each book forming a cycle. Each cycle shows the same general dynamics, a loosely triadic development from woe through assailing doubt to final comfort and rejoicing. (A number of the poems show the same development when taken separately.) A thematic outline of the first book will show what is meant.

1–3: Man's sorry plight, but with the assurance that God will not forget His covenant: we are "written in His hand"—Biblical examples (Old Testament).

4–5: Vanitas mundi; pessimistic tone, dim hope of salvation—modern (secular) examples.

6–8: Prayers for deliverance—situation of the "I" of the odes.

9: A hymn on the vanity of the world, but now with emphasis on certainty of salvation—identification of "I" with body of believers.

10–12: Deliverance; I too am "written in His hand"—personal situation.

Many of the odes are paraphrases of passages from the Bible. These tend to be particularly enthusiastic, even exacer-

bated, in tone and ornate in diction. An example from the
first ode of the second book (*Werke* II, 33), based on Psalm
71, 20 f.:

> *Reiss Erde! reiss entzwey! Ihr Berge brecht und decket*
> *Den ganz verzagten Geist.*[3]
> *Den Blitz und ach und noth / und angst / und weh'*
> *erschrecket!*
> *Und herbe wehmutt beist!*
> *Ihr immerlichten stätten Himmel-Lichter!*
> *Ach bescheinet meine glieder! ach bescheint die glieder*
> *nicht!*
> *Die der Donnerkeil der schmertzen / die die krafft der*
> *Angst zubricht . . .*

Gryphius' odes have been occasionally admired but little
studied.[4] The poet himself seems to have thought highly of
them; he polished them with each successive edition and
seems to have lavished as much care on them as on his (today)
much more famous sonnets.

If we look about in the seventeenth century for another
spirit akin to Gryphius, we find one of his closest relatives in
Blaise Pascal (1623–62), almost his precise contemporary.
For both, *the* interpretation of man's condition is the Christian view, and for Pascal as for Gryphius the heart of the
Christian message is summed up in our corrupt nature balanced by the promise of redemption: "Car la foi chrestienne
ne va presque qu'à établir ces deux choses: la corruption de
la nature, et la rédemption de J. C." (*Pensées*, ed. Stewart,
p. 106.) Like Gryphius, Pascal is tortured by the paradox of
man's being both mind and body, one ever conflicting with
the other in such a way as to preclude all final knowledge.
Like Gryphius, Pascal sees life in the most sombre colors.
One of his striking images is that of a chain gang condemned
to death. Each day one member is throttled in sight of the
others and the survivors, looking at each other "avec douleur

et sans espérance, attendent à leur tour. C'est l'image de la condition humaine." (*Pensées*, p. 80.) But if there is one thing of which all men are certain—death, there are two things of which Pascal and Gryphius are certain: death and immortality. It is not the first so much as the second that gives their work vibrancy. Both would arouse us from "cette insensibilité," the state of unawareness of our true condition, which Pascal calls "la plus grande des maladies," that we may take thought of the eternal.[5] Gryphius is inexhaustible in the depiction of man's fallen state, which he typically sees under the image of instability or transiency, the uncanny nature of time (*Werke* II, 35):

> *Der schnellen Tage Traum /*
> *Der leichten Jahre Schaum*
> *Zerschlägt sich an der schwartzen Bahr /*
> *Eh wir die Zeit erkennt*
> *Verfleugt sie und verrennt;*
> *Wir dringen durch die Welt*
> *(Die weil [indem] sie wächst / zerfällt /)*
> *Nach längst erblaster Völcker Schar.*
> *Wir / die wir stets vol Noth*
> *Schwach / siech / und lebend-tod.*

Pascal's vision is no different. What Gryphius sees under the aspect of time, he sees under that of space. Compare his estimate of our state (*Pensées*, p. 24):

> Voilà nostre estat véritable . . . Nous vogons sur un milieu vaste, toujours incertains et flottans, poussés d'un bout vers l'autre. Quelque terme [fixed point] où nous pensions nous affermir, il bransle et nous quitte; et si nous suivons, il échappe à nos prises, nous glisse et fuit d'une fuite éternelle. Rien ne s'arreste pour nous. C'est l'estat qui nous est naturelle, et toutefois le plus contraire à nostre inclination; nous brûlons du désir de trouver une

assiette ferme [sure resting place], et une dernière base constante pour y édifier une tour qui s'elève à l'infiny, mais tout nostre fondement craque, et la terre s'ouvre jusqu'aux abismes.

For Pascal as for Gryphius, the only chance man has of "raising a tower to the infinite" is through faith, trust in God's promise. It may amaze us that both Pascal and Gryphius can still move us with this medieval view of man's condition. That their pathos still rings true is a measure not only of their sincerity but above all of their artistry. There is of course no doubt that Pascal is the more "modern." The first great stylist of modern French prose, nervous, problematic, keenly aware of the difficulties that beset the nonbeliever, Pascal is universally read even today, while Gryphius really lives only in a few sonnets included in the anthologies. And though it may seem an unfair comparison, the measure of Pascal's modernity and Gryphius' outdatedness lies precisely in the fact that Pascal could write modern prose and Gryphius could not. His German prose is still modeled on the ponderous *Kanzleistil* (the prose of official documents), which in comparison with Pascal's reminds one of a parody by Rabelais of a medieval lawyer's brief. German prose, despite Luther, was just beginning to become a supple instrument of expression. And prose, not verse, was to be the key to the modern age.

Nonetheless, both men are essentially alike. Both, we should remember, were fully cognizant of the most advanced thought of their day—Pascal was a famous mathematician, Gryphius, very learned, was offered the chair in mathematics at Frankfurt on Oder. The point of true contact, however, lies in their both *rejecting* science as having anything essential to say about the human condition, though Pascal regarded man as "visiblement fait pour penser" and Gryphius was deeply impressed by the great scientific discoveries of his time (see

95

his poem on Copernicus). In the end, this too was vanity, "Eitelkeit," "corruption de la nature." For Gryphius it seems to have been a hard pill to swallow. His poems on the vanity of human knowledge have a peculiarly bitter ring, as in these lines from "Letzte Rede eines Gelehrten aus seinem Grabe" (*Werke* II, 8 ff.):

> *Ach! was ist alles was uns zihret /*
> *Undt für der welt zum wunder macht!*
> *Wenn nun der todt sein recht ausführet*
> *Und unser geist in angst veschmacht.*
> *Was nützt doch / bitt ich / unser wissen:*
> *Wenn wir die lassen [müden] augen schlissen?*
>
> . . . . . . . . . . . . . .
>
> *Gott / dem wir rechnung übergeben /*
> *Schawt kein gelehrtes wissen an.*
> *Er forschet nur nach unserm leben /*
> *Und ob wir was er hies gethan:*
> *Er will zwar weisheit mit vielen kronen:*
> *Doch nur wenn sie ihm dient belohnen.*

An age that sees everything *sub specie aeternitatis* is bound to regard all science as vanity. And yet the seventeenth century was a great scientific age. This is one of its fundamental tensions and it is a tension clearly reflected in Gryphius. The difference in this respect between the age of the Baroque and the Middle Ages, which also saw the world from the standpoint of the eternal, is by no means as great as we might assume. The Middle Ages also gave much attention to things (*res*) and was intent upon discovering their properties. Indeed, there was a positive reverence for things (Spee's poetry is in this tradition), but not for the sake of the things themselves. The medieval bestiaries, lapidaries, and all kinds of handbooks dealing with things had a religious rather than a scientific basis. Things were to be read, they were the letters in God's book: *non solum voces, sed et res significativae sunt* (not only words but also things have meaning—Richard of St. Victor). Meaning, of course, meant *spiritual* meaning—there was no other kind. Furthermore, every separate thing had as many meanings at it had properties.[6] It was therefore important to discover the latter. The Middle Ages may have gone about this in a way that seems to us ludicrously childish, but not the seventeenth century, the age when modern science begins. And yet the science of the Baroque is intent upon the same pursuit as the "science" of the Middle Ages. Religion is its mother (and consequently the mother of modern science, though she may now have been disowned). The seventeenth century was still trying to read God's book. The *tension* that we feel in the Baroque between the eternal and the temporal, between the world of things and the world they signify, is the new nonmedieval element—it is typically baroque. To fully explain its causes would demand much more erudition than the present writer can command, but certainly the intervention of humanism between the Middle Ages and the seventeenth century played a role. There was a turning to the earthly and the pagan, a turning away from the heavenly and the Christian (Rabelais and Montaigne are two great examples). It may also be significant that Luther, in his interpretation of the Bible, hesitates to go beyond the word to the thing —it is one of his most unmedieval traits. The Baroque, however, is in this respect both antihumanistic and un-Lutheran; it returns to the interpretation of things and creates a poetry based on emblemism, i.e. a poetry that interprets all things metaphorically, or better, tropologically, in terms of the moral sense. But the tension between the flesh and the spirit remains. A complete return to the medieval harmony was not possible. The Baroque is an age of precarious balance, of extreme tensions, as is particularly evident in the plastic arts. The rights of the flesh had asserted themselves in Renaissance humanism at the expense of the spirit and they still demanded a voice. This gave rise to that dichotomy so typical of many

97

baroque poets: *carpe diem, carpe florem* on the one hand and *carpe coelum* on the other. (This dichotomy is as good as absent in the poetry of Ronsard, "the great Pan" of the Renaissance.) In Gryphius the spirit is definitely the victor still, but only at the cost of the harshest measures taken against the flesh, even against life itself. It is not for nothing that he does not sing of erotic love and reduces nature herself to a shadow.

We find a striking example of this tension between science and religion in a contemporary engraving of the anatomy theater in Leiden, constructed in 1616, probably the very room in which Gryphius himself pursued his anatomical studies and held his demonstrations. The engraving shows the usual sunken dissecting table with a corpse spread-eagled upon it and rising tiers of benches for the spectators. Posed upon the railings enclosing each tier of benches and intermingled with the elegantly dressed living onlookers are a number of skeletons, both human and animal. The former hold banners with such inscriptions as "Nosce te ipsum" (know thyself), "Pulvis et umbra sumus" (we are dust and shadow), "Nascentes morimur" (being born we die), etc. The figure of Death himself mounted on the skeleton of a horse and holding a great hammer overlooks the whole scene.[7] The baroque preoccupation with man's state as living death and the consequent fruitlessness of science could hardly be more clearly presented. But the conviction of the vanity of all knowledge did not preclude the search for it; as we have tried to show, it was, in paradoxical way, the reason for the search.

Gryphius' most excessive expression of the view of life as living death is found in his notorious—one hesitates to say famous—"Kirchhofsgedanken" (1657), a poem of fifty eight-line stanzas in four-beat iambics rhyming ababcddc, a variant of ottava rima, the chief narrative stanza of the Renaissance. The fictional situation is a visit (one thinks of it as nocturnal, but this is not indicated by the text) to a graveyard as to a "school in which we mortals are taught the highest art." The narrator comes to the school of death to learn the secret of life. The graveyard is the *res*, what is its *significatio*? This can be ascertained only by discovering its properties. The disposition of the poem is as follows:

Stanzas 1–8: Introductory—depiction of situation, graveyard as a "garden" in which the seed planted by God has not yet come up and as a grim "school" in which the narrator is to learn not the wisdom of the ancients (Socrates and Aristotle) but "wahre Weisheit"; the question is how?

9–33: The earth trembles, the graves open and reveal their horrifyingly repulsive contents—the "properties" of the tomb are discovered.

34–37: Transitional passage—speculations on narrator's own death and place of burial; it is of little moment where one lies, for the Judgment Day is not far.

38–47: Vision of the Last Judgment.

48–50: The moral: *Gedenke zu sterben, weil du noch kannst, damit du ewig lebst.*

If anything was for Gryphius "der Weissheit letzter Schluss," it was probably this. The theme had of course been treated before, notably by Gryphius' contemporary, the neo-Latin Jesuit poet Jacob Balde (1604–68), translations of two of whose "ecstasies in a graveyard" Gryphius appends to the "Kirchhofgedanken," thus emphasizing his indebtedness, a typical seventeenth-century gesture. Truth, not originality, is the aim. And the truth is known—it has been revealed to us —the striving is to present it in the most impressive form. Gryphius employs his favorite stylistic devices extravagantly: anaphora, rhetorical questions, exclamations, antitheses abound. As a homily in narrative form, the poem suffers from the anticlimactic nature of the final insight. We have known all along where the poet was heading. The mountain has labored and borne a mouse. It would, however, be hard to surpass the horror of the vision of the opened graves in the middle part of the poem. Not even the visions of the Expressionist Georg Heym, of Gottfried Benn in his "morgue" poetry, or the nauseous dishes William S. Burroughs sets before us in *Naked Lunch* much exceed those of Gryphius for gripping repulsiveness and none of them can arouse the same sense of metaphysical terror that is a function of belief. An example (*Werke* III, 13):

> *Der Därmer Wust reisst durch die Haut /*
> *So von den Maden gantz durchbissen;*
> *Ich schau die Därmer (ach mir graut!)*
> *In Eiter / Blutt und Wasser fliessen!*
> *Das Fleisch / das nicht die Zeit verletzt /*
> *Wird unter Schlangen-blauen Schimmel*
> *Von unersättlichem Gewimmel*
> *Vielfalter Würmer abgefretzt.*

The vision of the Last Judgment in the latter part of the poem has something approaching the Dantesque about it (III, 17):

> *Ich werd euch [die Erlösten] sehn / mehr denn das Licht*
> *Von zehnmal tausend Sonnen schimmern;*
> *Ich werd euch [die Verdammten] sehn / und mein*
>    *Gesicht*
> *Verbergen vor dem Jammer-wimmern.*
> *Ich werd euch sehn / mehr schön als schön /*
> *Euch mehr denn hässlich und elende!*
> *Euch zu dem Trost; euch in die Brände*
> *Gespenster-schwerer Nächte gehn.*

The underlying metaphor of the whole poem, let us stress once more, is life as death; we are the dying, if not the dead: "nascentes morimur." Decay is a metaphor for our fallen state; the graves open and reveal what we are as temporal beings (Stanza 34):

100

*Ach Todten! ach was lern ich hier!*
*Was bin ich / und was werd ich werden!*
*Was fühl und trag ich doch an mir*
*Als leichten Staub und wenig Erden.*

This devaluation of life as life is the dead hand that weighs on all of Gryphius' poetry.

As a work of art, one of Gryphius' most successful formulations of his constant theme is the poem called "Verleugnung der Welt" in the second book of odes. Its form is that of a sestina minus the envoy. The sestina is a complicated verse form of Provençal origin consisting of six stanzas of six lines each plus a three line envoy. It came into German via the Pléiade. The sestina is rhymeless, the function of rhyme being taken over by a recurrent pattern of end-words in a constantly shifting but fixed order. If we let the letters *A* through *F* stand for the end-words, the following scheme (disregarding the envoy) emerges: stanza 1: *ABCDEF*; 2: *FAEBDC*; 3: *CFDABE*; 4: *ECBFAD*; 5: *DEACFB*; 6: *BDFECA*. It will be noted that the end-word of the last line of each stanza is the same as the end-word of the first line of the next and that there is one end-word (*A*) which never occurs in conjunction with itself (also not in the envoy). It is this feature of the sestina that Gryphius (like Petrarch before him—see, e.g., *Canzoniere*, no. 30) exploits in a genial fashion in "Verleugnung der Welt" (*Werke*, II, 40 f.):

1) *Was frag ich nach der welt! sie wird in flammen stehn:*
   *Was acht ich reiche pracht: der Todt reisst alles hin!*
   *Was hilfft die wissenschaft / der mehr als falsche dunst?*
   *Der Liebe Zauberwerck ist tolle Phantasie:*
   *Die wollust ist fürwar nichts alss ein schneller Traum;*
   *Die Schönheit ist wie Schnee / diss Leben ist der Todt!*

2) *Diss alles stinckt mich an / drumb wündsch ich mir den*
   *Todt!*

101

*Weil nichts wie schön und starck / wie reich es sey / kan stehn*
*Oft / eh man leben wil / ist schon diss Leben hin.*
*Wer Schätz' und Reichtumb sucht: was sucht er mehr alss dunst.*
*Wenn dem / der Ehrenrauch entsteckt die Phantasie /*
*So traumt ihm wenn er wacht / er wacht und sorgt im traum.*

3 ) *Auff meine Seel / auf! auf! entwach aus diesem traum /*
*Verwirff was irrdisch ist / und trotze Noth und Todt!*
*Was wird dir / wenn du wirst für jenem throne stehn /*
*Die welt behülfflich seyn? wo dencken wir doch hin?*
*Was blendet den verstandt? soll dieser leichte dunst*
*Bezaubern mein gemüth mit solcher Phantasie?*

4 ) *Biss her! und weiter nicht! verfluchte Phantasie!*
*Nichts werthes Gauckelwerck. Verblendung-voller traum /*
*Du schmertzen-reiche Lust! du folter-hartter Todt!*
*Ade! ich wil nunmehr auf freyen Füssen stehn*
*Und tretten was mich tratt! Ich eyle schon dahin;*
*Wo nichts als warheit ist. Kein bald verschwindent dunst.*

5 ) *Treib ewig helles Licht der dicken Nebel dunst*
*Die blinde Lust der welt: die tolle Phantasie*
*Die flüchtige begierd' und dieser gütter traum*
*Hinweg und lehre mich recht sterben vor dem Todt.*
*Lass mich die eitelkeit der Erden recht verstehn*
*Entbinde mein gemüth / und nimb die Ketten hin.*

6 ) *Nimb was mich und die welt verkuppelt! nimb doch hin*
*Der Sünden schwere Last: lass ferner keinen dunst*
*Verhüllen mein Gemütt / und alle Phantasie*
*Der Eitel-leeren welt sey für mich alss ein traum /*
*Von dem ich nun erwacht! und lass nach diesem tod*
*Wenn hin / Dunst / Phantasie / Traum / Tod mich ewig stehn.*[8]

102

We of course recognize at once that the end-words *hin, Dunst, Phantasie, Traum, Tod* characterize the phenomenal, the fallen world of time, while *stehn*, an expression of longing for stability, for cessation of time and change, characterizes the noumenal. Only end-words with a negative valence occur in conjunction, thus emphasizing the utter nothingness of the worldly. Life as a dream, a favorite image of the whole baroque age (*la vida es sueño*) and an especially significant expression of the ontological lack of substance of this life, occurs frequently in Gryphius (*Werke* II, 83):

*Diss Lebenlose Leben*
*Fällt / als ein Traum entweicht /*
*Wenn sich die Nacht begeben*
*Und nun der Mond erbleicht!*

Name, praise, honor, and fame disappear "Gleich wie ein eitel Traum leicht aus der Acht hinfällt" (*Werke* I, 35), etc., etc. *Dunst, Phantasie, Tod* (*hin* is more or less neutral) have here approximately the same significance as *Traum*.

The movement of the poem is (1) growing insight into the dream-like insubstantiality of wordly values (Stanzas 1–2), followed by (2) an admonition to the self to reject these values and the resolve to do so (Stanzas 3–4), which is then reinforced (3) by a prayer for divine aid in carrying out this resolution (Stanzas 5–6). Man cannot save himself. The dialectic that works itself out stanza by stanza places a large burden on the concept of *stehn* and symbolizes the precariousness of man's position in this world of shifting transitoriness. *Stehn* constantly assumes an ever more positive (i.e. an ever more metaphysical) value as the other end-words are given an ever more negative connotation.

Stanza 1) "[Die Welt] wird in Flammen stehn"—statement of insight into negative value of the worldly.

2) "Nichts . . . kann stehn."

3) "Was wird dir [die Welt helfen] wenn du wirst für

jenem [Gottes] Throne stehn"— in a question, *stehn* begins
to assume transcendental valence.

4) "Auf freyen Füssen stehn"—moral decision: necessary first step that the soul may "*be*stehn" before God.

5) "Die Eitelkeit der Erden recht *ver*stehn"—in prayer
for internalization of insight attained.

6) "Ewig stehn"—in prayer: the transformation is complete, the vision of permanency won, though only in hope.

Gryphius is far too convinced a Lutheran to ever go
further than the *hope* of salvation. Man's state is by definition
sinful, and his sin not taken away except in hope, so that the
most he can be is *simul peccator ac iustus*, at once a sinner
and righteous. We will find in Gryphius no heavenly ecstasies,
he remains true to his youthful prophecy:

*Ich will die Saiten rühren /*
*Und Augen-klar die Angst der herben Welt ausführen.*
*Mehr schlägt mir Phoebus ab. . . .*

"Verleugnung der Welt," by substituting in the final
verse the summation scheme for the three-line envoy of the
standard sestina, calls attention to its hexadic form. This insistence on "sixness" is underlined by the use of the hexameter
with its six beats per line. Everything here is sixes. It is
very likely that this is meant symbolically. Marian Szyrocki
has shown that Gryphius' first sonnet cycle (the so-called
"Lissaer Sonette") is structured on the hexadic principle.[9]
He argues, not unconvincingly, that six symbolizes the
"Vergänglichkeitsgedanken." This sestina provides a supporting argument, for that six here has a negative valence
is hardly disputable: 666 is of course "the number of the
beast" according to Rev. 13, 18, but in our context it is
undoubtedly more important that the world was created in
six days (and man on the sixth!)—six is the number of creation, of the world of time, of *Dunst, Phantasie, Traum* and
*Tod*, where there is no stability, where man finds it so hard

to *stand*. The only true *Stehen* is before God, "ewig stehn." By exploiting the structure of the sestina and making *stehn* the only end-word not to occur in self-conjunction, thus not "cancelling itself out," Gryphius points to its metaphysical value.

Gryphius' present reputation rests almost entirely upon his sonnets. Most of them he wrote during his earlier years, or, as one can perhaps more accurately say, most of them he *began* to write then, for he never regarded them as finished but continued to file and polish with each successive edition. His first collection of 31 sonnets appeared in 1637 (in Polish-Lissa, as we have noted) before he went to Holland. In the prefatory dedicatory verses he promises: "Ich will in kurtzem mich noch gar viel höher schwingen," which is probably a reference to the 100 "Sonn- und Feiertagssonette" on which he was then working and which were published two years later in Leiden. In 1643, also in Leiden, he published the fifty poems contained in "Sonnete: Das erste Buch," which incorporates twenty-nine of the Lissa sonnets in revised form. In 1650, this time in Frankfurt a.M., a collection containing these fifty sonnets (revised) plus a second book of fifty new sonnets appeared. Finally, in 1657, a complete and carefully printed edition of his collected sonnets was published in Breslau. This volume contains 100 secular poems, i.e., sonnets Books I & II, and 100 sacred poems, i.e., the Sonn- und Feiertagssonette, which are likewise divided into two books, one with sixty-four, the other with thirty-six poems. In 1663, shortly before the poet's death, still another edition with still further revisions was brought out.[10] It is above all of these poems that we think when we think of Gryphius. Among them are some of the noblest poetical achievements of the Baroque.

It is interesting and instructive to see with what care and to what effect Gryphius revised his poetry. The editor of the critical edition of Gryphius' lyrics holds that the earlier or earliest versions of the sonnets are better, as being fresher, less artificial, stylistically more unified and making a more original impression.[11] This view has been strongly and successfully challenged by Günther Weydt.[12] It may be worth our while to take a page from Weydt and attempt a comparative analysis of an earlier and a later version of one of the sonnets. The famous poem now known as "Thränen des Vaterlandes / Anno 1636" was called in the Lissa sonnets of 1637 (*Werke*, I, 19):

## TRAWRKLAGE DES VERWÜSTETEN DEUTSCHLANDES

*Wir sind doch nunmehr gantz / ja mehr alss gantz vertorben.*

*Der frechen Völcker Schar / die rasende Posaun /*
*Das vom Blutt feiste Schwert / die donnernde Carthaun /*
*Hat alles diss hinweg / was mancher sawr erworben /*

*Die alte Redligkeit und Tugend ist gestorben;*
*Die Kirchen sind verheert / die Starcken umbgehawen /*
*Die Jungfrawn sind geschändt; und wo wir hin nur schawen /*
*Ist Fewr / Pest / Mord und Todt / hier zwischen Schantz und Korben*

*Dort zwischen Mawr und Stadt / rinnt allzeit frisches Blutt*
*Dreymal sind schon sechs Jahr als unser Ströme Flutt*
*Von so viel Leichen schwer / sich langsam fortgedrungen.*

*Ich schweige noch von dem / was stärcker als der Todt /*
*(Du Strassburg weisst es wol) der grimmen Hungersnoth ,*
*Und dass der Seelen-Schatz gar vielen abgezwungen.*

106

The version of 1663 (*Werke*, I, 48) reads:

*THRENEN DES VATTERLANDES / ANNO 1636*

*Wir sind doch nunmehr gantz / ja mehr denn gantz
    verheeret!*
*Der frechen völcker schar / die rasende posaun*
*Das vom blut fette schwerdt / die donnernde
    Carthaun*
*Hat aller schweis / und fleis und vorraht auff gezehret.*

*Die türme stehn in glutt / die Kirch ist umgekehret.*
*Das Rahthaus liegt im graus / die starcken sind
    zerhawn.*
*Die Jungfern sindt geschändt / und wo wir hin nur
    schawn*
*Ist fewer / pest und todt der hertz und geist durchfehret.*

*Hier durch die schantz und Stadt / rinnt allzeit
    frisches blutt.*
*Dreymal sindt schon sechs jahr als unser ströme flutt*
*Von Leichen fast verstopfft / sich langsam
    fortgedrungen.*

*Doch schweig ich noch von dem was ärger als der todt.*
*Was grimmer denn die pest / und glutt und hungers
    noth*
*Dass auch der Seelen schatz / so vielen abgezwungen.*

(Explanation of unusual terms: "Trawrklage": *Völcker*, Soldaten; *Carthaun*, a kind of howitzer; *verheert*, durch Heere
zerstört; *zwischen Schantz und Korben*, between the earth-
work defenses and the reinforcing rolls of wickerwork; Protestant *Strassburg* was neutral during the Thirty Years War
—here an example of those who have lost their *Seelen-Schatz.*
"Threnen": *graus*, Schutt.)

Obviously many changes have been made in the course
of successive revisions. Does the final version still "say" the

same thing as the first? Is it the same poem? It is Weydt's thesis that each revision comes nearer to giving convincing expression to the underlying theme and that it does so by becoming ever more artful, i.e. in a sense, ever more artificial. "Stylistic unity and poetic originality" are not, as Szyrocki claims, lost through repeated revision, rather they are the result of it.

The theme is for the baroque poet what the "experience" is for the romantic. The former strives to particularize a general truth emblematically, the latter to show forth a general truth in the particular symbolically. What is the basic theme that Gryphius here seeks to particularize through this concatenation of apocalyptic images? Undoubtedly it is war as an image of man's fallen state, this world, which, in Pascal's words, God only lets subsist as a test of faith. That Gryphius means his poem to be so interpreted is shown by the final tercet. Those whom war has forced to give up their "Seelen-Schatz" are those who have not stood the test. The tone of the sonnet may betray sympathy with those who have failed under such extreme circumstances, but it does not condone them. If this is indeed the basic theme, then our question must be whether it is more forcefully and artistically formulated in the first version or the last.

We can point out only a few significant details of the revision. Let us look at the rhyme in the first version: *vertorben* [verdorben], *erworben*, *gestorben*, *Korben*; versus that in the final one: *verheeret*, *auff gezehret*, *umgekehret*, *durchfehret* [durchfährt]. It is immediately apparent that the rhyme in the later version is unified by the same idea, that of destruction, whereas in the earlier version *erworben* intrudes itself between *vertorben* and *gestorben*, weakening the idea of *Verderben*, while *Korben* is merely for the sake of the rhyme and in itself meaningless. Furthermore, and even more importantly, *vertorben-gestorben*, especially the line, "Die alte Redligkeit und Tugend ist *gestorben*," anticipates in a

108

disturbing way the idea to be brought out in the final tercet as the "Sinngebung des Ganzen" (Erich Trunz). The point of the sonnet is given away beforehand—for the baroque art of sonnet-making a sad failing. Like so many baroque sonnets, this one is built on the emblematic principle of *imago* plus *significatio*. In the final version all is *imago* up to the final tercet, which then states the *significatio*, whereas in the first version the two are (con)fused already in the octave. One can probably assume that it was the insight into the not yet fulfilled emblematic structure that brought the revisions in its wake.

The final tercet, in terms of emblemism, the *significatio*, the moral sense, is much more skillfully, clearly, and powerfully phrased in the later than the earlier version:

> *Ich schweige noch von dem was* stärcker *als der Todt*
> *(Du Strassburg weisst es wol) der grimmen*
> Hungersnoth
> *Und dass der Seelen-Schatz gar vielen abgezwungen.*

(I still have said nothing about that which is *stronger* than death / [You Strassburg know it well!] nothing about the grim hunger / And that in submitting to force so many have lost their inmost treasure.)

> Doch *schweig ich noch von dem was* ärger *als der todt.*
> *Was* grimmer *denn die pest und glutt und hungers noth*
> *Dass auch der Seelen schatz so vielen abgezwungen.*

(*And yet* I have still said nothing about that which is *worse* than death, / *more grim* than pestilence, fire and starvation, / (namely) that in submitting to force so many have lost their inmost treasure.) In the first version, the sense, though we can penetrate it, is illogically put; later it comes through with all clarity. Furthermore, by deleting the reference to Strassburg, the poet is able to bring in an abbreviated "summation" of the images of first eleven lines: *Pest, Glut, Hun-*

*gersnot* are a kind of shorthand recalling what has gone before. All that tests faith is present at once.

We have compared Gryphius with himself. Perhaps even more revealing is a comparison of Gryphius' kind of poetry with another and one aesthetic with another. Following Manfred Windfuhr in his instructive book, *Die barocke Bildlichkeit und ihre Kritiker* (Stuttgart, 1966, pp. 84 ff.), we will attempt a comparison between one of Gryphius' numerous poems using the metaphor of life as a sea voyage and Goethe's "Seefahrt." Gryphius' sonnet (*Werke* I, 61 f.):

### AN DIE WELT

*Mein offt bestürmtes Schiff / der grimmen winde spiel /*
*Der frechen wellen ball / das schier die flutt getrennet /*
*Das über klipp auff klipp / und schaum / und sand*
*gerennet;*
   *Kommt vor der zeit an port / den meine Seele will.*

*Offt wenn uns schwartze nacht im mittag überfiel:*
*Hat der geschwinde plitz die Seegel schier verbrennet!*
*Wie offt hab ich den Windt / und Nord und Sud*
*verkennet!*
   *Wie schadthafft ist der Mast / Steur-ruder /*
   *Schwerdt[13] und Kiel.*

*Steig aus du müder Geist! steig aus! wir sind am Lande!*
*Was graut dir für dem port / itzt wirstu aller bande*
   *Und angst / und herber pein / und schwerer*
   *schmertzen los.*

*Ade / verfluchte welt: du see voll rauer stürme:*
*Glück zu mein vaterland / das stätte ruh im schirme*
   *Und schutz und frieden hält / du ewigliches schlos.*

Goethe also uses the metaphor of the sea voyage frequently. His poem:

110

## SEEFAHRT

*1 ) Lange Tag' und Nächte stand mein Schiff befrachtet;*
*Günst' ger Winde harrend, sass mit treuen Freunden,*
*Mir Geduld und guten Mut erzechend,*
*Ich im Hafen.*

*2 ) Und sie waren doppelt ungeduldig:*
*Gerne gönnen wir die schnellste Reise,*
*Gern die hohe Fahrt dir; Güterfülle*
*Wartet drüben in den Welten deiner,*
*Wird Rückkehrendem in unsern Armen*
*Lieb' und Preis dir.*

*3 ) Und am frühen Morgen ward's Getümmel,*
*Und dem Schlaf entjauchzt uns der Matrose,*
*Alles wimmelt, alles lebet, webet,*
*Mit dem ersten Segenshauch zu schiffen.*

*4 ) Und die Segel blühen in dem Hauche,*
*Und die Sonne lockt mit Feuerliebe;*
*Ziehn die Segel, ziehn die hohen Wolken,*
*Jauchzen an dem Ufer alle Freunde*
*Hoffnungslieder nach, im Freudentaumel*
*Reisefreuden wähnend, wie des Einschiffsmorgens,*
*Wie der ersten hohen Sternennächte.*

*5 ) Aber gottgesandte Wechselwinde treiben*
*Seitwärts ihn der vorgesteckten Fahrt ab,*
*Und er scheint sich ihnen hinzugeben,*
*Strebet leise sie zu überlisten,*
*Treu dem Zweck auch auf dem schiefen Wege.*

*6 ) Aber aus der dumpfen grauen Ferne*
*Kündet leisewandelnd sich der Sturm an,*
*Drückt die Vögel nieder auf's Gewässer,*
*Drückt der Menschen schwellend Herz darnieder,*

Und er kommt. Vor seinem starren Wüten
Streckt der Schiffer weis' die Segel nieder,
Mit dem angsterfüllten Balle spielen
Wind und Wellen.

7) Und an jenem Ufer drüben stehen
Freund' und Lieben, beben auf dem Festen:
Ach, warum ist er nicht hier geblieben!
Ach, der Sturm! Verschlagen weg vom Glücke!
Soll der Gute so zu Grunde gehen?
Ach, er sollte, ach, er könnte! Götter!

8) Doch er stehet männlich an dem Steuer;
Mit dem Schiffe spielen Wind und Wellen;
Wind und Wellen nicht mit seinem Herzen:
Herrschend blickt er auf die grimme Tiefe,
Und vertrauet, scheiternd oder landend,
Seinen Göttern.

Both of these poems are *allegorical* in the baroque understanding of allegory as extended metaphor. Gryphius' is of course pronouncedly so; Goethe's teases us with an allegorical form while withholding the key to the meaning, thus inviting interpretation at many levels. We may be inclined to call Goethe's poem symbolical rather than allegorical, but as Windfuhr correctly points out (pp. 83 f.), the boundary between allegory and symbol is much less distinct than we —especially German critics—are usually willing to admit. Windfuhr's own formulation of the basic difference between the two is summarized in his statement (p. 89) to the effect that allegory *points out* (ausdeutet) the relationship between metaphor and theme, while symbolism only *hints* (andeutet) at it.

Already in the title of his sonnet, Gryphius keys us in on the meaning of the imagery, while Goethe leaves us to surmise: "An die Welt" immediately tells us what to look for; "Seefahrt" is neutral, it could stand for many things or simply be purely descriptive. We see at once that in Gryphius the stormy sea equals the world, the ship the body, the port death, the land the beyond or heaven. A number of details, it is true, are left without specific equivalencies. We cannot say exactly what, or if anything in particular, is pointed to by mast, rudder, keel and "Schwert." Very likely they are merely makeweights meant to give verisimilitude. Gryphius offers a summary in an easily decipherable metaphorical shorthand of the meaning of temporality—as always, a trial of strength and faith. We can hardly mistake the meaning nor be confused about the chief equivalencies.

Goethe's poem is a very different matter. What, first of all, *is* the basic theme for which the sea voyage is a metaphor? For that it must be meant metaphorically there can be no real doubt; to interpret it purely as an empirical description of putting out to sea would be to overlook a number of hints that face us in other directions. The most important of these is the remarkable way the voyage itself is framed by the friends on shore, like spectators in a grandstand watching some kind of contest. The last line of Stanza 5 also seems to call attention to some metaphorical meaning: "Treu dem Zweck auch auf dem schiefen Wege." And striking is the way the "I" seems to combine within itself the roles of merchant, skipper, steersman. Yet these references are so general that one hesitates to tie them down to a specific interpretation. From Goethe's biography we know that "Seefahrt" was written shortly after his entry into the new life at the court of Weimar (1776), the great caesura of his early years and for him the beginning of a new epoch. The persons on shore could be his old Frankfurt friends anxiously following his new career, the storm the unexpected difficulties the poet had to face in a very different environment, and so on. The trouble with interpretations of this kind, even when subtly and expertly worked out, is, first, that the points of reference stand *outside* the poem, and, second, that they trivialize the poem as such. In concerning ourselves with such things we are talking about Goethe's life, not his art.

Nonetheless, who can doubt that the poet has here taken a specific experience from his own life and objectified it metaphorically? His method, however, is approximately the opposite of that of the baroque poet. Instead of particularizing the general, he generalizes the particular, raising the autobiographical to the level of the paradigmatic, yet without robbing it of its vital particularity. "Seefahrt" can be read not only biographically but also as a poem about the nature of decision, as a parable of the entry into manhood, as a paradigm illustrating the beginning of every new venture of momentous import. Gryphius' sonnet, on the other hand, though the subject is his own life, does not admit of any strictly biographical interpretation. All particulars are mediate, i.e. applied to generals, and though his life too becomes life pure and simple, it at the same time ceases to be *his* life. It can be read only allegorically.

Windfuhr points out that Goethe's poem tells a story, it presents a *moment* of life and we delight in its details. Gryphius tells no story: his poem is a concentrated résumé of the meaning of life. Life itself in his hands is reduced to signs and emblems that jerk like amputated froglegs under the application of the electrodes of his pathos-laden rhetoric—but in effect dead, mere seeming. We will look in vain in Gryphius for such images as that of the sails "blooming" in the breath of the morning breeze, of the sun tempting with its fiery love ("Seefahrt," Stanza 4)—these things are possible only in poetry that sees life as an end in itself. This was not the view of the Baroque.

As the book by Dietrich Walter Jöns, *Das "Sinnen-Bild": Studien zur allegorischen Bildlichkeit bei A. G.* (Stuttgart, 1966) shows beyond any reasonable doubt, the fundament of Gryphius' symbolism, i.e., his allegorical view of nature, is derived from a theological rather than a poetic

114

tradition. In the Baroque, poetry takes over the medieval theological-allegorical interpretation of nature as a *mundus symbolicus* and erects on the basis of this world an interpretive superstructure of parabolic poetry. *Mundus symbolicus— poesis parabolica* is Jöns's apt formulation (p. 83). We have had occasion to refer to this method a number of times. Gryphius, along with Spee, is a paradigmatic example and Greiffenberg is not basically different. The striking difference in *attitude* toward nature between Gryphius on the one hand and Spee and Greiffenberg on the other is due perhaps above all to the fact that the latter love the world because it is God's, while Gryphius despises it for the sake of the godly. For him it is a snare of Satan, for them a revelation of the divine. This is, among other reasons, because Gryphius primarily sees the world in the light of power, politics, fame, they as nature. When Gryphius uses nature symbolism, as he does occasionally, he tends to reduce it to a system of schematic signs that have a peculiar unreality and lack of density, the precise counterpart of his view of this life as an uncannily transient proving ground of the spirit. We cannot conceive of Gryphius writing a line betraying such love of creation as Greiffenberg's about the sweetness of God in the fruits of this earth: "Sein' Süssheit sich zu Mund will aus den Früchten schwingen . . ." The mystery of the Incarnation, so central to both Spee and Greiffenberg, reveals to them God in the world and leads to love of it for His sake, but Gryphius, for all his poems on the birth of the Saviour, primarily interprets this world not as an incarnation of the divine but as a passing shadow, the night of time and sin. The deeper meaning of the Saviour's birth seems closed to him.

Though it has long been recognized, or at least suspected, that Gryphius arranged his books of sonnets in some kind of cyclic order, the compositional principle of the two books of secular sonnets (i.e., Books I and II) has not yet been demonstrated.[14] It cannot be our task here to go into this fascinating

115

question in detail, but close inspection would seem to show that, though it may not be possible to find a neat underlying scheme, some cyclic principle is indeed present. The mere fact that Books I and II contain fifty sonnets each, bringing the total to the "perfect" number of one hundred, is significant and seems to ask us to look for an underlying principle. Certainly, it is not hard to show that there are definite subcycles within the larger framework and that these subcycles complement and comment each other. Let us look at Book II from this standpoint.[15]

1–4: Times of day as states of the soul: (1) morning—hope (dawn of the light of God's grace); (2) midday—fear (of the light of God's justice); (3) evening—hope (of eternal salvation, symbol of the stars); (4) midnight—fear (night of vanity and sin, fear of dawn of Judgment Day). (Taken as a whole, this cycle reflects man's perilous state in the world of time.)

7–13: Servitude vs. freedom: (7) acceptance of servitude—example of the Saviour; (8) acceptance of the bonds of marriage as freedom from love's servitude; (9) faith's constancy brings freedom from the world's tyranny—ironic example of the martyrs; (10) epitaph on the Temple of Mortality—error binds man as long as life lasts; (11) to Dicaeus in prison—life as a prison, only identification with the transcendent can free us; (12) moral constancy can overcome the world's inconstancy and make us free; (13) freedom is most surely gained by rejection of servitude to the world's vanity, in order that we may freely honor God (the word "frei" occurs in this sonnet eight times).

17–20: Time and change conquered by friendship and love.

26–28, 29–32, 33–38: Three sub-cycles mutually illuminating each other: (26–28) "Dominus de me cogitat"—poems of praise and gratitude for God's mercy in liberation from "Angst"; the note of hope seems justified by (29–32) wedding poems celebrating the renewal of life, but ironically followed (33–38) by five epitaphs on the demise of persons of various ages and conditions (from the queen of Byzantium to a child) plus a sixth poem on the five foregoing ones on the vanity of all epitaphs.

39–42: Rome (one of the most interesting sub-cycles): (39–40) on two persons, who, though living in Rome, are blind to its glories and deaf to its learning—*Rome invisible*; (41) the poet's farewell to the Eternal City; its meaning for him: height of this world's glory—*Rome visible*; (42) the catacombs beneath Rome: foundation of the New Rome, the Church of God and the true Eternal City—*Rome invisible*.

46–49: On the Last Things: (46) death as door to Last Judgment; (47) Last Judgment; (48) Hell—death without dying; (49) Heaven—life without death.

In Sonnets 46–49, the alternation between hope and fear, the theme of the four opening sonnets, is resolved in the light of eternity. But alternation between hope and fear is not only the theme of the opening poems, it is the ground theme of the whole cycle: "Wenn David Lob will singen / . . . Zuckt Saul den schnellen Spiess." "Die Angst der herben Welt" is the theme of Gryphius' poetry as a whole but especially of his two cycles of secular sonnets, which reflect the dubious battle between the powers of light and darkness for the trembling soul of man.

But the cycle does not end with the 49th sonnet. The 50th is on the "man of fire," the prophet Elijah (*Werke* I, 92):

### ELIAS

*Der Flammen aus der Brust der Mutter hat gezogen;*
*Der von der heilgen Flam des eifers heiss entbrandt /*
*Der Fürsten Grimm verlacht / und dem verführten*
*Land*
*Durch flammen hat entdeckt / wie Kron und Haus*
*betrogen:**

*Der Mann / auff dessen wortt die flammen abgeflogen*
  *Durch die erhitzte Lufft / und die der König sandt*
  *Mit schneller glutt verzehrt,† ist / als ihn* GOTT
    *entbandt /*
*Auch in dem Fewr'gen Sturm aus dieser welt gezogen.‡*

  *Er fehrt / doch unversehrt / kein fewrig Ross und*
    *Wagen*
  *Letzt den / der Fewr im Mund und Hertzen pflag zu*
    *tragen*
*Mit dem Er Hertzen mehr denn marmorhart zusprengt /*

*Der gantz von Fewr war / muss mit dem Fewr*
    *hinscheiden:*
*Fragt ihr warum sein kleidt nichts kan von flammen*
    *leiden:*
  *Mich wundert / dass es nicht / weil er es trug /*
    *versengt.*
  [*Cf. 1 Kings 18, 23 ff. †Cf. 2 Kings 1, 9 ff. ‡Cf. 2 Kings
  2, 11–12.]

The position of this sonnet as the copestone of the cycle lends
it unusual importance. It is interesting to compare it with the
final sonnet of Book I, "Über seines Herrn Bruders P. Gryphii
Grab." Book I contains four sonnets (nos. 15, 17, 37, 50) on
Gryphius' half-brother Paul, a courageous Lutheran pastor
who suffered much from religious persecution and who was
probably the person whom the poet admired most and loved
best. Is there a connection between the seventeenth-century
Lutheran pastor and the Old Testament prophet? The answer is obviously, yes. It lies above all in their fearlessness
and their burning zeal for the Lord's cause. Of Paul Gryphius
we read in I, no. 15, that he was one

*Der eifers voll von Gott hat tag und nacht gelehret /*
  *Den Christus Lieb entzündt / den Gottes Geist*
    *regirt . . .*

118

and that, like Elijah, he was not to be intimidated: "Der keiner feinde glimpf noch schnauben je gehöret . . ." In I, no. 50, it is again said of him that he was inflamed by the holy spirit— "den Gottes Geist entzündt." His eloquence, the sign of his divine inspiration, is called almost incomparable: "des beredsamkeit kaum einer wird erreichen." Paul Gryphius and Elijah quite obviously represent two aspects of the realization of an ideal dear to the poet. Both are types of religious heroism, "men of fire," fire being here a metaphor for divine possession.[16] (In a prayer to the Holy Ghost, the poet cries: "O Flamme / die wir Gott und lebend-machend nennen / O komm und zünd in mir dein schütternd Feuer an!"—*Werke* I, 99.) Fire appears in the Lutheran pastor in his eloquent preaching (he is divinely "inflamed"), in the prophet in the physical fire of God's wrath with which he destroys his enemies and in which God reveals himself to him at crucial stages of his career.

In regard to the position of the Elijah sonnet within the cycle, it is not improbable that the number fifty, which plays such a prominent part in the prophet's story (1 Kings 18, 13; 2 Kings 1, 2 ff.), is significant, though it is hard to say precisely what connection the poet may be implying between his fifties (two times fifty sonnets) and those in the Bible. Perfectly evident, on the other hand, is the connection between Elijah as the type of the divine herald who comes before the final judgment to warn the people to turn from their evil ways (Malachi 4, 5) and Gryphius' sonnets, which seek to awaken us to our sinful state and to turn our hearts to the eternal before it is too late (I, p. 67):

*Sterbliche! Sterbliche! lasset diss dichten! Morgen! ach!*
*morgen ach! muss man hin zihn!*

The poet identifies himself with the great prophet in his role of herald and warner. He too would "burst hearts harder than marble." There can be no doubt that Gryphius under-

119

stands his poetry primarily as the art of persuasion, a way of moving men's hearts, or even as shock: "dein *schütternd Feuer.*" He too is a preacher and a prophet, a Paul Gryphius and an Elijah. For this reason he places their poems in an emphatic position at the end of his cycles: they are ideal projections of his own poetic persona.

CHAPTER FOUR

# MANNERISTS AND EROTICISTS

A separation of the poets of the German Baroque into categories such as those that form some of our chapter headings is not without its problems. Greiffenberg, for example, whom we have discussed primarily as a meditative religious poet, is in her way fully as manneristic as Klaj, whom we intend to discuss as a mannerist, and Klaj, in his turn, is undoubtedly also a religious poet. Kuhlmann, also treated along with the religious poets, is at least outwardly almost unbearably manneristic, paronomasial conceits of great complexity being one of the ruling features of his work and indeed the very basis of his fundamental image of the "Cool Kingdom." Weckherlin even, with his emphasis on wit and over-ingeniousness ("Scharfsinnigkeit"), whom we have assigned to the Renaissance or pre-Baroque rather than to the Baroque proper, might with reason be called a mannerist, if we take the term to mean something like classicism in decay or the elaborately conspicuous and self-conscious use of formal means for the sake of effect. Obviously, categorization in literary history is as problematic as it is necessary. Any category narrow enough to be meaningful is almost bound to do the particular

121

poet some injustice, yet without categories we cannot organize our material. In the end, it must be a matter of emphasis and, to a considerable degree also, of individual point of view. One can only hope that one's own point of view is defensible.

Whatever else we may choose to call them, the poets discussed in this chapter can, I think, also be called mannerists. In all of them we find conscious play and experimentation with formal aspects primarily for their own sake, the baroque version, one might almost say, of "absolute poetry," though this may be disguised (as in the case of the Nürnberg poets) by highflown theory about the "genius" of the German language. All of them are what Günther Müller aptly calls *virtuosi*, for though any poet worth his salt must naturally have control of his means of expression, it is the overt emphasis on formal aspects that makes us apply the term in its Italian sense of a supremely skillful performer. There is sometimes a trace of charlatanism in this virtuosity, a tendency to exploit technical skill for its own sake, to play the magician and to bluff. But it is hard to judge a young literature harshly. We must remember that these poets were just beginning to discover the possibilities of their own tongue. If seventeenth-century Germany did not produce a Milton, it is hardly to be wondered at.

By the middle of the century, the members of the generation of Martin Opitz were already considered by the burgeoning versifiers born a decade or two later as classics, for them the only classics in German, for the Middle Ages were as good as forgotten and the preceding age despised. But while the Opitzians were still widely imitated and universally admired, the striving of the new generation, the avant garde of the day, was to go beyond Opitz and the Renaissance manner. It was felt that German poetry had by no means reached its peak, and that especially in regard to form much still remained to be done.

122

In post-Opitzian theory we find a great deal of woolly, semi-mystical expatiation on the mysterious affinities of the sounds of German as an "ancient" language—second only to Hebrew and therefore superior to both Latin and Greek!—and the sounds of nature. In English, a lion may roar, but in German *ein Löwe brüllt* and that is a much more exact linguistic equivalent of the sound a lion really makes. Luckily, the poetry is more respectable than the theory. What these poets were actually stumbling onto of course was the magic of aural suggestion, sound symbolism and onomatopoeia, an ancient feature of poetry, but up to then little exploited in German.

Another patented feature of the poetry of the avant garde was the use of dactylic meter, to which Opitz had given no place in his *Poeterey*. It was popularized and propagated by August Buchner (1591–1661), an influential professor of poetry in Wittenberg, and by his students, among whom were numbered such men as Paul Gerhardt, Johann Klaj, Philipp von Zesen, David Schirmer and Justus Georg Schottel, the leading language theorist of the day. Buchner had a sensitive ear and a strong feeling for rhythms. His influence must, on the whole, be accounted positive and his innovations an enrichment of the German lyric, though the use of the dactylic measure tended to degenerate into a fad in the hands of some of his pupils.

Three typical poets of the mid century are customarily lumped together as the "Nürnberg School": Georg Phillip Harsdörffer (1607–58), Johann Klaj (1616–56) and Sigmund von Birken (Betulius) (1626–81) whom we have already met as the propagandist of Catharina von Greiffenberg. Each is a distinct poetic personality, but only Klaj, as the most interesting of the three, will occupy us here.[1]

123

Klaj's fame rests on a fascinating innovation which remained essentially without sequel, the so-called "Redeoratorien," oratorios without music but suggesting a musical composition by linguistic means. Flemming calls the form a "declamatory oratorio," Cysarz speaks of a "barockes Gesamtkunstwerk," and Wiedemann of "barockes Worttheater." As the name implies, the Redeoratorien were meant to be recited or declaimed, not merely read, and they were recited by Klaj himself, apparently with great success and before large audiences. A mere description can scarcely give an adequate impression of these works, and the difficulty is increased by the fact that, because of their unique character, no critical vocabulary has been evolved to describe them.

The thematic material is religious and there is a vague connection with the medieval "mysteries," though only the vaguest, for the reciter or "orator" takes all the parts himself and there is no real acting out of a "story." It is obvious that the *Rezitator* had to be a virtuoso indeed, and lack of capable actors may have been one of the reasons why the form fell so quickly into desuetude. It could hardly have been because of the works themselves, which are veritable verbal fireworks that still have great appeal, even when read in the privacy of one's study.

The genesis of the form is still unclear, but Wiedemann's suggestion (*Friedensdichtungen*, pp. 13*f.) that it is connected with the rise of "figural music," which reached its peak in the Italian oratorical manner (cultivated also in Nürnberg) and which was in fact a kind of musical rhetoric, would seem to have much to say for it. Wiedemann sees Klaj as striving, as it were, to turn the process around: to do with language what music was trying to do with pure sound, the latter taking its inspiration from rhetoric, rhetoric from music—the poet as his own Hans Leo Hassler and Heinrich Schütz.

Klaj's six Redeoratorien appeared between 1644 and 1650: *Aufferstehung Jesu Christi*, 1644; *Höllen- und Himmel-*

*fahrt Jesu Christi*, 1644; *Herodes der Kindermörder*, 1645; *Der leidende Christus*, 1645; *Engel- und Drachen-Streit*, n.d. [1649–50]; *Freudengedichte, der seligmachenden Geburt Jesu Christi zu Ehren gesungen*, 1650. Only a slight developmental line is apparent, though the last work, the *Geburt Jesu Christi*, is generally considered the best. A cursory analysis of one of these pieces may provide some kind of impression of their unique quality. We have chosen *Höllen- und Himmelfahrt Jesu Christi*, Christ's Harrowing of Hell and Ascension.

The poem, 542 lines in length, *looks* like a miniature drama, with speeches assigned to the various characters. But the persons do not actually speak *to* each other, they merely *make* speeches characterizing themselves, their actions and their situation. There is no dramatic development; where this possibility seems on the point of occurring, there is a change, if not of scene, then of mood or approach, strongly reminiscent of a Brechtian "Verfremdungseffekt." The style is purely deictic, i.e., it points out and portrays; there is no real dialectic. The impression is that of a large baroque painting, full of figures and sometimes frantic action, in which we move from one part to another guided by the poet, who actually assigns speeches to himself in his role of master of ceremonies and openly implements the transitions. All this, plus verbal sound effects. Cysarz was not wrong in speaking of a "Gesamtkunstwerk." Elements of lyric, epic and dramatic poetry, music, painting and oratory are here combined to form a unique linguistic product.

The poem falls into three main parts: the first deals with the Harrowing of Hell, the second with the rejoicing of heaven and earth over the defeat of sin and death, the third with the Ascension. The parts are of approximately equal length. There is a wide spectrum of stylistic levels, ranging from the scurrilous to the sublime, a most unusual procedure in a baroque work, and due, it would seem, to Klaj's desire to attain "realism," his own extreme application of the doctrine of decorum, or the fitting of style to subject matter. It was precisely this potpourri of styles that was to be attacked by the neoclassicists (in so far as they took any notice of Klaj at all), but which a later age is likely to find attractive—the Romantics have not lived in vain. Changes in levels of decorum are matched by changes in meter and rhythm, the meters being noted in the "stage directions," another "alienation effect," at least for the reader.

The "Eingang," spoken by the poet, and set in various meters, is an impressionistic vision of Hell, not Dantesque so much as Breughelesque, and provided with sound effects:

> *Wie geschicht mir? Das Geblüte kaltet /*
> *Das Herze pocht / die Haut veraltet /*
>
> . . . . . . . . . . . . . . . . . .
>
> *Was hör ich? beyde Ohren gellen /*
> *Ach wer greifet mich zu fällen /*
>
> . . . . . . . . . . . . . . . . . .
>
> *Grab / Grab / der schwartze Rabe schreit.*
> *Höret / Uhu / Uhu tut. Ach die Nachtverdambten*
>     *Eulen /*
> *Die Gespenste poltern / Ach / Ach dem unerhörten*
>     *Heulen /*
>
> . . . . . . . . . . . . . . . . . .
>
> *Stille! wer brült?*
> *Wer schilt?*
> *Harnisch / beschildet die Wagen /*
> *Heute müssen wir schlagen . . .*

These lines give some idea of the way Klaj achieves identification of reader (or listener) with the situation, an identification, however, that is continually being interrupted, "alienated," by the various devices already mentioned, though not in order that we may stand back and draw the moral à la Brecht, but so that we may admire the art with which the effect is achieved. In the following speech, assigned to Lucifer and set in confident alexandrines, there is no mention of the martial preparations referred to at some length in the opening lines; instead, Lucifer brags about how splendidly things are going in Hell. Only yesterday Satan added Judas to the number of the damned. Lucifer gives specific—and highly scurrilous—instructions for his torture. We are in the *malebolge* of the medieval hell of popular art and superstition.

In the next fifty-five lines, assigned to the "Poet" and using "Neue Trocheische Weiblicher Art / welcher er [who? Klaj? the "Poet"?] sich in der Höllenfahrt durch und durch gebrauchet," we return to the main theme, the Harrowing of Hell. Note the use of the epic rather than the dramatic mode:

> *Weil [während] diss tolle Fastnachtspiel mit dem Judas*
> *wird gespielet*
> *Und die Geister allesamt ihre Mühtlein abgekühlet /*
> *Kömmet die betrübte Post / numehr sey zu Feld*
> *gegangen*
> *Der belaubte Siegesfürst . . .*

The legions of the Crucified are on their way to do battle with the legions of Hell. Furious, grotesque preparations on the part of the latter:

> *Das beschwartzte Reich schreit laut: Holla / Lermen /*
> *Lermen / Lermen*
> *Die berauchten Geisterlein wie die grossen Hummeln*
> *schwermen . . .*

It is significant, however, that though this speech begins in the narrative mode and is assigned wholly to the Poet, after fourteen lines it fades into Lucifer's direct words (who gives commands for warding off the imminent attack), and then, twenty lines later, returns to the mode of the beginning. What has happened to the point of view? What *is* the point of view? A glance at the way Klaj handles the Poet's speeches (not always specifically designated as such) may afford significant clues about the ontology of the poem, its way of being.

First, in the opening lines of the work, the Poet seems to be himself a soul in torment, freshly delivered to the nether regions, then, in such a line as "Heute müssen *wir* schlagen," he seems to include himself among the minions of Lucifer. In the beginning of his second speech he maintains a cool epic distance, disassociating himself from the infernal tumult, which he calls a "tolles Fastnachtspiel." Then, as we pointed out, he lets Lucifer speak directly, in the middle of his own speech, returning again in the final section to the epic point of view, but now associating himself with the powers of Heaven: "Aber *unser* Simson [i.e., Christ] hebt der Bley-schweren Thore Flügel [the gates of Hell] / Mit Macht aus den Angeln aus . . ." The fact would seem to be that the poet (or "Poet") is every person and everywhere, ominpresent. He is the embodiment of what Thomas Mann calls "der Geist der Erzählung," the Narrative Spirit, though in Klaj this spirit may also be dramatic or lyric. His function is to continually call our attention to the work of art per se. By introducing constant changes in point of view, he makes us see the work from many perspectives and *as* a work (of art). By identifying with everything, he identifies with nothing in particular.

It is easy to over-interpret baroque poetry, because it offers itself so willingly to interpretation, and many an exegete has fallen into this trap. We can perhaps reinforce our own interpretation by a quotation from Klaj himself. In the *Lobrede der Teutschen Poeterey* (p. 5) we read:

> Es muss ein Poet ein vielwissender / in den Sprachen durchtriebener und allerdinge erfahrener Mann seyn: Er hebt die Last seines Leibes von der Erden / er durchwandert mit seinen Gedanken die Länder der Himmel /

die Strassen der Kreise / die Sitze der Planeten / die
Grentzen der Sterne / die Stände der Elementen. Ja er
schwinget die Flügel seiner Sinne / und fleugt an die
Stellen / da es regnet und schneiet / nebelt und hagelt /
stürmet und streitet. Er durchkreucht den Bauch der
Erden / er durchwädet die Tiefen.

To return to our poem. No battle between Heaven and
Hell takes place. Klaj knows his Luther: "Ein Wörtlein kann
ihn fällen":

*Ich bin es / ein einig Wort sie zu Gottes Boden rennet ...*

. . . . . . . . . . . . . . . . . . .
*Das geschlagne Teufelsheer stürzt sich in die
   Schwefelflüsse /
Lekket den vergifften Schwanz / beist die Bokgefüsten
   Füsse.*

The Harrowing of Hell is followed by the rejoicing of
heaven and earth. There is a change of tempo, a change of
tone and mood. If the first part was predominantly *con brio*,
with scherzo-like passages characterizing satanic activity, the
second is *moderato, con sentimento*. The pervasive note is
lyrical. Alexandrines and vers communs, dactyls (or anapests)
and trochees, fitted to lines of varying length, spell each
other off. This variety is matched by variations in mood and
content. God addresses the heavenly hosts, outlining the plan
of salvation; allegorical figures (Joy, Hope, Faith, Peace)
appear; Christ takes his way toward the Mount of Olives for
the Ascension, while flowers—particularly the passion flower
—spring up beneath his feet, and nature joins in the general
rejoicing in verses with interior rhyme that are the trade mark
of the Nürnberg School:

*Die Blätter vom Wetter sehr lieblichen spielen /
Es nisten und pisten die Vogel im Kühlen /
Es hertzet und scherzet das flüchtige Reh /
Es setzet und hetzet durch Kräuter und Klee.*

These springy anapests soon change into elegantly handled trochees of great suggestiveness:

> Die begilbte Sommersaat sich in Stamm und Strauch
> erhebet /
> Der fastreiffe Halme schallt / ein Geräusche von sich
> webet /
> Auch die Palme blühet schön /
> Alles gibet ein Gethön /
> Das Gewässer
> Und die Flösser
> Säuseln / murmeln durch die Sträucher /
> Jordan rinnet rein und reicher.

One of the most charming passages in this division of the work describes the phoenix, a "figure" of Christ, in terms of an example of the Byzantine goldsmith's art, "of hammered gold and gold enamelling," and frames for the mythical bird a self-characterizing speech in vers communs. Truly, everything has a place in this poem. It is not for nothing that the flower "sacred" to Klaj in the Blumenorden was the clover blossom (Klee), which he associates with the great god Pan, that is, "All" (*Fortzetzung der Pegnitz-Schäferey*, p. 66):

> Wie der Bokkgefüste Pan dieses Gantze deutet an
> Welt und See /
> Feld und Klee /
> Alles / was man nennen kan:
> Also / was ein Dichter kan / ist diss Gantze üm und an
> Glut und Luft
> Fluht und Gruft
> und der Horngefüste Pan.
> Weil der hufgefüste Pan Klee mit Tritten pflantzen kan /
> Nimt mit Ruhm
> Klee zur Blum
> Unser Schäfer Klajus an.

The final section of the oratorio begins *allegro, ma maestoso* with a passage describing the angelic army descending to the Mount of Olives to accompany the Saviour on His Ascension. On their way down to earth the heavenly hosts hold jousts of joy in the skies and the passage ends in wildly exulting anapests as Christ approaches the Mount:

*Trommeten / Clareten Taratantara singen /*
*Es dröhnet und thönet der Waffen Erklingen /*
*Es siegen und fliegen die silbernen Fahnen /*
*Die Truppen die klopfen / zur Freuden aufmahnen.*

The major portion of this section, however, does not pronouncedly suggest music; it is visually rather than aurally oriented. Klaj here suggests the meaning of Christ's victory by description of the symbolic banners borne by the angels: Mary with the Child, the Agnus Dei, the Rainbow of Promise, the Lion of Juda, the Eagle (the Risen Christ) soaring triumphant through the firmament. A Counter-Reformation procession raised to the angelic power with all doctrine transformed into images.

In a short, simple lyric almost *volksliedhaft* in tone, Christ takes leave of the eleven remaining disciples (the "nochgeeilfte Schaar"). Then, in a close paraphrase of the words of Acts 1, 9, we are told that "eine Wolke kam / Die ihn je mehr und mehr von ihren Augen nahm." There is an almost startling change of tone and mood between this passage and the one immediately preceding. Once more, the poem points to itself and invites us to consider art as art. At the same time, a deeper symbolism may well be present: It seems not improbable that the poet may have also wished to contrast the simplicity of the language of the New Testament and the humility of the historical Jesus with the pomp and circumstance and the elaborate language with which his deeds have come to be celebrated by the Church militant. If the poem as a whole makes an impression of Jesuit gran-

131

deur, still Klaj does not wholly deny his Lutheranism. Both are included in his universalistic view.

An echo poem prophesying Christ's return to judge the quick and the dead functions as a bridge passage leading to the arrival of the Son in the house of the Father. What began in hell, took its way through the realm of man and nature, ends in jubilant dactyls in heaven. Klaj pulls out all the stops:

> *Engel / Ertzengel und Cherubinnen /*
> *Herrschaften / Thronen und Serafinnen /*
> *Englische Stimmen Wolkenan schwingen /*
>       *Lieblichen singen.*
> *Singet und klinget süsser im Chore /*
> *Flöten / Posaunen / rühren Pandore /*
> *Führen die Weisen höher zu Höhen*
>       *Prächtig zu gehen.*
> *Haltet in / stille! Himmlische Flammen*
> *Höret / die Chöre fallen zusammen /*
> *Messen der Lieder flüchtigen Zügel*
>       *Mit dem Geflügel.**

[*I.e., beat time with their wings.]

God the Father Himself conducts the final chorus and we too are invited to join in the general rejoicing:

> *Singet ietzt und immerdar*
> *Halleluja mit der Schaar /*
> *Sünd und Höll sind überwunden /*
> *Tod und Teufel sind gebunden.*

Are the Redeoratorien great poetry? No. But they are true poetry nonetheless, poetry of charm, verve, humor and great technical skill. Above all, they fascinate because of the aesthetic problem the poet has posed for himself and the way he goes about solving it. We may summarize the problem thus: how is it possible to extend the bounds of poetry by suggesting, in poetry itself, the effects achieved by non-linguistic arts? Beyond even this: how is it possible to write a "pan-poem"? How Klaj attempts to deal with this problem we have tried to suggest, though in a necessarily limited fashion. Discussion of further works by Klaj would be supererogatory. Wherever we open him, he is essentially the same.

In Klaj, as in some other formalists, there is a tendency to underplay rhetorical figures and emphasize aural aspects of poetry. Concettism, play with "conceits," though it had by no means run its course, was beginning to lose some of its novelty: the new thing was sound effects and sound symbolism. This too soon degenerated into a mere game, but not before it had produced some delightfully suggestive lyrics. Both concettism and sound symbolism are of course germane to the nature of poetry and neither can ever disappear entirely; it is only when they appear in self-conscious excess and constantly force themselves upon our attention that we think of them as manneristic.

Philipp [Filip] von Zesen (1619–89)[2] is another member of the middle generation whose endeavors to surpass the "classics" led him to mannerism. Historians of literature usually see Zesen as forming the point of articulation between "pre-Baroque," i.e. the Opitzians with their Renaissance classicism, and "High Baroque," i.e. the bombastic excess of poets writing toward the end of the century, and there is certainly something to be said for this classification. But one must also remember that no poet can be fathomed in his individuality by this kind of schematization. Zesen, as Zesen, was not trying to form a bridge from the Opitzians to the High Baroque; he was trying to write verse in his own way, according to his own temperament and insights. Literature is made by poets, *Geistesgeschichte* is constructed by professors. The history of literature should be an attempt to understand the poets in terms of their own individuality, as well as in terms of intellectual categories. In dealing with the Baroque this is not always an easy task. The overriding rhetorical spirit of the age, with its ideal of impersonality and general applicability (as contrasted with our concern for ultimate situations and the individual experience), lends the productions of this period a certain "joint-stock" character that tends to obscure the individual voice.

Yet Zesen's voice, if we listen for it, is unmistakably his own: a cultivated countertenor of great elegance. Gracefulness, airiness, and a kind of fervent sweetness, though also, often enough, affectation, characterize Zesen, who stands at the opposite end of the emotional scale from Gryphius. Zesen's favorite words to describe poetry in positive terms are "ammutig" and "lieblich" and this is the effect he especially strives for. His words of dispraise are "gekünstelt" and "gezwungen," "wider die angebohrenheit und natur der sprache" (cf. *Helikon* [1656], 3. Teil, p. 6). Weber (p. 44) points out that Zesen's poetry lacks the intensity and dialectical rhetoric of the Petrarchists, even when he composes in the Petrarchan manner: his sensibility tends rather toward the style of the social song (*Gesellschaftslied*), which conveys one emotion rather than confronting in dialectic argument conflicting emotions. Zesen is not, at least not typically, a mannerist in the sense of being a concettist. His mannerism, like that of Klaj, springs from other roots.

The *Helikon* shows that Zesen regarded himself as a better Opitz, the successor and surpasser of the master. In temperament and aim, however, the two poets are almost diametrically opposed: Opitz is a cool reckoner, Zesen is warm and *gemüthaft*; one emphasizes social values, the other emotional. Unlike Opitz, Zesen has almost no interest in the

134

central problem of the initiator of the New Poetry, namely, the Germanization of Renaissance forms and modes; his standpoint is strictly native and he consequently operates from within the language to a much greater degree than Opitz.[3] Above all, Zesen's view of the *function* of (secular) poetry differs basically from that of his famous predecessor. Opitz strove to maintain a Horatian balance between *prodesse et delectare* (instruction and delight, *Nützen* und *Ergötzen*), Zesen is outspokenly on the side of *delectare*, contrary though this was to the attitude of his honored teacher Buchner, who emphasized *prodesse*. What a thoroughly hedonistic function Zesen attributes to poetry is abundantly clear from his foreword to *Dichterisches Rosen- und Liljenthal*, where he stresses his desire to appeal to *all* the senses (but *not* the intellect!) through his songs:

> Siehestu hierinnen etwas zierliches; so weide deine augen sat. Höhrestu etwas anmuhtiges; so fülle nun deine ohren vol. Schmäkkestu / ja riechestu etwas angenehmes; so labe nun deine Zunge / samt der nase / wohl. Empfindestu etwas / das deinem griffe belieblich; so ergetze nun deine finger nach genügen. Ja siehe / höhre / koste / singe und spiele dich nun sat und über sat. Also lass alle deine sinnen hierinnen lustmahl halten. Ich lade sie zu gaste.

Poetry is here seen as what Brecht would call "culinary" art, and with a vengeance. It is from this striving for pansensualism that Zesen's own kind of mannerism springs. His aim is not essentially different from Klaj's, though the poetic voice and its effect on the reader (or should one say "user"?) is quite different. Klaj is like a brass band, Zesen a woodwind trio. Both regard poetry as a kind of better hallucinogen.

It comes as no surprise to learn that a poet with this view of his art saw in music and dance the true sisters of poetry: "die tantzkunst [ist] der Dichterei schwester so wohl, als die Singekunst, und eine ohne die andere, wan man zur folkom-

135

menheit gelangen wil, [kan] fast nicht sein," he says in the *Helikon* (cited by Ibel, p. 30). His practice is in harmony with his theory. Not only were his poems published with accompanying melodies, but a number of them were also meant to be performed as dances. Zesen is strongly motor and aurally oriented and this is reflected in his unerring sense of rhythm and his cultivation of vocal effects, especially in his overfondness for rhyme, though play with vocalism also has another root in his work, as will be seen shortly.

Zesen was especially proud of having introduced into German many different strophic forms. These range from simple folksong-like stanzas to complicated structures using as many as three different meters with a varying number of beats per line. Naturally not all the stanza forms he uses are new. An example of Zesen at his simplest will also serve to illustrate his use of sound symbolism. These verses are the first two stanzas of a four-stanza song of parting (quoted after Ibel, p. 105):

> *Ich scheide zwar von hinnen:*
> *doch bleib ich ewig Dein*
> *mit hertze, muht und sinnen;*
> *und wil Dein Bruder sein.*
>
> *Dein Bruder wil ich bleiben*
> *in fester lieb und treu,*
> *so lange man wird schreiben,*
> *was treue liebe sey.*

This is appealing and almost unbelievable within the context of learned baroque poetry. It sounds more like something by Novalis than by the man who reputedly ushered in the bombastic era in German literature. In spite of this, there is almost certainly something learnedly baroque about it and this is the use of sound symbolism or, as Weber (pp. 200 ff.) prefers to call it, sound analogy. I have said *almost* certainly,

136

for it is hard to prove beyond doubt whether Zesen was in a particular instance making use of the system of sound analogy. In any event, it is not hard to see what happens here. The theme is parting which is yet not parting: *scheiden und doch bleiben.* The /ai/-sound, belonging to both *scheiden* and *bleiben,* dominates both stanzas (it occurs eleven times) and culminates in the word *treu* (which Zesen in his Meissen speech pronounced /trai/) and it is "Treue" that constitutes the "message" of these lines: *dein sein* equals *treu sein* equals *scheiden und doch bleiben.* Weber has shown that Zesen was very interested in outré circular arguments about the nature and origin of language, rampant throughout the seventeenth century and stemming in large part from Jakob Böhme. To somewhat oversimplify the argument that interests us here: One might "show" or "prove" the "Adamic" character of a word or sound, i.e. its "natural significance," by associating sound and meaning on the basis of some pregnant example (not by any means always a sound or word imitative of a sound in nature—that would be too simple). In the present instance "treu" is the pregnant word, /ai/ the symbolic sound. We may take it that for Zesen "treu" *naturally* meant faithfulness, naive as this may strike us. On the basis of the vowel /ai/ an analogical complex is built up reenforcing the idea of "Treue" or, if one prefers, symbolizing this idea. The woolly linguistic mysticism on which the process is based does not necessarily keep it from being effective, though one may feel that it would work better if kept at a subliminal level. With Zesen it was a conscious process and consequently often carried to extremes. Weber, who has given the problem much thought, is convinced that sound analogy "affords the key to the understanding of Zesen's lyric composition" (p. 200), and though her proof is not completely convincing, it is convincing enough to give one pause.[4] It is often hard to determine *what* is supposed to be symbolized by Zesen's sound analogies—here lies the subjective element: we cannot

137

fathom his "etymologies." (For this whole problem, see also pp. 83–84.)

In describing the performance of a dance song in the *Helikon*, Zesen ascribes psychological values to the three basic meters. Iambs, which are said to have a "rising" rhythm, correspond to a sedate gait, and are to be danced (naturally also sung and played) "mit ernsthaftiger liebligkeit." Trochees have a "falling" rhythm, are "lighter and swifter" than iambs, and danced correspondingly. Dactyls "skip and hop," their rhythm is "neat and of charming sweetness" (färtig und lieblich), and they are danced with "as it were trembling yet cheerful steps" (Maché, pp. 74 ff., and Ibel, pp. 30 f.). All this shows once more Zesen's strong motor orientation. Poetry is for him something that one *does* and that does something *to* one—physically. Seldom is he primarily interested in the argument of a poem; he is interested in its sensual effect. A poem is for him a bodily and an aural experience.

Zesen's thematic material—he characteristically deals with erotic or encomiastic themes—is thoroughly unoriginal, the veriest clichés for the most part, but so skillfully organized rhythmically and vocally as to be almost unfailingly successful, at least as "music." A poem by Zesen hardly deepens our understanding intellectually, nor is it meant to, but it can delight, and that is its aim. This one-sided emphasis on *delectare* is the measure of his art and ranks him as a definitely minor poet. The quality of the experience afforded by Zesen's verse lacks depth. The comparison with a pleasant drug is almost inevitable. These rhythmically delightful lines from "Mahrholds Scheidelied," using a combination of dactyls and trochees in each line ($-\cup\cup-\cup-\cup\cup-[\cup]$) are perhaps as "profound" as anything in Zesen (*Rosen- u. Liljenthal*, p. 166):

> *Meinstu / wir sind nun gäntzlich geschieden?*
> *Gib Dich / o Anemone / zu frieden.*

*Unsere Seelen scheiden sich nicht |*
*ob ich schon scheid' aus deinem gesicht.*
*Unsere Seelen | deine von meiner |*
*meine von deiner | scheidet nun keiner.*

Zesen's interest in sensual effect and his characteristic disinterest in discursive "sense" is the source of his form of mannerism. As an example of the neglect of (logical) meaning for the sake of vocal effect, consider these lines from an echo-song (quoted after Weber, p. 128):

*Wie mag das Rosen-kind verzühen?*
*(Gegen-stimme:) Es wird blühen.*
*Wan sol es dan die blüht erreichen?*
        *zeit mus weichen.*
*Wie würd die zeit uns noch erfreuen?*
        *gantz verneuen.*

Sound, not meaning (or sound *as* meaning), is likewise the key to the following dactyls with their double rhymes at the beginning and end of the line (quoted after Weber, p. 145):

*Glimmert ihr sterne |*
*schimmert von ferne |*
*blinkert nicht trübe |*
*flinkert zu liebe*
*dieser erfreulichen lieblichen zeit.*
*Lachet ihr himmel |*
*machet getümmel |*
*regnet uns segen |*
*segnet uns regen |*
*der uns in freude verwandelt das leid.*

In this song, which contains eight stanzas, the stanzas (with the exception of the last) might come in almost any order, so slight is the thematic development, so exclusive the emphasis on the rhythmic-aural effect; nor is this by any means

139

an isolated case. Weber (p. 152) points out that the more Zesen makes use of the expressive forms of music, the more the words lose a logically definable meaning. They become mere sound-carriers and stand under a different expressive principle, that of pure sensuous appeal.

Zesen was particularly proud of his strophic forms in mixed meters. These poems tend to show with special clarity his purely sensual use of language. One must also remember that these poems were often meant to be danced and sung, which naturally contributed to the reduction of the value of the word as a conveyer of discursive meaning. An example from a dance song (quoted after Weber, pp. 124–25):

> *Platz! platz! höret auff zu tantzen /*
> *Schliesst den Reyhen / reumt den Saal /*
> *Seht der Liebe güldne Lantzen!*
> *Seht der Pfeile Blitz und Straal!*
> *Wie tantzen die Lantzen / wie eylen die Pfeile /*
> *Wie blitzen die Augen der beyden allhier!*
> *Sie funkeln im dunkeln bey nächtlicher weile /*
> *Wie sonsten die Sterne von ferne voll Zier.*
> *Sie winken und blinken und wollen zur Ruh /*
> *Drümb stille! fein stille! helfft imer dazu.*

These lines are of course an admonition to a company of dancers celebrating a wedding to break off their festivities and allow the young couple to go to bed. But far more attention is paid to the ancient conceit of Love's arrows darting from the eyes of the newlyweds and seen in terms of sparkling light, the sparkling quality being reflected in the dancing anapests with interior rhyme. The overt content is secondary to the virtuosity of the presentation. The effect of the stanza as a whole, however, is thoroughly unified and not dependent on intellectual analysis. It begins with the measured trumpet calls of the imperatives in the first four lines, modulates to the swift anapests of the next five lines, which one thinks of as being given to fiddles, and ends with a verse, which though still anapestic, has a much slower rhythm and would be marked *piano*. The whole is a subtly constructed rhythmic delight that moves one viscerally; at the same time it is the despair of discursive description.

Not all of Zesen's poems in mixed meters reduce the semantic value of the word so radically. The following "Sprach-lied," the first third of a wedding song, subordinates vocalism and rhythm to the development of theme and imagery (*Helikon*, 1656, 3. Teil, 35 f.):

### DIE JUNGFER BRAUT REDET IHREN LIEBSTEN AN

#### 1

*Es bricht herfür der nächte licht*
*ach! Liebster / kommt: sein angesicht*
    *soll meine sonne werden.*
*Die nacht / das sehr verschwiegne kind /*
*erwekt den kühlen suden-wind*
    *der fast [schier] erhitzten erden.*
        *Es wehn und gehn*
    *alle Winde sanft und linde;*
        *mond und sterne*
    *winken durch die luft von ferne.*

#### 2

*Der Liebe stern ziht erstlich auf /*
*und wil durch seinen sanften lauf*
    *uns beide selbst begleiten /*
*dem folgt das andre sternen-heer /*
*und hengt das gold ie mehr und mehr*
    *am himmel auf vom weiten;*
        *ja ich wil mich*
    *o mein Leben / Ihm nun eben*
        *gantz ergeben:*
    *Nun wil ich nach freuden streben!*

The strophic structure, a baroque version of the scheme used by the Meistersinger, is quite sophisticated. Stanza 1 has this structure:

"Aufgesang"

| line 1: | 4-stress iambs | a masc. | |
|---------|----------------|---------|---|
| 2: | 4-stress iambs | a masc. | 1st "Stollen" |
| 3: | 3-stress iambs | b. fem. | |
| line 4: | 4-stress iambs | c masc. | |
| 5: | 4-stress iambs | c masc. | 2nd "Stollen" |
| 6: | 3-stress iambs | b fem. | |

"Abgesang"

| line 7: | 2-stress iambs | interior rhyme only (masc.) |
|---------|----------------|----------------------------|
| 8: | 4-stress trochees | interior rhyme only (fem.) |
| 9: | 2-stress trochees | d fem. |
| 10: | 4-stress trochees | d fem. |

(The second stanza shows a slight, but significant, variation in the Abgesang.)

The more obviously "poetical" aspect of the poem is the personification of nature, which, however, in contrast to many baroque examples, is by no means extreme or bizarre. Modern sensibility, in fact, may well admire such a line as "Die Nacht, das sehr verschwiegne Kind," and it will probably find it hard to resist the Brentanoesque quality of lines 7–10 (Stanza 1). But there is more to these two stanzas than mere rhymed description of personified nature. The poem becomes truly poetic in a way one is tempted to call "romantic," dangerous as it is to use this term in speaking of baroque verse, through the identification of the speaker, the "Jungfer Braut," *with* nature and the reflection of the spiritual in the phenomenal on a different and more subtle plane than that of personification. The first Stollen of Stanza 1 expresses the will of the speaker: "Kommt (!)" "soll." These lines find their correspondence not in the first Stollen of the second stanza, but in the Abgesang (i.e. the last four lines) of this stanza, which again express the will of the young bride: "will mich . . . ergeben" "will . . . streben." What stands between the opening verses of Stanza 1 and the final lines of Stanza 2 is personified nature: the night, the wind and the stars, especially Venus, "der Liebe Stern," which literally oversees the whole scene. The lines depicting nocturnal nature show a constant process of expansion: the awakening of the south wind, the beckoning heavenly bodies, the appearance, first of Venus, then of the whole multitude of stars, until the whole night is aglow. With this expansion in the phenomenal world the speaker then identifies herself spiritually: "Ja, ich will mich . . . ganz ergeben" and this giving (Geben) of herself is reflected in the enjambement and especially in the high incidence of *eben*-rhymes, the change in function bringing with it a slight modification in the structure of the second Abgesang in the form of an additional end rhyme.

As a final example of Zesen's art and his intense preoccupation with the motor aspect of poetry, we quote two stanzas from a "Tantzlied" for a performing horse ("das edle Weisschen") (*Rosen- und Liljenthal*, p. 309):

> *Auf / Weisschen! richte brust und köpfchen in die höh';*
> *lass fliegen üm den Hals der blanken mähne schnee;*
> *lass spielen aug- und ohren;*
> *lass spielen fuss und bein.*
> *Du bist zur lust erkohren.*
> *Auf / Weisschen! trit herein.*
>
> *Auf / Weisschen! auf! ich seh / dein' ohren werden*
> *spitz;*
> *dein' euglein spielen süss / und flinkern / wie der blitz.*
> *Hüpf' auf! mein Röschen / hüpfe!*
> *du weist der sprünge schnit:*
> *und / dass dein fuss nicht schlüpfe /*
> *versetze trit üm trit.*

Highly conscious artistry and an emphasis on *delectare* are also characteristic of the Saxon David Schirmer (1623–87),[5] though Schirmer's tone is earthier than Zesen's and he remains nearer to the manner of Opitz, whom he frequently imitates. Schirmer is almost exclusively an erotic poet, but not in the strictly Petrarchan tradition—any deeper dialectic is largely lacking. In his foreword to the *Rosengepüsche* he at once defends erotic poetry and denies its seriousness: the truth about poets' loves is that they are mostly fictions, a point of view taken by a number of poets in the Baroque and also later. Love is his theme, it may have been his experience as well, but that is beside the point. In Schirmer "Brunst" rhymes with "Kunst." For Schirmer, as for Zesen, the aim of poetry is "Ergötzlichkeit," and this is best realized through formal grace, "Anmutigkeit." But where Zesen is graceful and inward, appealing to sentiment, Schirmer is vehement, exaggeratedly elaborate and half-mocking—his poems characteristically have a touch of self-irony.

If one may judge by the "Ehrengedichte" that precede the *Rosengepüsche*, Schirmer's contemporaries seem to have regarded him above all as a "fiery spirit" (references to "Feuer," "Flammen," "glühen," etc., occur in almost every congratulatory poem) and his work shows that this is not an unjust characterization. Yet despite his fire and his technical finish, Schirmer can be dull and incredibly repetitious. One "Rosengepüsch" contains ten poems in the pastoral vein (fifty pages), all of them imitations of Opitz's "Galathee" ("Coridon der gieng betrübet"). Reading 400 pages of his work is no unalloyed pleasure. But the same can be said even of Fleming, and, at its best, Schirmer's verse has a charm and freshness not often equaled in the seventeenth century German lyric. And, in spite of his repetitiousness, his formal range is wide, extending from simple song to poetry of elaborate conceits, from verse that relies almost wholly on its "music" for its effects to poetry of witty pseudo-argument, from simple to mixed meters in the manner of Zesen, from longer pastorals and elegies to madrigals, sonnets, and epigrams.

As for his dominant theme, it is, as later with Hofmannswaldau, slavery to love, or perhaps better: slavery to longing. Unlike Hofmannswaldau, however, Schirmer is not lascivious, not "galant," even though some of his poems were reprinted toward the end of the century in the so-called "Neukirchsche Sammlung," which specialized in lascivious erotica. Schirmer does not regard the female as mere prey to be trapped by any means possible or as a plump, fleshly fruit to be lusted over and then devoured. The salacious interests him only peripherally. The emotion that stands at the center of his work and the one he knows how to convey most convincingly is the intensity, but also the sadness, of erotic longing. One is tempted to see something quasi-metaphysical, parareligious, about Schirmer's love poetry, though at the same time it cannot be properly called Petrarchan, for the poet does not luxuriate in his pain nor interpret it as a sign of the heavenly. The underlying feeling is perhaps a sense of the impossibility of perfect fulfillment. Only the intensity of his longing (and even this he characteristically treats half mockingly) betrays a "mystical" quality.

It is revealing that "Marnia," to whom he devotes a cycle of sonnets, dies halfway through the cycle. To interpret this purely biographically, as Sonnenberg (pp. 5 f.) would have us do, is to miss the point. It is not a matter of Marnia the person, whoever she may have been (Sonnenberg, while insisting on her reality, never says who she was), but of what she stands for, namely, erotic fulfillment, that Schirmer is concerned with. But fulfillment is not possible, or, to put it another way, erotic fulfillment is the mother of desire. The motor that drives his poetry is longing itself. Hence Marnia dies only to be resurrected immediately in another love who resembles her to a hair—and the longing begins anew. "Ich bleibe voller Treue / senck dich nur her

145

in sie / so lieb ich dich auffs neue," he begs his deceased mistress in telling her of his new love. A true Petrarchan would love Marnia dead better than Marnia living; her influence, purified of sensuality, would lift him to a higher plane—of this there is no hint in Schirmer.

Like Zesen's, Schirmer's poems, with the exception naturally of the pastorals, elegies, sonnets, and epigrams, are primarily songs. An example of his simpler song style is the rhythmically compelling "Sie soll bey ihm bleiben" from the fourth part of the second book of the *Rosengepüsche*:

> *Sonne der Freuden /*
> *Flamme der Liebe /*
> *Wilstu denn scheiden*
> *Unter das trübe?*
> *Bleibe mein Licht.*
> *Liebe verbindet*
> *Hertzen und Hertzen.*
> *Liebe bezündet*
> *Duppelt die Schmertzen /*
> *Scheide doch nicht.*
>
> . . . . . . . .
>
> *Unsre Zeitlosen*
> *Grünen am Strande /*
> *Blumen und Rosen*
> *Blühen im Lande.*
> *Bleibe mein Licht.*
> *Leben und Jugend /*
> *Jugend und Leben*
> *Reiffen zur Tugend*
> *Sich zu erheben.*
> *Scheide doch nicht.*

The adonics ($-\cup\cup-\cup$), symbolizing the inevitability of separation, time's ceaseless flow, have just time to pick up speed when they are interrupted by the prayer that time may stop:

146

"Bleibe mein Licht . . . Scheide doch nicht" ($-\smile\smile-$). But the overall tone is one of sadness, one feels that the prayer will be in vain. The imagery is composed of pale stereotypes employed as mere counters, one might almost say merely as sounds that embody the rhythm. They fleetingly arouse one fleeting idea after another. There is nothing to linger over. Thus rhythm and imagery say the same thing. As in a number of Zesen's songs, the stanzas (there are five) are, except for the first and last, interchangeable.

Schirmer's most attractive madrigal is "Über die aufmachende Anemone," found in the fifth "Rosengepüsch" of the second book. Like the song quoted above, it is often anthologized.

> *Der Abend war ankommen.*
> *Ich hatte meinen Weg bereit zu ihr genommen /*
> *Zu Ihr / zu meiner Anemonen.*
> *Ich klopfet an.*
> *Bald ward mir aufgethan.*
> *Die rechte Hand trug Ihr das Licht.*
> *Die Lincke deckt ihr Angesicht.*
> *So balde war das tiefst in meinem Hertzen*
> *Verletzt von ihren göldnen Kertzen.*
> *Wo kam ich hin? Sah ich denn in die Ferne?*
> *Das kann ich itzund nicht aussprechen.*
> *Jedoch die mir das Licht getragen /*
> *Die war die Venus ohne Tagen [ohne Zweifel?]*
> *Selbselbst mit ihrem Abendsterne.*

The charm of these lines lies above all in the way they employ the tone and rhythm of everyday speech only slightly heightened and stylized. Even the realization that an epiphany has been experienced, that Anemone was Venus herself, though the tone is fervent and lyrical, is not couched in excessive language. The worn baroque comparison of the loved one to the goddess of love assumes new life—it is, as it were, taken literally, and thus becomes truly poetical. There is a fine sense of emotional progression from complete self-possession to total loss of self-possession, followed by the insight into the deeper nature of the experience, positive in tone, yet uttered with an almost unbelieving shake of the head. It would be extremely difficult to place this poem out of context. It rings of the mid-eighteenth rather than of the mid-seventeenth century. It is not for nothing that Schirmer has been called a precursor of the Anacreontic poets of the next century.

Schirmer's characteristic tone of intense longing mixed with self-irony is heard in "Nacht-Lied," the first poem of the *Rosengepüsche*. To understand the first two stanzas one must be familiar with the myth of Danae, the daughter of Acrisius, shut away in a brazen tower by her father so that the prophecy that her son should murder his grandfather might not be fulfilled. Whereupon Zeus visited her in the form of a golden rain and begot Perseus.

*Meine Burg ist nun erstürmt*
*Und mit Feuer eingenommen /*
*Du / du aber bist bethürmt /*
*und zu Danaen hinkommen.*
*Ist Acrisius darinnen /*
*der / Asterie / vor dich /*
*Härter noch zu quälen mich /*
*Eingeschlossen deine Sinnen?*

*Regne doch du Sternen-Heer /*
*Nur zum Zeugen des Verlangen /*
*Das vergöldte Liebes-Meer*
*Auf den Glantz der Purpur-Wangen.*
*Oder / fürchstu dich zu fliessen?*
*Ach so tröpfle mich zu ihr!*
*Ich will eine neue Zier*
*Umb den zarten Leib hergiessen.*

*O wie sanffte schläffst doch du*
*Bey dem Spiel der süssen Träume!*
*Mich nur decken sonder Ruh /*
*Die verdorten Mandel-Bäume.*
*Wie der Pan / so vor der Sonnen*
*Offt in ungebähnter Flucht*
*Die zu schnellen Nymphen sucht:*
*So bin ich dir nachgeronnen.*

*Stelle mir die Tugend frey*[6] */*
*Dir ein Opffer anzustellen /*
*solte / Göttin / meine Treu /*
*Tödten mich auff deiner Schwellen.*
*Ja / ich wolt das Mörder-Eysen /*
*Dafür manchen offt gegraust /*
*Alsobald mit eigner Faust*
*selber durch mein Hertze weisen.*

*Aber Tugend / die du hast /*
*hält mich allzeit noch zurücke /*
*biss mich unter meiner Last*
*dein Anschaüen einst erquicke.*
*Kan zu letzt ich was erlangen /*
*ach / so gib mir einen Blick /*
*deine Tugend ist der Strick /*
*der mich itzund führt gefangen.*

*Nun schlaff wohl / ich bin gesund /*
*o Asterie / du Schöne!*
*ich schwehr dir auff deinen Mund /*
*dass ich alle Falschheit höne.*
*Mir ist ewig angestorben*
*der sehr herbe Lorbeer-Krantz;*
*Bring ich dich auch an den Tantz /*
*ey so hab ich gnug erworben.*

The image underlying the whole is of course that of exclusion, the source of the longing that provides the motor power of the poem: Danae shut away in the brazen tower, the poet outside beneath the withered almond trees, the imagined immolation on the threshold, Asterie's unyielding virtue, and finally, in a surprising turn, the state of being a *poet* as a final, crowning factor. The implication seems clear: my true office is to sing of longing, not fulfillment: "ich bin gesund," bitter as is my laurel wreath. If I can bring you to also feel a touch of longing, that is as much as I can hope for: "Bring ich dich auch an den Tantz / ey so hab ich gnug erworben."

"Sie liebet ihn," the poem immediately following, is a burst of wild exultation, packed with the energy that in his best flights Schirmer knows so well how to convey—Asterie has heard his prayer after all, she is willing to "condemn herself to love":

> *Funkelt ihr göldnen Himmels-Sternen!*
> *blitzet ihr hellen Nacht-Laternen!*
> *Jauchtzet ihr Stralen an der Sonnen!*
> *rauschet ihr kühlen Wasser-Bronnen;*
> *Asterie will sich zur liebe verdammen /*
> *die keusche Brust fühlet die blinckenden Flammen;*
> *Tugend und Gunst*
> *mehret die Brunst /*
> *welche die rauchenden Geister anbrennet.*
> *Hertzgen und Mund*
> *stehen verwund /*
> *dass sich Asterie selber nicht kennet.*

Both these poems show Schirmer's masterly use of rhythm to convey emotion: the first, with its not infrequently unrealized stresses, or realized only in the emotionally important words, as in

> *Ich will eine néue Zíer*
> *Umb den zárten Leíb hergièssen*[7]

which lends such lines fervency, stands in strong contrast to the unfailingly realized stresses of the exulting dactyls and trochees of "Sie liebet ihn," where certainty, at least for the time being, has been attained.

"Seine tödliche Schmerzen an Rosomenen," the sixth poem of the first book, is another characteristic expression of intense longing, excessive and dark in its imagery, as though the poet were straining to drain the last drop out of the "cruel mistress" convention. It goes considerably beyond anything the Opitzians would dare. The first stanza runs:

*Brand / Feuer / Flammen und Hagelsteine*
*betäuben / O Schöne / mein Angesicht /*
*dass ich täglich weine.*
*meine matten Glieder*
*schlagen mich darnieder /*
*ob ich sey der deine /*
*Gut / Muth / Blut vergehen.*

Perhaps the best, as well as the best known, sonnet in the Marnia cycle is no. 54, "An seine neue Buhlschaft" (To his new mistress). Its light, humorous touch, which yet has a serious undertone of slavery to Eros, is very typical of one aspect of Schirmer's art. Typical also, not only of Schirmer but of the age, is the almost complete reduction of the beloved to her merely physical properties, while the spiritual is virtually ignored. Marnia the person is nothing in comparison to Marnia the erotic object, and thus interchangeable with her successor when the latter acquires her outward seeming.

*Sie / meine Marnia / kam an das todte Meer /*
*der Charon solte sie mit andern überführen /*
*du / Schöne / wer du bist / rief er / hier gilt kein zieren.*
*Leg deine Schönheit ab / und denn kom wieder her.*

*Sie that / was er befahl. Was ich nicht mehr begehr /*
*sprach sie / das nim nur hin. Hier liegt des Hertzens*
*rühren /*

*hier liegt der Wangen Blut / hier liegt der Pracht
  dupliren\* /
hier liegt mein gantzer Lieb / ja hier / hier lieget er.*

  *Mercur† der sah ihr zu / und sprach: soll denn dein
    lachen /
der Mund / der Hals / diss Haar so gar verdorben seyn?
nein / edle Marnia / nein / edle Nymphe / nein /
sie sollen deinen Schatz noch oftermahls anlachen.*

  *Drauf hub er alles auf / und bracht es / Nymphe / dir.
Nun lieb ich dupelt dich von wegen dein und ihr.*

[\*I. e., her breasts. †As psychopompos, conductor of souls.]

Schirmer's attitude toward love, however, is by no means as frankly materialistic as that of Kaspar Stieler (1632–1707),[8] who affirms the physical without reservation and with no hint of transcendent yearning. Such at least is the attitude assumed in the songs of the *Geharnschte Venus*, and though there is naturally a strong element of role-playing in all socially oriented poetry, *what* role is assumed is indicative. Here the mask is that of the soldier lover, who takes his pleasure where he finds it. The emphasis, however, is not on the warrior, of whom we catch only a fleeting glimpse, but, contrary to what one might gather from some histories of German literature, on the lover.[9] I do not sing arms and the man, Stieler says in effect in the opening poem, but love and love's fire in the midst of war:

  *Ich brenne. Wer nicht brennen kan,
    fang' ein berühmter Wesen an.
  (I burn. Who does not feel love's fire,
    to higher things may tune his lyre.)*

The only war that interests Stieler is the war between the sexes. (Das Lieben ist auch ein Kriegen.)

But though Stieler posits the physical as the essential element in love, he is not coarse (merely frank) and seldom actually lewd, except in some of the epigrams, which are private, rather than public, poetry, i.e., not meant for social production. His predominant theme is not sex but desire; he is in love with the idea of being in love—a more knowing Cherubino (*G.V.*, p. 69):

> *O süsser wahnwiz! ach! wie gerne,*
> *wolt' ich noch iezt so rasend sein.*
> *Diss ist die Seeligkeit der Sterne*
> *und aller Götter ins gemein:*
> *dass sie in Wollust so verführet*
> *nicht merken, wenn sie Schmerzen rühret.*

Eros, who in Stieler sometimes appears under the guise of Priapus, is a servant of Dionysus and releases us from the bonds of individuation. The love that Stieler longs for is a supreme intoxication, "Sinnen-raub." "Catonic," i.e., puritanical, natures cannot of course understand this, but the poet in the Foreword expressly forbids them to read his verse! And he closes his book with these words to the "Over-Zealous" (*G.V.*, p. 137):

> *Der ist geschossen im Gehirn,*
> *wer murrt und runzelt denn die Stirn,*
> *Wenn Amor singt und Venus schlägt die Laute.*

The impression one gains from the book as a whole is that of joyous sensuality. The face of Eros is not disfigured either by the roué's sad satiety or the pallor of the transcendentalizing Petrarchan. These are songs meant to be sung during the "Florische Feste," i.e., they are dedicated to the spirit of fertility, the life principle.

The *G.V.* consists of seven books of ten poems each,

called "Zehen" or decades. Appended are fifty "Sinnreden," jesting riddles that always have a sexually oriented solution. Appended to these are eighteen madrigals, added "damit der Käuffer nicht ledige Blätter bezahle," i.e. to complete the signature.[10] Some of the decades have a definite dominant theme. The first defines and defends the general theme of the whole book: I sing because I am inflamed by desire.[11] (Not, be it noted, in order to inflame *others*. Stieler is not interested in pornography, and seduction and the carpe diem motif play only a subsidiary role.) The second decade treats of woman's fickleness and the war of the sexes; the theme of the third is the pangs of love—here one finds some poems of surprising tenderness. The leading theme of the fourth decade is love's omnipotence. The fifth and sixth do not seem to have a predominant theme, though that of the interconnection between eros and poetry is important. The final decade is dedicated specifically to Priapus, "dem unbehobeltem und nakkendem Garten-Gözzen," and is above all in praise of "der beste Sinn, das Fühlen."

Though the formal spectrum of *G.V.* is considerable, ranging from the folksong strophe and the ballad to quite complicated, typically "baroque" structures in the manner of Zesen and the Nürnberg poets, it is the thematic rather than formal aspect of Stieler's book that forces itself on one's attention. When, as is not infrequently the case, Stieler gives us a set piece in the concettistic, Renaissance manner, he leaves us cold. (See, e.g., II, 1, 2; III, 1, 6, 8; IV, 9; VI, 6.) His forms live from his themes, especially from his central theme: the inebriation of desire. Unlike Klaj and Zesen, he is no experimenter and he has no avant-garde ambitions. His appeal lies in his freshness, which is a function of his unabashed sensuality, and in his humor, which is largely a function of his half-ironic attitude toward the conventions in which he feels so much at home (I, 6, "Der Hass küsset ja nicht," is an excellent example). He does not conquer a

154

new field for the lyric, rather he exploits the genre of the Gesellschaftslied in the name of "das Fühlen" (rather than "das Gefühl"). In this he is a continuator of the style and attitude of such minor lights as Finckelthaus and Greflinger, whose revolt against Petrarchanism he shares. The difference is that he perfects this style, that is to say he is a better poet. In this regard he may fairly be called a "virtuoso."

While of course based on a well worn convention, Stieler's insistence on the connection between eros and poetry has the ring of sincerity, almost indeed of a "problem," if one may speak of problems in connection with such an unproblematic figure. As we have stressed, the persona of the *Geharnschte Venus* is the Cherubinesque lover, not the soldier, but we must add: above all of the lover *as poet*. It might even be possible to argue that the poet as lover (or vice versa) is the true theme of *G.V.*, as it is the theme of much of Ronsard. In any event, it is a motif to which Stieler constantly adverts (see, e.g., I, 6, 10; II, 3; V, 1, 3, 10; VI, 2). With his worth as a lover his worth as a poet stands and falls (p. 22):

> *Ich habe die Schöne mit nichten gewonnen*
> *mit Solde von Golde, mit Perlenem Wehrt,*
> *und scheinenden Steinen in Bergen geronnen,*
> *den Tyrischen Purpur hat sie nie begehrt.*
>    *Die Zeilen, die süssen*
>    *aus Pegasus Flüssen*
> *die haben ihr härtliches Hertze gerührt:*
> *Nu stehet mein Lorber mit Myrten geziert.*

Indeed Apollo's laurel wreath is worthless unless accompanied by the myrtle of Venus (p. 17):

> *Ich achte keiner Lorber-Kron'*
> *im fall ich nicht der Myrten Lohn*
> . . . . . . . . . . .
> *aus ihren Händen solt' empfangen.*

155

It is love and love alone, however earthly, that has taught him to sing (p. 15):

> *Ist wo ihr Leib entblösset:*
> *so bin ich schon beflösset*
> *mit Wasser auss dem Pferde-Guss.* [*Hippocrene*]
> *Auff ihr Bewegen, Regen,*
> *wächst mir geschwind entgegen*
> *ein Buch, das Troja trozzen muss.*

If we cannot call Stieler's motives "pure" and his song "ein Hauch um nichts," we also cannot say that he places his art solely in the service of seduction. If love teaches him to put his talent to very practical uses and "auf Kunst-gemachten Lettern / zur Liebsten Fenster ein zu klettern" (p. 87), it is, after all, *love* that teaches him. In II, 3, "Dumme Leute sein dumm," he says, neatly turning the tables, that to heed my song is to hearken to love itself: I am the voice of love. To turn a deaf ear is proof of insensibility and stupidity.

Stieler's best poem is perhaps the justly well-known showpiece called "Nacht-Glükke" ("Willkommen Fürstin aller Nächte!" *G.V.*, p. 103). It is a poem fairly throbbing with sweet desire—sweet because assured of fulfillment, no vain pallid longing, no lovelorn dialectic, earthy and yet firmly placed within a higher order: the heavenly bodies, representatives of the macrocosmos, are called upon to be present at this union, as are the deities of love and fruition. The whole is seen as a stage setting with man as the principal actor and the macrocosmos, personified in the stars and the moon, as a sympathetic spectator. The breeze, the flowers, the vegetation are cast in supporting roles. "Priapus Plazz" is the omphalos of the cosmos, the center of creation. This love has no doubts about its justification. I quote the third stanza and the final one:

> *Es seuselt Zefyr auss dem Weste*
> *durch Pomonen-äste,*

*es seufzet sein verliebter Wind*
*nach meinem Kind.*
*Ich seh es gerne dass er spielet*
*und sie fühlet,*
*weil sie mir*
*folgt durch die Garten-Thür,*
*und doppelt den geschwinden Liebes-tritt.*
*Bring, West, sie bald und tausend Küsse mit!*

. . . . . . . . . . . . . .

*Komm, Flora, streue dein Vermügen*
*darhin, wo wir liegen.*
*Es soll ein bunter Rosen-hauf'*
*uns nehmen auff,*
*und, Venus, du solst in den Myrten*
*uns bewirten,*
*biss das Blut*
*der Röht' herfür sich tuht.*
*Was Schein ist das? die Schatten werden klar.*
*Still! Lauten-klang, mein Liebchen ist schon dar.*

The point of the poem, and by extension of Stieler's verse as a whole, is that the physical, if it is honest and wholehearted, has the approval of the metaphysical; indeed, it is man's way of lending meaning to the universe, a self-justified and justifying part of the whole. Thus Stieler points forward to Günther and the overcoming of the "galant" convention rather than to Hofmanswaldau and the exacerbated eroticists around the turn of the century.

Christian Hofman[n] von Hofman[n]swaldau (1617–79),[12] with whom we close this chapter, represents the peak of the "High Baroque" and is the one true lyric genius of the so-called "Second Silesian School."[13] Other poets there were of

157

course, and indeed in great number, but they have predominantly historical, not poetical, significance.

In his forthright earthiness Stieler is in revolt against the Petrarchan convention, though this is of course only another way of recognizing its all-pervasive influence. Hofmanswaldau, on the other hand, is a submissive Petrarchan, though his poetry shows the convention in its most decadent and problematic form. Stieler is an eroticist with a clear conscience, Hofmanswaldau an eroticist with a bad conscience, and this makes him a much more interesting poet.

A bad conscience, however, is an integral part of Petrarchism, indeed its very *movens*, in so far as the poet seeks to come to grips existentially with its underlying problem and does not merely play with its outward forms. The underlying problem did not originate with Petrarch; it is the problem of all serious erotic poetry from the time of the troubadours to the final secularization of religious values, a period of roughly seven hundred years. In essence it is this: how to reconcile (illicit) passion and religious sentiment? It is perhaps the most continuous theme of our literature and the story has often been told.[14] Petrarchism is only one of its manifestations, though by far the most influential for modern (i.e. Renaissance and post-Renaissance) literature. For centuries it eclipsed all other conventions.

The bad conscience arises from the insight, usually suppressed as long as possible, that one is, or has been, worshipping a false god. In the next to the last sonnet of the *Canzoniere* (no. 364) Petrarch confesses that he knows his sin, and does not excuse it: "ch'i' conosco 'l mio fallo, e non lo scuso." For twenty-one years Love kept him "burning" and ten more years "weeping," now he turns in his last years to the one true God. In the final canzone the lover begs the Blessed Virgin "on the knees of his heart" (con le ginnochia de la mente inchine) to be his guide in these last days and set straight his crooked path:

158

*Vergine dolce e pia*

. . . . . . . . . .

*prego che sia mia scorta,*
*e la mia torta     via drizzi a buon fine.*

The attempt to reconcile Eros and Religion is finally vain. In Dante's *Vita Nova* it succeeds, but only at the price of dehumanization: Beatrice, the woman, dies and her place is taken by an angel, a messenger of the divine. The dialectic then revolves about the poet's attempt to realize the divine nature of his love.

The medieval church did not ignore the problem. The view of Albertus Magnus, who says that man, in his fallen state, cannot enjoy pleasure without danger of losing sight of the First Good, is especially revealing in our context. Not that pleasure per se is sinful—in Paradise it would have been even greater—but in our present condition it leads to the loss of the only thing worth having.[15] It can become a religion in its own right, just as the doctrine of courtly love proclaimed, a para-religion and parody of the Christian scheme, with its own heaven, hell, and purgatory, ruled over by the God of Love.[16]

This is what happens in Hofmanswaldau. Dante's idealistic treatment of the love relationship was a conscious effort to avoid this pitfall. Petrarch leaves the issue unsettled, unless we give his *revocatio* more weight than all the rest of his book. The outcome of the struggle waged upon the stage of his heart is indecisive, and his mind remains deeply troubled by the mortal passion he vainly strives to idealize. This is the root of his poetry. Hofmanswaldau, on the other hand, does what Dante does, but in an opposite sense: he too absolutizes his passion, but in the direction of Hell, not Heaven. In Hofmanswaldau, slavery to passion is a metaphor for man's fallen state. It is literally *passio*, suffering, though it goes without saying that fulfillment is seen in terms of Paradise (Neukirch I, *Neudr.*, p. 79):

*Es schlägt itzt über mir die wollust-fluth zusammen /*
*So mir die höllen-angst ins paradiess verkehrt.*

Especially in his less "official" poems, those he held back
from publication and which were later included in Neukirch's
anthology, the poet seems to be worshipping at the altar of
pure sensuality. Here the only reality is that of lust, and the
world, a narrow one but a complete one, is eroticized. The
imagery is at times deliberately blasphemous; it is the blasphemy of the black mass. All values are reversed (Neukirch
II, *Neudr.*, p. 15):

*Hat das verhängniss mir den steg zu dir verzehrt /*
*Kan ich / o Göttin! nicht dein rein altar berühren /*
*Soll auf dein heiligthum ich keinen finger führen /*
*So hat mir doch die pflicht noch keine zeit verwehrt.*
*Mein geist muss opfer sein / mein hertze wird der herd /*
*Ich thue / was ich Kan / und was sich will gebühren*
*Ich weiss / du wirst itzund mehr als genug verspüren /*
*Was vor ein reiner dampf zu deinem throne fährt.*

The "pure altar" the lover longs to "touch" (!) is of course
the pudendum. Naturally there is irony in such poems, which
usually end in a disillusioning *pointe*, but that should not
blind us to the underlying seriousness, in some cases even
desperation, that speaks in such verse in the guise of decadent
Petrarchism. Unlike Sade, Hofmanswaldau is a believer.[17]
This gives his work a dimension the nonbeliever can never
achieve: it makes blasphemy possible. Hofmanswaldau's desperation is not that of nihilism, which is the case of Sade, but
of slavery to irresistible lust. Again and again passion is seen
as slavery, and though the lover glories in his degradation
(as the Petrarchan must), he realizes nonetheless that it *is*
degradation, loss of "il ben dell' intelletto," the power of
right judgment, that is freedom, which as Virgil explains to
Dante (*Inferno* III, 16 ff.), is hell itself. One needs to read
Hofmanswaldau against the grain. Was it perhaps because he

160

was dubious whether he would be read in this way that he refrained from giving his "Lust-Gedichte" to the printer ("[um] zu ungleichem Urtheil nicht anlass zugeben")? Was it because what was meant as a warning against the toils of Venus was all too open to interpretation as an invitation to succumb to lust? Eichendorff offers a parallel case: the warner against the siren voice of romantic self-loss can be (and often is) read as the voice itself. Self-loss, which brings with it loss of the First Good, is the theme of the lines entitled "Gedancken über die eitelkeit." They are perhaps Hoffmanswaldau's most convincingly formulated insight into the nature of his slavery (Neukirch I, Neudr., p. 364; emphasis added):

*Was ist dis thun / so dein gemüthe liebet?*
*Dem liebe sich so leichtlich übergiebet?*
*Ein weisser koth / der farb und masque trägt /*
*Den ieder wind der eitelkeit bewegt /*
*Den mehr dein gold / als deine bitte lencket /*
*Der sinnen-koth um andern koth verschencket.*
*Die stirne / so dein freuden-spiegel ist /*
*Bleibt schlüprig eiss; und so du das erkiest /*
*So wird dein fuss mit deiner freyheit fallen.*
*Die stimme / so du stündlich hör'st erschallen /*
*Ist dieser gleich / so die Sirene bringt /*
*Und tödten kan / wie süsse sie auch klingt.*
Die küsse / so du von den lippen stiehlest /
Die stehlen dich / so wenig du es fühlest;
*Ja lieb' ist wohl mehr knecht / als frey zu seyn....*

As for the other side of the medal, the glorying in sensual slavery, we find examples everywhere. This "Welt-Sebastian / den Venus Schütze trifft" ("Abriss eines Verliebten") seeks his perdition with the same fervency that a saint seeks salvation. In the "Brunstgedichte," a term we might render as "poems in heat," the satisfaction of lust is of course seen as salvation, i.e. anti-salvation. I quote from a rhythmically par-

ticularly successful poem on his mistress's breasts, a favorite
subject (Neukirch, I, *Neudr.*, p. 403):

> *Du milch-brunn süsser anmuths-triebe;*
> *Berg / der mit flammen um sich schlägt;*
> *Du zauber-kreyss der grimmen liebe;*
> *Sarg / der des buhlers freyheit trägt;*
> *Ihr purpur-lippen /*
> *Und brust / wohlan!*
> *An euren klippen*
> *Fährt itzt mein kahn*
> *Der wollust an.*

(It goes without saying that Hofmanswaldau's contemporaries exploit the same themes as the master. The difference
between them and Hofmanswaldau lies in the note of desperation and the power to convey a sense of authenticity.
It is the difference between a man possessed by Eros and a
pornographer.)

The anti-heaven of lust has its own ethic, not unfittingly
denominated a "Brunstethik" by Rudolf Ibel.[18] It is most
thoroughly developed in one of Hofmanswaldau's "public"
works, the famous *Heldenbriefe*, on which the poet's reputation, at least among literary historians, has largely rested
until recently. The *Heldenbriefe* are modeled on Ovid's
*Heroides*, which are fictitious love letters from mythical
Greek heroines. Hofmanswaldau's correspondents are pairs
of historical personages, though sometimes under disguised
names. The theme of these letters is the "heroism" of (illicit)
love, which conquers all obstacles fate or society may place
in its path. All is justifiable in the name of passion: deception, adultery, bigamy, breaking the vow of chastity, even
murder. Reading these letters—each of which is exactly a
hundred alexandrines in length—is like walking through a
waxworks museum. These fourteen pairs of lovers constitute, as it were, exhibits *A* through *N* of man's slavery to lust.

Most of these disciples of Venus, intent on nothing but the satisfaction of their passion, make a peculiarly cold and unsympathetic impression. Lust is a joyless, all-consuming, despiritualizing business: if there is any "message" to be had from the *Heldenbriefe* it is this.

Is this work also meant to be read against the grain? According to the author's foreword, yes. Here he states that it is to be taken as a series of horrible examples of the lengths to which passion can lead. According to Ibel (*Studien*, p. 140) this is not the last word. Ibel points out that in the historical introduction to the thirteenth pair of letters Hofmanswaldau speaks in a tone of irritation about the necessity of taking morality into account when writing about "erlauchte Brunst" (noble lust): "Ich habe mit der Liebe hier und nicht mit den scharfen Sitten-Regeln zuthun . . . Wer aber Geistliches von mir begehrt, der soll es auch haben . . . itzt aber schreibe ich nach Eigenschafft dessen, was ich unter der Hand habe und entschuldige mich nicht weiter." However, this by no means has to mean what Ibel implies, namely, that Hofmanswaldau's sole aim is to indulge his erotic fantasy and offer the reader an "esca lasciva" (salacious bait) in the manner of Marino. Rather, the poet is here defending his good poetic right, indeed duty, to make the style suit the content, i.e. he is defending the *decorum* of his work. That Hofmanswaldau had a strong erotic imagination is undeniable, but it is a distortion or a half-truth to maintain that the " 'Irrungen' seiner sinnlich-erotischen Phantasie, dem wahren Wesen seiner Dichtung entsprechen." This is but one aspect of the "Wesen seiner Dichtung." It is the tension between his powerfully erotic nature and his religious conscience that makes Hofmanswaldau the fascinating poet that he is.

In his "Vermischte Gedichte," also contained in *Deutsche Übersetzungen und Gedichte* and thus "public" poetry, we find a series of "treatises" on the dangers of sensuality and the necessity of self-control. Typical is "Ein himmlisches

Gemüthe," from which I quote the first two stanzas (Bobertag, p. 80):

*Ein himmlisches Gemüthe, so Geist und Feuer hält,*
*Und nicht nur dem Geblüte zum Diener ist bestellt,*
    *Schaut des Glückes Gaben,*
    *Und alles, was wir haben,*
    *Mit halben Augen an.*

*Es reisst der Schönheit Gläntzen nicht seinen Fürsatz ein,*
*Er kennt der Liebe Gräntzen, und weiss den falschen*
    *Schein*
    *Dem Wesen abzuziehen,*
    *Und alles diss zu fliehen,*
    *So uns verleiten kan.*[19]

The point is, however, that Hofmanswaldau (i.e. of course the persona of his poems) *is* one who is "dem Geblüte zum Diener bestellt," a slave of his blood, whose firm resolve ("Fürsatz") is forever being put to naught by "der Schönheit Gläntzen," beauty's specious seeming. The insight into his servitude is of little avail. When did knowledge of the harmful effects of alcohol ever keep a drunkard from drinking? Even in the "Vermischte Gedichte" he admits as much (Bobertag, p. 83):

*Ich bin ein Ball, den das Verhängnis schläget;*
*Des Zufalls Spiel; ein Schertz der Zeit;*
*Des Kummers Zweck; ein Rohr durch Angst beweget;*
*Ein Zeughaus voller Angst und Leid.*
*Meine Seele lieget kranck;*
*Mein Hencker lacht; die Lieb ist Folterbanck.*

This tension is everywhere. We need insist no further.

One of Hofmanswaldau's most fervent objectifications of the tyranny of lust and at the same time probably the best carpe diem poem in German is "Albanie, gebrauche deiner zeit," a sensual-mystical prayer of seduction. Much of its smouldering intensity derives from the passionately urgent repetition of the name "Albanie" at the beginning of each stanza and again at the end in the echo-rhyme. This name, the embodiment of the woman to whom the prayer is addressed, encloses each stanza as the woman herself encloses his passion—for the moment there is nothing else in the world. We find here most of the essential elements of the poet's erotic mystique: worship of the flesh, the rights of passion versus the laws of society, the spirit as an aspect of the flesh, nature's example and God's will pleading the lover's cause, even Hofmanswaldau's characteristic culinary metaphors. The principle of intensification on which the poem is based is carefully carried out: from kiss to eyes to breast to "every limb" to pudendum to (anti-) spirit (i.e., self-loss as salvation) to blasphemous worship of the male organ before the female "altar." The spirit become flesh, the flesh become spirit. In its genre it is an astoundingly successful poem. The carpe diem motif can be carried no further (Neukirch I, *Neudr.*, pp. 70 f.):

*Albanie / gebrauche deiner zeit /*
*Und lass den liebes-lüsten freyen zügel /*
*Wenn uns der schnee der jahre hat beschneyt /*
*So schmeckt kein kuss / der liebe wahres siegel /*
*Im grünen may grünt nur der bunte klee.*
*Albanie.*

*Albanie / der schönen augen licht /*
*Der leib / und was auff den beliebten wangen /*
*Ist nicht vor dich / vor uns nur zugericht /*
*Die äpffel / so auff deinen brüsten prangen /*
*Sind unsre lust / und süsse anmuths-see.*
*Albanie.*

*Albanie / was quälen wir uns viel /*
*Und züchtigen die nieren und die lenden?*
*Nur frisch gewagt das angenehme spiel /*

165

*Jedwedes glied ist ja gemacht zum wenden /*
*Und wendet doch die sonn sich in die höh.*
Albanie.

*Albanie / soll denn dein warmer schooss*
*So öd und wüst / und unbebauet liegen?*
*Im paradiess da gieng man nackt und bloss /*
*Und durffte frey die liebes-äcker pflügen /*
*Welch menschen-satz macht uns diss neue weh?*
Albanie.

*Albanie / wer kan die süssigkeit*
*Der zwey vermischten geister recht entdecken?*
*Wenn lieb und lust ein essen uns bereit /*
*Das wiederholt am besten pflegt zu schmecken /*
*Wünscht nicht ein hertz / dass es dabey vergeh?*
Albanie.

*Albanie / weil noch der wollust-thau*
*Die glieder netzt / und das geblüte springet /*
*So lass doch zu / dass auf der Venus-au*
*Ein brünstger geist dir kniend opffer bringet /*
*Dass er vor dir in voller Andacht steh.*
Albanie.

The other side of the coin, love's poignant transiency and the weary mask of illicit love, is just as convincingly presented. "Wo sind die stunden der süssen zeit," Hofmanswaldau's most famous poem,[20] as well as "Gedancken über die eitelkeit," already quoted, may witness this. Transiency is Hofmanswaldau's other basic theme. The insight into the voluptuary's self-deception in creating an anti-heaven of the flesh is so moving because the deception is so fervent. Hofmanswaldau knows as well as Nietzsche that "alle Lust will Ewigkeit," but with his age he also knows that "Der Mensch ist Leichen-voll, wenn er sich recht beschaut." The only true

166

salvation, also for him, lies in the Christian faith (*Gedichte*, ed. Windfuhr, p. 104):

> *Was hier verfaulen wird, keimt zu dem neuen Leben;*
> *Der Höchste wird den Leib der Seelen wiedergeben*
> *Denn soll auf Ewigkeit ein neu Verlöbniss seyn.*

It must be admitted, however, that lines such as those just quoted (from the "Begräbnisgedichte") belong to the realm of eloquence rather than poetry, if it be true that "eloquence is *heard*, poetry is *overheard*." There is an unofficial, nonpublic air about Hofmanswaldau's most convincing poetry, impersonal and mask-like as it may seem when judged by later conventions. In such poems as "Wo sind die stunden" and "Gedancken über die eitelkeit" it is as though the mask had slipped. The "Lust der Welt" is after all (Bobertag, p. 88; emphasis added):

> *Nichts als ein Fastnachtsspiel,*
> *So lange Zeit gehofft, in kurtzer Zeit verschwindet,*
> Da unsre Masquen uns nicht hafften, wie man wil,
> *Und da der Anschlag nicht den Ausschlag recht*
> *empfindet.*

Baroque role-playing as an attempt to avoid the bitter truth: is this the key to Hofmanswaldau?

As a sonneteer Hofmanswaldau enjoys a considerable reputation in German literature. Ibel (*Studien*, p. 52) sees in him the fulfillment of the sonnet form for the seventeenth century, the perfecter of Opitz, Fleming, Zesen. Hedwig Geibel in her study, *Der Einfluss Marinos auf Chr. H. v. H.* (Giessen, 1938), is much more critical. She speaks of Hofmanswaldau's "filling out" the sonnet form rather than *ful*filling it (p. 78), and finds his sonnets inferior to those of Fleming and Schirmer (p. 82). Both critics are convinced that Hofmanswaldau builds his sonnets from the end, that is for the sake of the *pointe* or apothegmatic close (Ibel, p. 54;

Geibel, p. 75). There is undoubtedly something to be said for this view, though it does not do Hofmanswaldau's sonnets complete justice. Both Ibel and Geibel fail to recognize the tension in his poetry, interpreting him all too superficially as a mere rationalistic formalist.

Actually, two main stylistic tendencies of manneristic poetry are operative in Hofmanswaldau's sonnets, the first being the tendency to massive expansion, and the second the tendency toward the "sharp-minded" apothegm, sometimes formulated as a conceit. In Hofmanswaldau's sonnets the overweighted superstructure characteristically depicts his mistress's demonic erotic attractions, love's *terribilità*; the apothegmatic close formulates his bitterly half-humorous insight into the nature of his situation, his servitude. "Wo Phantasie und Urteilskraft sich berühren, entsteht Witz," Novalis tells us. These sonnets are witty in exactly this sense. Typical examples would be "Beschwörung vollkommener schönheit" ("Ein haar so kühnlich trotz . . ."), "Vergänglichkeit der schönheit" ("Es wird der bleiche tod . . ."), and in a lasciviously humorous vein "Er schauet der Lesbie durch ein loch zu" and "Straffe des Fürwitzes." The *pointe*, as though in revenge, can sometimes be turned against the goddess herself, which is something like blasphemy against the anti-religion of lust. Such a freedom the slave of Eros allows himself for example in "Er sahe sie zu pferde" (Neukirch II, *Neudr.*, p. 17):

> *Die lange Lesbia / so meine freyheit bindet /*
> *Erkühnte sich nechst hin zu schreiten auf ein pferd.*
> *Trug gleich ihr schöner leib nicht bogen / spiess und*
> *   schwerdt /*
> *So führte sie doch blitz / der alle welt entzündet.*
> *Ein etwas / so man fühlt und keiner recht ergründet /*
> *Dem kein Bucephalus sich recht und wol erwehrt /*
> *So Alexandern selbst und seinen muth verzehrt /*

*Macht dass ihr pferd den trieb / der himmlisch ist /*
    *empfindet;*
*Wie wirstu Heldin denn itzund von mir genant /*
*Der ich das erste mahl durch deine glut entbrant /*
*Ich / dessen asche noch soll deine wahlstatt zieren.*
*Reit / reit / Amazonin / getrost durch wald und feld:*
*Doch wiltu dass dein knecht die sehnen steiff behält /*
*So mustu / merck es wol / die brüste nicht verlieren.*

Certainly this is an eminently successful application of
manneristic style: expansion plus apothegm. The point is
well taken and we can imagine the delight of the poet's contemporaries. Hofmanswaldau's sonnets, however, if we compare them "absolutely" with the great sonnets of European
literature, will not stand the test. He is not in a class with
Petrarch and Ronsard; he is not even in a class with Marino,
certainly no sonnet of his can compare with Marino's magi-
cally evocative "Pon mente al mar, Cratone." Marino is
dynamic and spacious, Ronsard instinct with living detail,
Hofmanswaldau is ridiculously narrow and artificial by comparison. Ronsard's women come to life before the mind's
eye, Hofmanswaldau's are almost automatons, concatenations
of stylized physical details no one could possibly imagine as
living beings. All this can, however, be interpreted meaningfully. If our thesis concerning the basic configuration of his
work is correct, this is precisely the effect he was striving for.
In spite of the metaphoric material fetched from every corner
of the earth, the anti-heaven of lust is a narrow room, peopled
by monomaniac automatons, mechanical, atomistic.

Hofmanswaldau also cultivated with great virtuosity the
witty epigram, so admired by his age (*vide* Logau), and the
*blason,* called in German "Abriss" or "Icon."[21] His epigrams
can still arouse our admiration, we feel reminded of Pope or
Swift, but we stand pretty much at a loss before his *blasons.*
I quote two examples of his epigrammatic art, "An die
Phillis" (Neukirch II, *Neudr.*, p. 12):

169

> *Der und jener mag vor mir*
> *Das gelobte land ererben;*
> *Lass mich / Phillis / nur bey dir*
> *Auf den hohen hügeln sterben.*

and "Grabschrifft Henrici IV, Königs in Franckreich" (Neukirch I, *Neudr.*, p. 126):

> *Ich bin durch schimpff [Scherz] und ernst zu meinem*
> *reiche kommen /*
> *Ein unerhörter mord hat mir es weggenommen.*
> *Was halff mich / was ich lieb? was halff / was ich gethan?*
> *Nachdem ein messer mehr als eine messe kan.*

The last line is of course a play on Henri Quatre's famous words, "Paris vaut bien une messe" (Paris ist eine Messe wert), said to have been uttered when he abjured Protestantism to gain Paris in 1593. He was assassinated in 1610 ("ein unerhörter mord") by a fanatic. Compared to the efforts of the Nürnberger in this genre, Hofmanswaldau's epigrams make an impression of restraint; his punning and playing with names is usually truly witty, not merely childish. One of his neatest turns is the closing line of an epigram on his lack of success with the women of Paris: "Paris verachtet mich / weil ich nicht Paris bin."

The blasons or *Abrisse* tend to be lengthy. The longest (108 lines) and at the same time one of the best known is the first poem in the second volume of Neukirch's anthology: "Lobrede an das liebwertheste frauen-zimmer" (*frauen-zimmer* equals *Damen*), in which there occur some fifty or more metaphors for the breasts. Lines 14–22:

> *Die brüste sind mein zweck / die schönen marmel-ballen /*
> *Auf welchen Amor ihm [sich] ein lust-schloss hat*
> *gebaut;*
> *Die durch das athem-spiel sich heben und auch fallen /*
> *Auf die der sonne gold wohlriechend ambra thaut.*

*Sie sind ein paradiess | in welchem äpffel reiffen |*
*Nach derer süssen kost iedweder Adam lechst |*
*Zwey felsen | um die stets des Zephirs winde pfeiffen.*
*Ein garten schöner frucht | wo die vergnügung*
   *wächst.*
*Ein über-irrdisch bild | dem alle opffern müssen.*
*Ein ausgeputzt altar | für dem die welt sich beugt.*

Windfuhr (*Barocke Bildlichkeit*, p. 284) calls this poem "a
compendium of far-fetched comparisons or comparative relations." The comparisons come from everywhere: the breasts
are seen in relationship to such dissimilars as a skeleton key,
a pair of bellows, a compass, a coffin; they are compared with
cliffs (a standard metaphor), with a garden, a pond, towers;
they are also an altar, Paradise, a lighthouse, a julep; they are
sisters that sleep in the same bed, hunters, a mine, rooms,
bottles, a crystalline spring, unmeltable snowballs, springes,
panis angelorum, etc., etc. One asks oneself what is the point
of all this extravagance? Is it merely to arouse a sense of
astonishment, the notorious *stupore* or *meraviglia* recom-
mended in such strong terms by the Italian theoretician of
mannerism, Tesauro,[22] and neatly formulated in the oft-
quoted maxim by Marino?

*E del poeta il fin la meraviglia*
*(parlo de l'eccelente e non del goffo):*
*Chi non sa far stupir, vada alla striglia!*

(The aim of the poet is [to arouse] wonderment—I speak of
the true poet, not the bungler—: He who doesn't know how
to amaze, let him become a stable boy!) This seems to be the
opinion of reputable critics. In such a poem the poet lets his
*ingegno* (we would say imagination) run wild. The theme
serves only as a stimulus for the invention of metaphor; it sets
the imagination in motion (Friedrich, *Epochen*, pp. 630 f.).
Windfuhr (*Bildlichkeit*, p. 285) sees such poems as an exercise in "Scharfsinnigkeit." Perhaps no genre cultivated by

171

the Baroque is further from our own concept of poetry. For us, successful poetic description (as, say, in Coleridge's "Kubla Khan") conjures up a mood or a mood picture (inexact, but powerful) of the thing described. This is obviously not the object of the *blason*. There is no descriptive value in calling the breasts "ein see-compas / der hurtig rudern heisset / Eh man in hafen der vergnügung wird gebracht." There is, however, "ingeniousness," the free play of combinations, and the farther-fetched the metaphor, the more dissimilar the terms of the comparison, the more "stupefying."

It cannot be denied, to be sure, that there is a certain similarity between this attitude toward metaphor and that of the Romantics. August W. Schlegel regards metaphor as a way of relating everything with everything: "All things are related to all things; all things therefore signify all things; each part of the universe mirrors the whole." Thus metaphor can suggest "the great truth that each is all and all is each." But such a theory of correspondences is a far cry from the manneristic practice of the Baroque, though Schlegel specifically defends Hofmanswaldau and Lohenstein, saying that "poetry cannot be too fantastic; in a certain sense it can never exaggerate. No comparison of the most remote, of the largest and the smallest, *if it is only apt and meaningful*, can be too bold." This is a big "if." The practice of the baroque mannerists contravenes it and, more importantly, contravenes the ruling romantic doctrine of organic form. What the baroque poet actually does is characterized much more closely by Schlegel's own description of "mechanical form," typical of art in the last stages of decadence: "If works of art are to be looked at as organized wholes, then *the insurrection of individual parts against the unity of the whole* is exactly what in the organic world is putrefaction." And: "The form is mechanical when through outside influence it is imparted to a material merely as an accidental addition, without relation to its nature. . . . Organic form,

172

on the other hand, is innate, it unfolds itself from within."[23]

By any modern standards there is dross enough in Hofmanswaldau, though probably less than in most poets of the German Baroque. Especially in the lyrical epistles, which are closely related to the *Heldenbriefe*, does one find passages typical of "Schwulst" (the "swollen" style) at its worst. "Über einem Minimum von Aussage erhebt sich ein Berg von Metaphern" is Windfuhr's apt description of what happens (*Bildlichkeit*, p. 315). Content is buried in rhetoric, the means take precedence over the end, which is almost a definition of mannerism. A reference to "An Algerthen" (Neukirch I, *Neudr.*, pp. 80 ff.) will illustrate the process. In lines 49 f. we have this expression of the actual content:

> *Und können wir nicht stets der süssen frucht geniessen /*
> *So schmeckt doch nichts so gut / als wann mans selten*
> *schmeckt.*

This thought is elaborated for twenty-two more lines containing approximately eighteen metaphors paraphrasing the same idea. Even a poet of Hofmanswaldau's undoubted quality is not free from the vices of his time.

But it would be wrong to close our discussion of Hofmanswaldau on this note. If he has his poetic vices, his poetic virtues outweigh them. Though his range is quite narrow, he is—technically at least—a consummate master of the genres he cultivates. He knows what he can do. He uses sixty-six different strophic forms, matching each to the contentual material. A critic of stature (Wolfgang Kayser) considers him "den grössten Verskünstler, den die deutsche Literatur des 17. Jahrhunderts besitzt."[24]

In contrast to Zesen and the Nürnberger, Hofmanswaldau appears to despise aural decorativeness and "Klangmalerei." He neither plays with sound effects nor strives to body forth some esoteric doctrine of sound symbolism. Naturally this does not mean that his verse is harsh, as that

173

of Gryphius can be at times. On the contrary. It is smooth, flowing, urbane, but aurally unmannered. Hofmanswaldau's mannerism is largely a matter of his metaphoric usage. With the exception of the *blasons* it hardly inheres in the forms themselves (the *blason* is by definition the complete metaphorization of a given theme) and the excessive use of metaphor is thus a typical trait of the poet's style.

It is as a rhythmist that Hofmanswaldau shows greatest mastery. Consider these stanzas from "Wo sind die stunden" (Neukirch I, *Neudr.*, pp. 437 f.) with their rhythmically suggestive use of breath groups (*cola*), especially the effect of the heavily weighted last line (*pondus*):

> *Wo sind die stunden*
> *Der süssen zeit /*
> *Da ich zuerst empfunden /*
> *Wie deine lieblichkeit*
> *Mich dir verbunden?*
> *Sie sind verrauscht / es bleibet doch dabey /*
> *Dass alle lust vergänglich sey.*

> . . . . . . . . . . . . . . .

> *Empfangne küsse /*
> *Ambrierter safft /*
> *Verbleibt nicht lange süsse /*
> *Und kommt von aller krafft;*
> *Verrauschte flüsse*
> *Erquicken nicht. Was unsern geist erfreut /*
> *Entspringt aus gegenwärtigkeit.*

> *Ich schwamm in freude /*
> *Der liebe hand*
> *Spann mir ein kleid von seide /*
> *Das blat hat sich gewand /*
> *Ich geh' im leide /*
> *Ich wein' itzund / dass lieb und sonnenschein*
> *Stets voller angst und wolcken seyn.*

The cola are built up in groups of twos and threes. Schematically, the first stanza looks like this:

| | |
|---|---|
| x x́ x x́ x ⫶ | 2 |
| x x́ x x́\| | 2 |
| x x́ x x́ x x́ x\| | 3 |
| x x́ x x́ x x́ ⫶ | 3 |
| x x́ x x́ x\|\| | 2 |
| x x́ x x́\|\| x x́ x x́ x x́\| | 2 plus 3 |
| x x́ x x́⫶ x x́ x x́\|\| | 2 plus 2 |

The pattern of short cola suggestive of the "süsse zeit" is continually being crossed by the pattern of longer cola suggestive of the sad insight into transitoriness. These two patterns are then combined in the final lines, which bring the overt statement of the insight.

CHAPTER FIVE

# GÜNTHER AND THE BEGINNINGS OF A NEW SENSIBILITY

Hofmanswaldau and Lohenstein are the last poets of stature whom we can unhesitatingly assign to the Baroque. Not that the baroque manner suddenly ceased to be overnight—it was too firmly established as a poetic mode for that—but it did begin to undergo certain changes. What, for want of a better term, has been called the rhetorical mode, remained in force as the only way of writing poetry, unless one were to fall back on the primitiveness of the sixteenth century or the uncultured simplicity of the folksong. Recourse to either would have seemed the height of absurdity to the poets born in the latter part of the seventeenth century, who, when they express themselves on the point, thank their stars that the muse has at last come to make her home in the lands of German tongue and look back beyond Opitz only with a shudder.[1] The atmosphere remains intellectual and scholarly, the tone cultivated, the ideal "courtly"—it is the age of absolutism—and admiration for "das Volk" is still far in the future.

177

To be sure, there was opposition throughout the century to the intellectualistic, concettistic, manneristic poetry written by most of the poets we have considered. In the earlier part of the period this countercurrent even produced a writer of undisputed European stature: Hans Jacob Christoph von Grimmelshausen (c. 1622–76), the author of *Simplicissimus*. But Grimmelshausen is of course a prose writer and thus of little concern in our context. With the exception of Friedrich von Logau, himself a nobleman and a courtier, whose opposition is more a matter of content than form, and Simon Dach, who cultivates the *genus humile*, the verse writers of "anti-courtly" persuasion are aesthetically insignificant and have therefore been passed over in silence.[2] The hymnists, whose work rests on a firmly established tradition, belong in a somewhat different category. The most important of these, Paul Gerhardt, accepts the new poetry and adapts it to his own ends. Though he remains fundamentally unmanneristic, he cannot be said to belong to the opposition.

The Opitzian ideal was, as we have stressed, the humanistic golden mean, balanced and temperate. It was, however, an ideal based upon a conception of poetry as rhetorical artifice, in essence versified oratory, public in the extreme and anti-confessional. "It is not the individual who expresses himself in poetry," one critic has said, "but poetry that speaks to the individual as a member of society."[3] While still paying lip service to Opitz, the poets writing toward the middle of the century became more and more estranged from the Opitzian ideal. They became, that is, more and more imbalanced and intemperate, when judged by humanistic-Renaissance criteria. It is their work that we think of as typically "baroque." Fundamentally, it exemplifies the well known phenomenon of the priority of formal means over that which is to be expressed by these means, a reversal of values that occurs again and again in the history of art and literature. Zesen and the Nürnberg poets are outstanding

178

examples of this process, which now became the mainstream of German poetry.

To this type of poetry, but also to the Renaissance poetry of the Opitzians, the so-called "Old Germans" were vehemently opposed.[4] Their main argument was that such a manner of expression was a "lie" and "un-German," not in keeping with the ancient virtues of "deutsche Treu und Redlichkeit," which they of course traced back via Tacitus to their pagan forebears. Typical representatives of the Old German opposition are the prose satirist Johann Michael Moscherosch (1601–69) and Johann Lauremberg (1590–1658), a skillful and amusing writer of Low German verse depicting the social scene. Both satirize the German mania for aping foreign ways, and especially Lauremberg, in his *Scherzgedichte*, gets in many a telling blow at the metaphorical-periphrastic mode in contemporary poetry. Neither Moscherosch nor Lauremberg was a "man of the people." Moscherosch was highly educated, a translator of Quevedo, and addressed himself to the cultured upper classes; Lauremberg was professor of poetry in Rostock and could himself write in the courtly manner when occasion demanded. In fact, none of the opposition was "popular" in the present sense of word. It was the work of learned men, who spoke in the name of what they felt to be "truly German." (Even Grimmelshausen was no man of the masses; he was well educated and far from being the "Bauernpoet" of legend.)

Toward the end of the century a new wave of opposition to the excesses of the baroque manner—not the rhetorical mode itself—begins to make itself felt. An effort, and on the whole a successful one, is made to return to the "purer," more temperate style of the Opitzians. It is a movement which finds theoretical backing in the writings of Père Bouhours (died 1702) and the counter-baroque wave in France. The poets adhering to the new stylistic ideal are known as the "Galanten," after their catchword "galant," which signified

179

approximately "sophisticated," "up-to-date," "possessing savoir faire," often also with the implication of free manners in social intercourse between the sexes. The term and its classic exemplification was French. What the "galant" poets strove for above all was a certain lightness of touch, a tempering of metaphorical rankness, and greater nearness to actual speech. Their works are typically in the *genus mediocre*, though the doctrine of stylistic levels does not play a central role. The magic word is the "golden mean" (Mittelweg).[5] They are antipathos, antibombast, antihyperbole and highflown periphrasis, but only moderately so. Much emphasis is placed on smoothly flowing rhythms, the attainment of which involved a breaking up of the heavy periods typical of the High Baroque. The alexandrine, the baroque meter par excellence, begins to lose favor; madrigal verses and more lyric measures take its place. These had of course been used before, but not, so to speak, programmatically. The principal theorist of the movement is Erdmann Neumeister, whose poetics, *Die allerneueste Art zur Reinen und Galanten Poesie zu gelangen*, first appeared in 1707. By 1742, it had gone through eleven editions. The poets of this school are definitely minor figures, though at least one of them, Johann Burkhard Mencke ("Philander von der Linde"), was of influence on an important poet, Johann Christian Günther, who sat at Mencke's feet in Leipzig. Mencke was directly instrumental in helping Günther cure his "Phoebus" of baroque excesses.

In part overlapping with this group in aims and chronologically were the early classicists, later typified in Gottsched. It goes without saying that they too adhered to the rhetorical mode, but their reforms are much more radical than those of the "Galanten," i.e., they reveal a much more antibaroque spirit in their demands for lucidity, plain speaking, and common sense. Rhymed prose seems to be their ideal. Their bible is Boileau and his *Art poétique* (1674). Boileau demanded faithfulness to "nature," i.e., to the universally true, the norm: "Jamais de la nature il ne faut s'écarter." He demanded strict adherence to "truth": "Rien n'est beau que le vrai; le vrai seul est aimable." He defended the primacy of reason as the means of recognizing the true: "Aimez donc la raison; que toujours vos écrits / Empruntent d'elle seule et leur lustre et leur prix." The overriding purpose of art was still seen in the Horatian terms of *utile dulci*: "N'offrez rien au lecteur que ce qui peut lui plaire," but also: "Qu'en savantes leçons votre muse fertile / Partout joigne au plaisant le solide et l'utile."[6] On the whole a rather antipoetic doctrine, at least in our eyes. Certainly, its application in Germany produced very mediocre poetry. The trouble with it is of course that it is too sensible, too reasonable, for much as Boileau may pay lip service to the ancient doctrine of divine inspiration, the thrust of his teaching is to hobble Pegasus, not to free his wings. Such an attitude is understandable, however, as a reaction to the hyperbolic luxuriance of the Baroque, and it found a welcome in Germany with perhaps better reason than in France.

It is above all the "Schwulststil" that the classicists as well as the "Galanten" criticize. Christian Weise's (1641–1708) famous injunction: "Welche *Construction in prosa* nicht gelitten wird, die soll man auch in Versen davon lassen," was widely echoed. Weise was determined, he said, to "maintain his simplicity of speech" in verse as in prose, and his early book of verse, *Der grünenden Jugend überflüssige Gedancken* (Leipzig, 1678), exemplifies this doctrine.[7] It is characteristic of the poets of the counterbaroque that they insist on regarding their poetry as a mere side line. Weise's poetic "Gedancken" are "überflüssig," others call their collected poems *Nebenstunden* (Canitz, *Nebenstunden unterschiedener Gedichte*; Hunold, *Akademische Nebenstunden*, etc.), something that would never have occurred to a poet like Günther, who was married to the muse. Partly, no

181

doubt, this is a pose, partly it is self-irony, partly a way of securing a place for poetry at all in a basically antipoetic environment. Masked as social entertainment or a private pastime, it could not give offense: "de petits vers galants, que je compose en me peignant" (Ronsard). Yet on the whole this self-judgment was correct—this poetry *is* a sideline; fundamentally, it lacks seriousness. Nonetheless, it played a useful role, for the German language profited from these efforts: it began to gain a suppleness and naturalness it had signally lacked. Günther's work is the reward given to German poetry for its long days in school, a work that is neither baroque nor classicistic nor galant, but which derives its supple strength from all that has gone before, in so far, that is, as the work of a genius can be said to "derive" from anything. Before turning to Günther, however, we must glance briefly at a few of his contemporaries.

Friedrich Rudolf Freihherr von Canitz (1654–99), a Prussian nobleman of ancient lineage, was a diplomat in the service of Friedrich Wilhelm, the Great Elector. An ardent admirer of French manners and literature, he translated Boileau and attempted to follow the latter's principles in his own writing. He was without poetic ambitions, and did not, in fact, even consider himself a poet—his work is truly the product of his "Nebenstunden." A fairly slim volume of his verse appeared posthumously in 1700.[8] It struck a responsive chord that would probably have surprised Canitz himself: between 1700 and 1719 ten printings were necessary. Günther said he "found gold" in Canitz, but it is very hard for us to do so. Flat, sober, prosaic, the antithesis of all that is truly poetic, this is likely to be our reaction. But fresh water tastes good when one has had nothing to drink but julep for a long time, and the enthusiasm for Canitz after the oversweet exuberances of the late Silesians can be accounted for on such grounds. In his "Satire von der Poesie" (Fulda, pp. 404 ff.), Canitz has some harsh things to say about the late baroque manner, though he also praises, quite illogically, Hofmanswaldau and Lohenstein. (These two poets were sacred cows; even those in revolt against their manner felt it necessary to bow before them.) The German Helicon, according to Canitz, has become a Blocksberg, "Auf welchem das Geheul des wilden Pans ertönt" (Pan on the Blocksberg!); poets' praise has become cheap, it is not a patron's worth but his willingness to pay that counts. But the fundamental failing is that the dictates of reason and the criteria of naturalness and clarity (one hears Boileau speaking) are disregarded:

> Man denkt und schreibt nicht mehr, was sich zur Sache
> schicket,
> Es wird nach der Vernunft kein Einfall ausgedrücket,
> Der Bogen ist gefüllt, eh man an sie gedacht;
> Was gross ist, das wird klein, was klein ist, gross gemacht,
> Da doch ein jeder weiss, dass in den Schildereien
> Allein die Ähnlichkeit das Auge kann erfreuen ...

Virgil is held up as the unsurpassed but now neglected model:

> So künstlich trifft itzund kein Dichter die Natur;
> Sie ist ihm viel zu schlecht, er sucht ihm neue Spur,
> Geusst solche Thränen aus, die lachenswürdig scheinen,
> Und wenn er lachen will, so möchten andre weinen.
> Ein Teutscher ist gelehrt, wenn er solch Teutsch
> versteht;
> Kein Wort kömmt für den Tag, das nicht auf Stelzen
> geht.

Obviously, a new attitude toward the *function* of poetry is evident here: the emphasis on reason and "nature" is in conflict with the decorative element, hitherto regarded as primary. The baldness of the classicists is the direct result of this change in attitude: it is no longer a matter, as in the Baroque proper, of presenting traditional themes in splendid dress—

this splendor was the "new" element for the baroque poet: "er sucht ihm neue Spur"—but of finding new or at least "true" aspects of the world through direct observation and presenting them in the sober garb of reason.[9]

The poets born after the middle of the century, if they remain productive for a considerable period, characteristically undergo a development from the florid style to the sober. In their earlier work they typically adhere to the late baroque manner, in their later, they become classicistic-galant. This was the case of Johann von Besser (1654–1729), master of ceremonies first at the court in Berlin, then in Dresden at the court of August the Strong. Besser, in so far as one can judge from the seventy-nine entries in the first two volumes of the Neukirch anthology,[10] is a poet of real ability, at least in the sense that he seems capable of writing a poem on any subject. He is the poet as manufacturer, impersonal and non-confessional, a man who has developed a dependable routine and can always turn out an acceptable product. Much of his verse, as is natural for a court poet, is *Gebrauchspoesie*, made to order and meant to be consumed on the spot. Except for his erotic poetry, which still retains considerable charm as witty pornography, there is little in Besser that has anything but historical interest. His best known erotic poem, contained in the first volume of Neukirch's anthology, is called "Ruhestatt der Liebe oder die Schooss der Geliebten" (240 lines). It is already in the galant vein rather than in the highly florid manner of Lohenstein's "Venus," a monstrous production of 1,888 lines, contained in the same volume. The theme of both poems is the all-powerful might of love. But while Lohenstein relates with great decorative detail the myth of Venus and her cult, Besser tells us a piquant story of how Celadon found Chloris asleep on the grass with her clothing in very revealing disarray, what he did, her reaction, and what arrangements were finally made between the lovers after Celadon had pled love's case

"mit rechten weissheits-gründen." Lohenstein can still relate
the myth itself with conviction. Besser's Celadon merely
mentions the myth to his Chloris, adding specific physio-
logical references and personal speculations which sharpen
the vividness of the recital and maintain the lubricous tone,
which is the main point of the poem (Neukirch I, *Neudr.*,
p. 225, lines 169–80):

> *Man sagt: die Venus sey / ihr wesen zu verstellen /*
> *Nicht nach gemeiner art / besondern aus den wellen*
> *In einer muschel helm empfangen und gezeugt /*
> *Wo sie des meeres schaum gewieget und gesäugt.*
> *Wer glaubet solches nicht / der Venus thun erweget?*
> *Weil aber eine schooss der muschel bildniss träget /*
> *Glaub ich / dass Venus gar / was sie ans licht gebracht /*
> *Hernach zu einer schooss der gantzen welt gemacht.*
> *Dass / als die herrscherin ihr muschel-schiff verlassen /*
> *Sie / aller menschen hertz in diesen schrein zu fassen /*
> *Die muschel in die schooss der weiber eingeschrenckt /*
> *Und sich nachgehends selbst / zur wohnung /*
>     *nachgesenckt.*

Perhaps we shall not be going too far if we see in the difference between Lohenstein's and Besser's treatments of the
theme a sign of the tendency of the age to turn away from
the general and traditional and to find its poetic subjects in
the direct observation of "nature"? Be this as it may, Besser
seems to have had great success with his "Ruhestatt der
Liebe." No less a man than Leibniz admired it for presenting
the indecent with such decency (a judgment that may give us
pause) and showed it to the Princess of Hannover, who immediately sent a copy to the Duchess of Orleans.[11] Besser
obviously understood the taste of his age, which, being neither
sentimental nor prudish, judged everything by the propriety
of its form: a lewd poem should be lewd but not coarse, and
only the rhymes need be pure.

185

Benjamin Neukirch (1665–1729), the anthologist, was also a popular poet and propagandist of poetry. A Silesian himself, he began as an ardent admirer and imitator of Hofmanswaldau and Lohenstein, but turned away from them around 1700 under the influence of Canitz-Boileau to try his hand at satire. We catch a glimpse of the power of his name in the following passage from a poem by Günther written in 1718 (*Werke* IV, 158, lines 65–70):

> *Was hör ich manchmal nicht vor Thorheit oder Neid,*
> *Wenn ohngefähr mein Kiel [pen] ein Tagewerck*
> *verstreut!*
> *Da kriegt das Maul zur thun, da schwazt ein Tisch voll*
> *Richter,*
> *Da schiert und foltert man den unbekandten Dichter,*
> *Da heists: Wer macht den Vers? Ists Neukirch? Ja.*
> *O schön!*
> *Nein, nein. Wer denn? Kehr um! Pfuy, las den Bettel*
> *gehn!*

In the "Vorrede" to the first volume of his famous anthology, Neukirch categorizes poets as "blosse verssmacher," "galante dichter" and those who hope to become truly great poets. The products of the first are mere waste of paper, those of the second require "feurige und auffgeweckte gemüther / welche in der galanterie wohl erfahren / im erfinden kurtz / in der ausarbeitung hurtig / und in allen ihren gedancken seltzam seyn" (p. 18). The models are Ovid, Martial, Claudian, Boileau, Bouhours, Hofmanswaldau. Besides genius, much free time and deep learning is necessary, if one would become a truly great poet and follow in the steps of Homer, Sophocles, Virgil (pp. 18 f.). This is apparently an impossible expectation. In any event, Neukirch plumps for the second category: "Dannenhero thun diejenigen am besten / welche die mittel-strasse halten / sich bloss auf galante gedichte legen / und die geheimnisse der hohen Poesie unbekümmert lassen" (p. 20). It is interesting to observe, however, that an analysis of the poems by Neukirch included in the first volume of his anthology shows him acting against his own advice or at any rate following it in the breach as often as in the observance. I count 1,332 lines under the rubrics "Galante Gedichte" (9 poems, 172 lines), "Verliebte Gedichte" (11 poems, 662 lines), "Verliebte Arien" (17 poems, 498 lines), but under the rubric "Begräbnis-Gedichte" alone 1,504 lines and under the "Hochzeit-Gedichte" 216, though Neukirch has just said: "Die hochzeiten und begräbnisse würden doch wohl vollzogen werden / wenn man nicht gleich allemahl dabey reimte . . ." (p. 18). Believe the poem, not the poet.

Neukirch is the born epigone, the follower, not the setter, of taste. So far as I can discern, there is not a poem among the 4,368 lines from his own work included in the first volume of his anthology that even approaches the calibre of his heroes, Hofmanswaldau and Lohenstein, though there is often great superficial resemblance. According to his own witness, it cost him his popularity when he later turned away from the decorative style of most of his earlier poems to the sober, flat style of those who sought to follow "nature" and "reason":

> So lang ich meinen Vers nach gleicher Art gewogen,
> Dem Bilde der Natur die Schmincke fürgezogen,
> Der Reime dürren Leib mit Purpur ausgeschmückt,
> Und abgeborgte Krafft den Wörtern angeflickt,
> So war ich auch ein Mann von hohen Dichter-Gaben;
> Allein, so bald ich nur der Spuhre nachgegraben,
> Auf der man zur Vernunfft beschämt zurücke kreucht,
> Und endlich nach und nach nur den Parnass erreicht,
> So ist es aus mit mir. . . .[12]

But it is a question, as we have seen, whether he can be believed. The passage from Günther quoted earlier would seem

187

to show the opposite, as well as the growing popularity of
Canitz and Boileau, his new models. The likelihood is rather
that Neukirch, as always, was merely trying to strike the
median taste.

In all respects the opposite of an epigone is the poet with
whom we close our book. Johann Christian Günther (1695–
1723), "the last Silesian," was born in the year in which
the first volume of Neukirch's anthology appeared. Because
Günther's life and work are so intimately connected, it is
necessary to sketch his biography in some detail. He was
born April 8, 1695, in Striegau, a once flourishing but at that
date poverty-stricken and underpopulated town about fifty
kilometers southwest of Breslau, whither his father, a physician, had moved from Aschersleben in Saxony in 1689. The
family was poor but proud and respected. Günther senior
was a man of considerable learning, if not liberal culture, a
passionate gardener and naturalist and a compassionate doctor. Johann Christian's early education was entirely in his
hands. Believing that he would not be able to send his son to
the university, he had determined that he should learn a trade,
but rather illogically he nonetheless taught him to read out of
Virgil and Ovid. The boy caught fire at once. Under his
father's tutelage and through his own initiative, he had acquired a thorough grasp of Latin and Greek by the time he
was twelve and by the age of seven was writing German
verse and composing plays for his playmates.

When his father saw the result of his instruction, he was
alarmed and angry. Poetry was a way to starve. Besides, poets,
as he conceived them, and in the seventeenth century not
without some justification, were immoral sycophants. But
threats and beatings were of no avail: the son's love of poetry
was stronger than his love and respect for his father, which

188

was great indeed. He had already married the muse, forsaking all others. As a boy he wished that he might suffer the fate of Ovid banished to frigid Tomi, if he might also be granted Ovid's gift of song. His wish was fulfilled. It is not too much to say that he at least subconsciously stylized his life as a victim of poetry, making his boyhood dream come true. "Was man in der Jugend wünscht, hat man im Alter die Fülle."

Through the generosity of a philanthropic colleague of Günther senior, a Dr. Johann Caspar Thiem, Johann Christian was able to attend school after all. In 1710, at fourteen years of age, he entered the newly opened *Gnadenschule* in nearby Schweidnitz, one of the "grace schools" recently granted the Protestants (who under the Habsburgs had the status of second class citizens) at the vigorous insistence of the Swedes. His preparation was so superior that he was placed in the highest class available. The atmosphere of the school and of the Lutheran community in general was strait-laced and puritanical, but there was a small and very active liberal element, representative of the dawning Enlightenment. Through his benefactor, Dr. Thiem, and more especially through the kindness of one of his teachers, Christian Leubscher, a progressive and liberal-minded man, who favored his brilliant pupil, young Günther came into intimate touch with this group. At school he was like a fish in water—the books his father had torn out of his hands were now part of the assignments. Leubscher, who believed in bringing out individual talent rather than in making it conform to a pre-determined pattern, encouraged Günther's poetic bent, even to the extent of producing one of his plays when Günther left school for the university. In Schweidnitz Günther made many friends, a number of whom were to stand him in good stead in his almost constant need, but he also made some relentless enemies. This town he was always to think of as a kind of New Jerusalem, a consecrated spot and his heart's

189

true home, but it was also the seat of many of his later misfortunes.

It was in Schweidnitz that Günther met Leonore Jachmann, who is as firmly associated with his name as Laura with Petrarch's, though she was by no means the only love of his highly susceptible heart. Leonore was the sister of one of Günther's fellow pupils and the daughter of a local physician, George Jachmann, another of whose daughters was the wife of Christian Leubscher. Günther was nineteen when he fell in love with Leonore; she was twenty-five, a handsome and much desired woman, who was at first understandably cool toward the impoverished if brilliant schoolboy, who could offer her nothing but devotion and passionate verses and the promise that she would live in his songs. But in the end that seems to have been enough. They became lovers and some months later were secretly engaged. Leonore even turned down a prosperous young doctor to share an uncertain fate with Günther. (Her younger sister quickly snapped up the doctor.) If the course of true love ever ran rough, it was that between Leonore and Günther. As soon as it was evident that his intentions were serious, he became the laughing stock of his circle, and she was censored by her family. Furthermore, they were in actual danger, for Schweidnitz had strict laws against immorality and against engagements entered into without parental consent. They could meet only secretly, in constant fear of detection. In spite of all precautions, their liaison did not remain unknown. Tongues wagged. One of them belonged to a local hypocrite and busybody by the name of Theodor Krause, an independent scholar who occupied his leisure by editing a periodical called *Vergnügung Müssiger Stunden* (Occupation of Idle Hours), which was partly devoted to gossip, formulated in such a way as to just avoid libel. Krause and Günther remained at swords' points for years. Some of the poet's most devastating satire is directed against this Silesian Tartuffe. One of his most telling blows, in fact, was incorporated in his baroque tragedy *Theodosius*, the play Leubscher produced when Günther left school. It contained pointed references to local figures, among them Krause as "Polylogus" ("blabberer," "forked tongue"), a widower given to the bottle and seeking a new spouse, who sang a song, a parody of a well known hymn, on the joys of losing his first wife: "Freu dich sehr, o meine Seele, / Und versauf all Angst und Qual . . ." Schweidnitz held its sides with laughter, but not all Schweidnitz. There were those who were not amused, including, besides Krause, members of the clergy and Günther senior. Johann Christian had succeeded in making enemies for life with his all too lively muse.

In November 1715, Günther matriculated at Wittenberg as a student of medicine. The university was one of the most medievally minded in Germany. Medical studies were a cruel farce, and members of the theological faculty of this Lutheran Rome were heretic hunters, who spent much of their time ranting against the Pietists at the newly established, liberally oriented Prussian university in Halle. On April 30, 1716, about six months after entering Wittenberg, Günther took a step which characterizes his whole life: he went head over heels in debt to have himself crowned as an imperial poet (poeta laureatus, Kaiserlicher Dichter). The Faculty of Philosophy had the right to grant this empty honor—for a stiff fee—to suitable candidates and Günther could not resist. After submitting a Latin poem recounting his curriculum vitae and some verses in German and Greek, he was officially admitted into the ranks of Petrarch, Johannes Secundus, Opitz, but also into the ranks of many a third-rate versifier, for the title had become almost meaningless. In short, he was now a Kentucky colonel, with all the rights and privileges thereof. His meager funds exhausted by the payment of the fee, Günther went into debt for food and lodging and one year after receiving his title, when his creditors began to press him, he found himself in debtors' prison. Here he seems to have spent most of his time

191

furiously composing laudatory poems, funeral odes, and wedding *carmina* in an attempt to raise money, but such work was paid for in Groschen and Günther owed many Taler. Finally, his friends satisfied his creditors and he was released.

News of this scrape naturally soon reached the ears of his father and his ill-wishers in Schweidnitz. Once more he had made himself the victim of his poetry. In an epistolary poem of the period, Günther, comparing himself first to the author of Revelation and then to Ovid, calls Wittenberg his "Patmos" and his "Pontisches Gestade," where his lyre is his sole comfort. The comparison is very revealing: it shows that Günther, like so many geniuses, experienced his life as a quotation, as the fulfillment of a predestined design. What else, indeed, was his *Dichterkrönung* but a ridiculously immature attempt to follow a sublime pattern?

In the late summer of 1717, Günther came to Leipzig, but did not matriculate in the university until the following summer. Destitute and largely dependent on the charity of friends (there were a number of Schweidnitzers studying in Leipzig), Günther seems nonetheless to have spent his happiest student days in the Saxon city. His poetic talents gained him entrance into lively intellectual and musical circles, and he found an influential protector in Johann Burchard (or Burkhard) Mencke, the rector of the university and a well known scholar, satirist, translator, and writer of light verse. The Leipzig group was devoted to Horace, Ovid, and Anacreon. Günther made a number of translations at this time, trying to enter into the classical spirit. The translations are lost, but the purifying effect on his own style is evident. It is the period of his student songs and the rococo-like poems to "Rosette" (Anna Rosina Lange), a young woman so far above him socially that his love—if such it was—was hopeless from the beginning.

In the spring of 1718, Günther fell sick of a pestilential fever. Believing himself on his deathbed, he made his last will and testament in the form of a poem entitled "Letzte Gedan-ken." He recovered, but in the meantime his circle of friends had largely dispersed, and his meager patrimony, his birth-place in Striegau, had been destroyed by a fire that reduced much of the half-empty town to rubble and ashes. During his sickness he appears to have received not a line from his father. He resumed his medical studies and plunged again into intense poetic activity. He wrote a long satire against his old enemy Krause and, encouraged by Mencke, a stirring ode to Prince Eugene of Savoy, the famous general of Charles VI and a statesman of the first rank. The ode made him famous, but it improved his finances only slightly. The court at Vienna ig-nored him and his ode, while admiring friends in Breslau took up a collection for him. On the strength of his fame, however, and at the urging of Mencke, Günther went to Dresden to compete for the post of assistant court poet ("Pritschmei-ster," a kind of master of ceremonies who had to be able to compose verse extemporaneously). The court of August the Strong, Elector of Saxony and King of Poland, was the most splendid of German baroque courts and Dresden Germany's most beautiful city. Günther was Germany's greatest living poet. Nonetheless, he did not get the post, which later fell to Ulrich König. His failure in Dresden may have crushed and disgusted Günther, but it allowed him to remain himself—the singer doomed to stand before closed doors, the man outside looking in, Ovid in Tomi.

In Leipzig Günther devoted considerable time to love as well as to poetry and medicine. Besides Rosette, there was a more serious affair with another Leonore (we do not know her family name), though she was by all accounts a poor sub-stitute for the "true" Leonore, Leonore Jachmann. In the cemetery, which was their meeting place, they pledged each other eternal faithfulness, but after the downfall in Dresden, the relationship was quickly dissolved. Günther's poems to this Leonore have at once a sultry and a schoolmasterish air; they are among the few examples of his art that make an unpleasant impression of disingenuousness.

September 1719, Günther left Saxony to return to Silesia. He had been away four years. What did this prodigal son hope to find in his homeland? Leonore's arms? Reconciliation with his father? A living of some kind? The house where he was born lay in ashes, his father refused even to admit him to his presence, and Leonore had long since left Schweidnitz. His bad reputation had of course preceded him and he met with a cool, not to say disdainful, reception at most doors. For his father's harsh attitude there was some reason: he had repeatedly begged his son not to neglect medicine for poetry, pleas that fell on deaf ears; in addition, he could not help giving some credence to the tales about Johann Christian's wild behavior assiduously circulated by his enemies. In his desperate striving to find some niche in society, Günther even went to Krause and offered to bury the hatchet. But what was he? A profligate rejected by his own father. Leonore was gone and Schweidnitz was Schweidnitz no more. He turned his steps toward Breslau.

Here he was well received by Ferdinand von Bressler and his wife Marianne, herself a poetess. Bressler had been the chief contributor to the purse sent to him in Leipzig. For a while it looked as though his luck might change. The Bresslers made every effort to find him a position, to fit him into society. But in the end nothing came of it. Again in debt and leading a hand to mouth existence, pursued still by his ill-wishers, mainly persons whom he had offended by his biting satire, he was forced once more to take to the road. Bressler redeemed his coat from the pawnbroker and gave him some traveling money.

While in Breslau, however, he had been able to see Leonore again. She had taken a position as housekeeper in a castle on the outskirts of the city. To this reunion and the parting

194

that followed we owe some of the most moving love poems in German. His "Schreiben an seine Leonore," dated from Breslau, December 22, 1719, is a kind of celebration of their marriage in the virtuality of poetry.

Günther was now determined to leave Silesia forever. Together with an impecunious student named Schubart, he set out in late winter for Leipzig, stopping with friends en route. Schubart was sure they could make a stake in Lauban, his home town on the Saxon-Silesian border. But they arrived in the midst of a severe famine, Günther with a badly infected foot that forced him to take to bed immediately. (It goes without saying that the journeys were on foot.) As a welcome, Günther was greeted in Lauban by a lampoon by a certain Fritsche, a clergyman who had mistakenly applied a satirical passage in one of Günther's poems to himself, and now blackened the poet's character in revenge. The Lauban poems are truly written *de profundis*—Ovid's fate was now Günther's and with a vengeance. But so was Ovid's power of lamentation—both had the divine gift of *saying* what they suffered. The only shelter Günther could find in Lauban was in the poorhouse ("der Stock"). (It would seem that he found a place here through Schubart's parents.) His suit was again in the pawnshop, but a kindly corporal's widow lent him her dead husband's overcoat. Feverish, half-starved, his swollen leg wrapped in straw, his shirt wrapped about his head, he sat propped on a wooden bench in an unheated attic, snow sifting through the tiles, and wrote some of his best poetry, indeed some of the best poetry in German before Klopstock and Goethe. He wrote constantly. In a Latin letter to a friend (Haas) begging for assistance, he says that he has composed more than two thousand verses in the last twenty-four hours! (*Werke*, III, 114, 12 ff.) It was here that he also passed through a religious crisis reminiscent of Hamann's in his London boarding house. (The centrality of this religious experience in Lauban has been underplayed and misinterpreted in

Günther criticism.) He was rescued from his misery by a "miracle," as he was himself convinced (see *Werke*, II, 143 f.). When he was able to walk again, he met a merchant by the name of Kirchhof, apparently at a funeral, and Kirchhof provided for him. Following his now firmly established pattern, he was no sooner out of difficulties than he made a new enemy, again a member of the clergy and again through his poetry. (In the name of the daughter of his protector he wrote a sarcastic poem in which she rejected the attentions of an unwanted suitor—the clergyman in question, a certain Minor: "Der *Kirchhof* unter meinem Kleide / Ist nicht für Ihren Leib bestimmt . . .")

In the same letter in which he mentions his prodigious productivity while lying in the poorhouse, Günther tells his friend that he has for the future determined to devote himself entirely to medicine. His friends in Lauban advised him to seek once more to reconcile himself with his father before continuing on to Leipzig to finish his degree. In the summer of 1720 he returned again to Striegau, his birthplace. His father remained adamant—he would have nothing to do with his son until the latter had proved that he had changed his ways by settling down as a doctor. In Schweidnitz he heard that Leonore was to become the wife of another. He succeeded in seeing her again and with his old charm seems to have dissuaded her from her purpose. His new determination to establish himself as a doctor no doubt gave her some hope. Friends advised him to go to Upper Silesia, near the Polish border, a thinly settled region, where, after taking an examination, he could practice as a "Physicus," i.e., as a doctor with training but no degree. (This was in fact what his father, unable to afford a degree, had done.) In Brieg, in Upper Silesia, where he had gone to take his examination, he lived as always half on charity and half by his pen. His efforts to find a practice at first met with no success. To add to his woes, he was publicly denounced by a Lutheran pastor by the name of

Lachmann, an associate of Fritsche, for spreading Pietistic doctrine through his verse, a serious charge, since the Habsburg regime was intent upon suppressing the Pietists. A sense of hopelessness begins to pervade Günther's work. He loses his hold over Leonore, who, worn out with waiting, finally leaves Silesia for Pomerania (Anklam, near Stettin). He hears that she has married. The report was not true: the death registry of the church of Maria Magdalena in Breslau shows that she died a spinster. Whether Günther ever learned the truth of the matter is uncertain. In any event, his last poem to her begins:

> *Sey immerhin der Hand entrissen,*
> *Im Herzen bleibstu dennoch mein . . .*

Constantly aided by his friends—did a man ever find more friends or complain more about friendlessness?—Günther finally established himself as doctor in Kreuzburg, a poor district with a half-Polish population. He seems to have been a first-rate physician and popular with his patients. Almost immediately he persuaded himself that he was in love again. This time it was the daughter of a pastor, Johanna Barbara Littmann, the "Phillis" of his song. Johanna Barbara was still smarting from having been jilted by her fiancé, a man by the name of Mennling (or Männling) who had married a woman with a larger dowry in order to advance himself more rapidly in the church (pastorates were often bought). Thus Barbara and Günther caught each other on the rebound. He had fond dreams of the blessings of a well-run home and a sensible wife to comfort his bed, a secure place in the social order. All his life he yearned desperately for the "Wonnen der Gewöhnlichkeit" with a yearning only the outcast can know. But this dream was not to be realized. (How should it be? The meaning of his life was to be the man outside.) Pastor Littmann made marriage with his daughter dependent on two conditions: that Günther reconcile himself with his father and that he obtain a medical degree. The fulfillment of the first condition was thwarted by the elder Günther's stern unforgivingness, the fulfillment of the second—which might eventually have brought about the fulfillment of the first—by death. Rejected by his father for the fifth time, Johann Christian was ashamed to return to Kreuzburg. The last epoch of his wanderings begins. We find him now in one Silesian town after another, sponging on friends and patrons, frantically seeking to scrape together enough money to re-enter the university. In Landeshut, one of the stations of his wanderings, he finds an appreciative patron in Hans Gottfried von Beuchelt, a rich man's son with an interest in the arts, who encourages Günther to begin collecting his scattered poems. Here he also enjoys the hospitality of Theodor Speer, a friend from Leipzig days and indeed the very one who, though himself poor as a church mouse, had sheltered him when he came to Leipzig from Wittenberg. Prosperous now, he introduces Günther into the best circles. Naturally, things do not go well for long. Günther soon falls in love with Speer's sister, Johanna Eleonore Dauling, who is married to a man seventeen years her senior. The situation, which resulted in some beautiful love lyrics thinly disguised as expressions of friendship and gratitude, quickly became socially intolerable.

Günther's poetry after leaving Landeshut is in large part a casting up of inner accounts, an attempt to make sense of his chaotic life. Two of the most important productions of this period are the famous 416-line letter to his father ("Quid feci? quid commerui aut peccavi, Pater?") and a verse epistle to Beuchelt—both are self-interpretations. Günther returned to Landeshut once more before leaving Silesia forever. He even tried once more to enter under the wing of Count Sporck, an enormously rich and eccentric *grand seigneur*, to whom he had already addressed one eulogy. The story of his relations with Sporck is complicated, but the long and short of it was that Günther went completely unrecognized and

unrewarded. By this time he was thoroughly sick of his homeland, where he had suffered one disappointment after another: "Betrogne Poesie, komm, pack den Plunder ein . . ."
The fall of 1722 found him in Jena—not Leipzig, whither
he had declared he meant to go—striving to complete his medical studies. Here too he found someone to give him food and
shelter (a young Silesian nobleman), otherwise he could not
have survived. In February, 1723, he fell sick, probably of an
upper respiratory ailment, and died March 15. He was not
quite twenty-eight years old. His fellow Silesians buried him
at their own expense in the graveyard before the Johannistor.
The church clerk entered him in the burial registry as a "student of theology." In a poem written in Leipzig in 1719, in a
fit of clairvoyant self-pity, Günther had composed his own
epitaph:

> *Hier starb ein Schlesier, weil Glück und Zeit nicht*
> *wollte,*
> *Dass seine Dichterkunst zur Reife kommen sollte;*
> *Mein Pilger, lis geschwind und wandre deine Bahn,*
> *Sonst steckt dich auch sein Staub mit Lieb und*
> *Unglück an.*

It is hardly possible to contemplate Günther's life objec-
tively without agreeing with the basic conclusions reached by
Günther senior in judging his son, namely, that he had few
enemies that he did not make for himself "mit seiner satiri-
schen Feder," that he did not lack influential benefactors, that
he failed to take advantage of many an opportunity, that he
was, in short, to blame for his own misery, "einzig und allein
*fortunae suae sinistrae faber.*" He refused to "accommodate
himself." Naturally, this does not excuse the father for playing the role of old Nobodaddy. Equally just is Goethe's judgment in the seventh book of *Dichtung und Wahrheit*, much
as Günther's biographer, Wilhelm Krämer, may fulminate
against it: "Er wusste sich nicht zu zähmen, und so zerrann

ihm sein Leben wie sein Dichten." The question is of course whether Günther in his inmost heart did not *desire* the fate he suffered, whether it was not necessary for him in order that he realize himself as a poet, the kind of poet he knew himself to be.

Günther was not in revolt against society. His dearest dream was to be integrated into it—but only on his own terms: as a poet who would not compromise with truth. With tiring regularity he reiterates his ideal of "sincerity" (*Redligkeit*). It is the *conditio sine qua non* of his poetry, which is always his prime consideration, the one thing he will not renounce or compromise. To his poetry he sacrifices his life. Or, as one could say with equal justice, he stylizes his life as a victim of poetry. The Ovidian *Urbild* of his childhood is never far to seek. To this question Günther scholarship has not yet addressed itself.[13]


Günther is too direct, too personal and too confessional to be called baroque, yet he cannot properly be placed in the Enlightenment. He is only remotely akin to poets like Haller, Brockes, Hagedorn, and Gellert. He is often called a poet "between the times." The question is: what times? The Baroque on the one hand to be sure, but what on the other? His attitude toward poetry is often compared to that of the *Sturm und Drang* with its cult of individual feeling and self-expression. In that case he cannot be said to be "between the times," but rather, like Georg Büchner at the beginning of the nineteenth century, ahead of his time. The comparison with Büchner also limps, however, for Günther is no formal innovator. He is avantgardistic only in respect to the content of his poetry. The tension between baroque form and extremely personal content is the trademark by which Günther's poetry is immediately recognizable.

When one comes to Günther after immersion in the impersonal, genre-oriented, decorative, generalizing verse of his predecessors and contemporaries, the immediacy of his confessional poetry is almost dismaying. Here is a man who writes directly about himself, who transforms his own life, not a general truth, into poetry! Günther lived his life in the name of poetry and wrote his poetry in the name of life. The linguistic habitus may be that of the Baroque modified by the new sobriety, but the point of view has changed, and changed much more radically than in Canitz or Besser. There is now a change from within, not without, truly a new concept of poetry. Tasso-like, Günther sees poetry as a way of saying what *he* suffers, seldom does he insist upon general applicability. The emblematic mode, though not entirely foreign to him, is atypical of his work. Thus his life as seen through his poetry becomes itself a symbol, especially a symbol of man's suffering, though it would probably be going too far to maintain that Günther consciously—in the manner of Goethe—thought of it in this light.

One of the more penetrating insights into the nature of Günther's poetry is found in Krämer's "Vorwort" to the first volume of his edition of the collected works (p. vi). Günther's poems, Krämer says, are to be regarded more as the limbs of a great organism than as independent individual structures, they are a "poetic report" on the way he became what he is. With only slight exaggeration one might say that Günther's noncommissioned work is one poem, his life as a poem. There is much in it that is second-rate; indeed, there is only a handful of "perfect" poems, but the production as a whole is very impressive and very moving. One cannot read Günther without becoming involved in the author as a person, so involved, in fact, that it is sometimes difficult to take his work simply as "art." How a poet nurtured in the baroque tradition arrived at the concept of poetry as an *apologia pro vita sua* is a problem scholarship has not yet investigated. It

201

explains nothing to see Günther merely as a "precursor" of Goethe.

As I have tried to indicate in the biographical sketch, Günther is without doubt the victim of his art, but the willing victim, for poetry is his life, more desirable finally than the well-ordered garden of bourgeois society for which he consciously longs. Whenever it is a question of gaining the latter at the expense of the former, Günther unfailingly chooses the role of the outcast. I have suggested that he chooses it (perhaps subconsciously) because it is the necessary concomitant of his greatest poetry. The tension established, he then sings of his longing for peace and security and of his suffering. At the same time, this self-created situation reflects his state existentially. His deepest wish is to win eternal fame through his verse, to join the "lorbeerreiche Schaar, / Virgil, Horaz, Petrarch, Secundus, Sannazar" (II, 51), that is, to be accepted into society as a great poet. But only on his own terms, never at the expense of his "sincerity" or his own peculiar individuality. The age mocked at such pretensions. It still demanded the submission of the individual to an order that ranked the poet approximately with a court jester and defined poetry itself strictly in terms of genre. There was no place for Günther and his new kind of poetry. His career thus becomes the tragedy of one born before his time.

Let me attempt to support some of these generalities by adducing passages from the work itself. The central fact of Günther's life for Günther himself is that he was born to be a poet and nothing else. With youthful exuberance (at nineteen) he proclaims (III, 18 f.):

> O höchstbeglückter Schluss, der Geist und Blut
>    gerührt,
> Dass ich dem Opiz schon in etwas nachgespürt!
> O höchstbeglückter Tag, der meine Dichterflöthen
> Das erste Mahl gehört! Der Hunger mag mich tödten,
>    Das Schwerd erwürge mich, dem Feuer mag der Leib

*An statt der Nahrung seyn, wenn nur mein*
*Zeitvertreib,*
*Das edle Harfenspiel, die Seele meines Lebens,*
*Nicht in dem Tode stirbt, ...*

After the debacle in Dresden, where he had failed to obtain
the post of assistant court poet, he claims that he is about
ready to agree with those who call poets fools; if he were
truly serious about gaining worldly honors and riches, he
would give up poetry for good; nonetheless (III, 75):

*Nichts desto weniger entzückt mich noch ihr [der*
*Poesie] Scherzen,*
*Und selbst mein Ungemach bringt mancher Einfall*
*bey;*
*Verschwör ich sie gleich oft, so geht es nicht vom*
*Herzen,*
*Denn weil der Mund noch flucht, so schreibt die Hand*
*aufs neu.*

Toward the close of this same poem, Günther finds a striking
image to characterize the lot of one who is a poet and nothing
else—his abandoned state which is yet the source of his true
happiness. Contrasting the pleasures of society with his own
simple, poverty-stricken existence, he says (III, 77 f.; emphasis added):

*Ich bleibe, was ich bin, und bleib ich auch verlassen,*

. . . . . . . . . . . . . . . . . . . .
*So siz ich bald daheim, bald aber in dem Grünen*
Und Phoebus und mein Creuz, sonst niemand, neben
mir.
*Da muss mir oft die Noth zum Seelenfrieden dienen,*
*Denn wenn die Muse spielt, weicht aller Schmerz von*
*hier.*

In a fragmentary epistolary poem to his patron and
mentor, Burkhard Mencke, written at the nadir of his career
from Lauban (April, 1720), he sees himself as the victim of his

poetry, admitting at the same time that the persecution he suffers in its name is his own doing (III, 106):

> *Warum mich nun der Zorn des Vaterlandes trift,*
> *Rührt, wie ich glauben muss, von mancher*
>    *Stachelschrift;*
> *Durch diese zeugt ich mir ein allgemeines Hassen.*
> *Der Kampf ist auch nicht jung, er fing schon in den*
>    *Classen*
> *Der letzten Schulzeit an....*

But he has been persecuted enough for the impulsiveness of youth; instead of kicking him when he is down, society should help him to his feet and allow him to make a fresh start. A fresh start, however, should it involve the renunciation of poetry, would be an impossibility, if Günther is to remain Günther (III, 109):

> *Man schreyt mir häufig zu: Verlas die Poesie!*
> *Was kan ich denn davor? So oft ich ihr entflieh,*
> *So oft erhascht sie mich mit allzeit grössrer Liebe,*
> *Die Reime fesseln mich, es sind nicht falsche Triebe,*
> *Es ist Natur und Hang ...*

The magic circle cannot be broken. Being Günther means being a poet. Furthermore, as he insists untold times, it means being "sincere," i.e. telling the truth as he sees and experiences it. Shortly after, in this same letter, he enlarges on the experiential basis of his poetry (III, 109):

> *Viel Dichter klagen blos, Gedancken anzubringen,*
> *Erbetteln ihren Schmerz, zu dem sie sich erst zwingen,*
> *Von fremder Traurigkeit und weinen künstlich toll*
> *Und glauben selber nicht, was uns bewegen soll.*
> *Wen aber rührt die Qual gemahlter armer Sünder,*
> *Es wäre denn ein Weib und noch nicht trockne Kinder.*
> *Die Noth erklärt sich schlecht [schlicht] und redet,*
>    *wie sie denckt.*

204

*Lis, prüfe, theures Haupt, was hier den [Günther]*
    *kränckt.*
*Die Wahrheit wird sich hier in keine Larve stecken,*
*Wohl aber überall ein treues Herz entdecken.*

This very quality of sincerity in turn he recognizes as the
source of all his misery, just as he knows it to be the source of
his deepest happiness, because it is the source of his best poetry (II, 193):

*Du mein Unglück auf der Erden,*
*Allerliebste Redligkeit,*
*Die du mich bey viel Beschwerden*
*Gleichwohl als mein Schaz erfreut . . .*

The circle is closed once more.

In his grimmer, and perhaps clearer, moments Günther
knows that it is absurd to expect an age which still regarded
the fulsome laud of a tyrant, the lewd quodlibet, Petrarchan
verses in praise of one's mistress as proper poetry to accept his
criterion of "sincerity": "Was Wahrheit? schreyt Marcolph,
die ist der Dichter Scham!" (IV, 161). Günther's own work,
which early discarded the florid style and demanded to be
taken in the name of "truth" and "Redligkeit," was bound to
meet with a mixed reception in times when

*. . . alle, wie man hört, verachten rechte Gaben,*
*Und wollen schlechterdings nur Lustigmacher haben.*
                                                        [IV,158.]

"Lustigmacher," jesters in a broader sense, were also those
who provided the "serious" poetry of the day, in whatever
guise it might appear, as ode, eulogy, funeral oration, or wedding "*carmen*." Günther's plaint is at bottom the plaint of a
man whom the world refuses to take seriously because it does
not take seriously that which is his existential expression, poetry itself.[14] We can regard him not only as the victim of his
own poetry, but also as the victim of the baroque taste and its

view of the art of poetry as rhymed oratory adhering strictly to generic conventions. What indeed did truth and sincerity have to do with that? But the times were changing and the view of the nature of poetry with them. Günther was perhaps the most popular poet of the generation that followed him.

In respect to the external form of his work and to his attitude toward his linguistic medium, Günther begins as a child of the Baroque. In respect to the former he remains essentially baroque throughout his short career, in respect to the latter he becomes, like Besser and Neukirch in the wake of Canitz, an adherent of the new sobriety. But rhymed prose, in the manner of Canitz, was never his ideal. As "naturalistically" as he may sometimes demean himself, he never becomes flat and unpoetic. The besetting sin of his work is not a prosaic attitude but prolixity. A born poet if there ever was one, he is far too facile. Even his correspondence he seems to have preferred to conduct in verse. To criticize Günther for his prolixity may, however, be somewhat unfair. It is to be remembered that he died before he had had a chance to complete the revision of his work, which appeared in a collected edition only posthumously (1724–35, in four parts). It is not unlikely that, had he been able to impose his will on the final form, he would have relegated much to limbo and would have shortened and tightened up much of the remainder.[15]

It has long been recognized that Günther's central poetry revolves about two main themes: love and misfortune; *his* love for this or that particular woman, and his *personal* misfortune in this or that particular situation. His other major themes, namely, the poet and society and man's relationship to God (his relationship to his father is an aspect of this), are interwoven with these two leading complexes. His satirical and encomiastic poetry is also important but not really central, being essentially a spin-off from the theme of the poet and society. The inchoate state of Günther criticism makes it difficult for the literary historian, whose task is rather to trans-

206

mit received opinion than to offer original views, to deal adequately with this poet. Perhaps, however, it is only slightly more difficult in the case of Günther (because of his relative complexity) than in the case of other baroque poets. For all the pounding of drums and the propounding of theories, the investigation of the German Baroque as a whole, not merely of Günther, is only in its beginnings.

How imperative was the linguistic habitus of the Baroque for a poet trying his wings at the beginning of the eighteenth century is abundantly clear from Günther's lament "On the Death of his Beloved Flavia" (I, 3), his foster-sister, Anna Maria Reinfelden, whom he had loved from childhood, first as a sister, then as a woman. The poem was written when Günther was nineteen. "Flavia," whom he also calls "Filindrene," was, together with Leonore Jachmann and "Phillis" (Barbara Littman), one of the three guiding stars of his erotic life. Of the genuineness of his affection there can be no doubt. In a late poem to "Phillis" he still speaks of "Filindrene" as being one of the "two hearts" he has already loved, the other being of course Leonore (I, 256, 133 ff.). The criteria of "truth" and "sincerity" thus being fulfilled, one can attribute such formulations as those in the following lines only to the weight of convention:

> *Stirbt meine Flavie, so klagen meine Flöthen,*
> *Der Schlag, so sie gefällt, muss mich auch selber tödten.*
> *Die Schönheit und ihr Kind, mein Leben, sinckt ins Grab,*
> *Das meine Lust vergräbt. Was mir der Himmel gab,*
> *Nimmt jezt die Erde hin. Der Zierrath aller Wälder,*
> *Der Ausbund aller Treu, macht der Elyser Felder*
> *Durch seinen Tod beglückt. Die ewig schwarze Nacht*
> *Verhüllt mein Sonnenlicht.*

The poem is so overloaded with baroque clichés as to seem almost a parody of the fashionable manner. It is strongly reminiscent of an elegy by B. Neukirch "on the supposed death" of his Sylvia (Neukirch I, 107), with its refrain, "O himmel / erd' und lufft / erhöret meine lieder! Schafft meine Sylvia / schafft meine liebste wieder," which Günther's opening lines, repeated at the beginning of each stanza, seem to echo. Both poems employ the pastoral convention, both strive—Neukirch rather more successfully than Günther, because somewhat more restrainedly—to raise the death of the beloved to the level of a cosmic event. Neukirch, for example, sings:

> *Wenn ich mein morgen-brod mit saltz und thränen*
>   *ass /*
> *So fiel sie neben mich in das bethaute gras /*
> *Und sang / ob wolte sie die gantze welt bewegen.*
> *Die winde musten sich auff ihre seuffzer legen:*
> *Die blitze stunden still / und Phöbus trat die bahn /*
> *So offt er sie ersah / mit vollen freuden an.*

Compare Günther:

> *... Der Parzen Urthelstab*
> *Reisst meiner Flavia den Schönheitspurpur ab.*
> *Die Äcker fühlen es. Die Zierligkeit der Blätter*
> *Verläst den dürren Stamm, ...*
> *... Es seufzen Feld und Wald,*
> *Da ein gebrochen Wort in seinen Thälern schallt*
> *Und ihren Tod beklagt. ...*

With the constant penchant of the Baroque never to leave well enough alone (to do so would have been "unpoetic"), a simple shepherdess is transformed into a half-goddess. The characteristic difference between the two poems—aside from the excessive length of Günther's product (236 lines)—lies in the fact that Günther's contains direct, homely touches reflecting actual experience. In the midst of all the baroque splendor and pastoral pretense we catch a glimpse of two simple children and devoted playmates, Anna Maria and Johann Christian, whose fondness for each other was to blossom into true love:

> *Der Kindheit Morgen warf den Zunder in die Brust,*
> *Der nach und nach entglamm; die erste Liebeslust*
> *War Spiel und Dockenwerck. Ich war dir schon*
>     *gewogen,*
> *Als aus den Wangen noch kein Haar die Milch gesogen.*
> *Wir waren schwach und klein, die Liebe starck und gross*
> *Und grösser als wir selbst. Oft trug uns eine Schoos,*
> *Oft führt' uns eine Hand, noch öfter das Verlangen.*
> *Wie öfters hat uns nicht ein kindliches Umfangen*
> *Die Armen schwer und blau wie selbsten lass gemacht!*

The attempt to give such lines a certain rhetorically decorative varnish is evident enough (e.g., the personification of "Kindheit," the use of the word "Zunder," the play on the verb "führen"), but it is also plain that they speak of a direct personal experience. Such realistic touches are foreign to Neukirch's plaint, just as they are foreign to the convention as a whole. The nearest Neukirch comes to anything similar is in the lines cited above ("Wenn ich mein morgen-brod . . ."), but this passage in no way oversteps the bounds of the pastoral. Günther, on the other hand, breaches the convention, while at the same time following it with an almost parodying fulsomeness that is itself suspicious—he insists too much. It is as though he cannot help telling the *true* story, ill as it may befit the costume he has assumed. The hallmark of Günther's verse—baroque form in conflict with the ethos of sincerity—is already apparent.

This tension remains characteristic of Günther's verse as a whole and marks him as a "transitional" figure. The excessively decorative element, however, so apparent in the poem on Flavia's death, was soon to be significantly reduced as inconsistent with his new ideal of poetry. In a verse epistle written in 1717 (III, 55) there occurs a famous passage which speaks of the poet's efforts to "cure his Phoebus" of baroque mannerisms:

> Mein Phoebus liegt noch kranck, ich hab ihn in der Cur
> Und will ihm nach und nach die schwülstige Natur,
> Die seine Jugend plagt, aus Blut und Gliedern treiben ...

This determination to jettison bombast was due in Günther's case not only to the influence of the new sobriety but also, and perhaps primarily, to his intense preoccupation with the classics during his Leipzig period. His striving and the method of his "cure" is, as he states in this same passage,

> ... die Minen und den Grund
> Worein die Poesie der Römer und der Griechen
> Den reichsten Schaz vergräbt, von neuem
> durchzukriechen ...

This bold metaphor is perhaps not immediately comprehensible. In classical poetry a treasure is buried (*Minen* are mines) which he means to rediscover and make valid for his own poetry. The subsequent development of Günther's verses shows that he does not mean to validate this treasure by outwardly imitating classical forms, as Klopstock was later to attempt to do, but rather by emulating its spirit of purity and sincerity. He seems already to be aware of the profound truth that Edward Young (in his "Conjectures on Original Composition") was to reveal to a later generation: that he could become a Greek only by being himself. At the same time, Günther's new poetic ideal—internal evidence indicates that it anticipates express announcement—does not involve the rejection of metaphor by any means. Rather, metaphor is restored to its true expressive function, as distinguished from a primarily decorative one. This does not take place suddenly. There is still fluctuation, especially in the earlier poetry, between the florid style and the new ideal, and we also find passages typical of the flat, sober style, associated with Canitz and Weise.[16]

The poems to Leonore Jachmann constitute Günther's most important love poetry. There are two main groups of Leonore poems, corresponding to periods in the poet's life and to his proximity to Leonore herself. The first group was written while he was still at school in Schweidnitz and during his first absence from Leonore in Wittenberg. Krämer dates this group Schweidnitz, June, 1714—Wittenberg, July, 1716, i.e., before Günther's announced determination to "cure his Phoebus." The second group is dated Dresden, August, 1719—Breslau, Autumn, 1720 and was composed between the time of Günther's return to Silesia and some time after Leonore's departure from her homeland for Pomerania.

Psychologically speaking, the great difference between this poetry and the erotic poetry that immediately precedes it or is even contemporary with it lies above all in the seriousness with which it takes the beloved as a *person*, not merely as an exchangeable erotic object. For the first time since Fleming, and to a much greater degree than in Fleming, we have the feeling that this poetry could have been written only to this particular woman. The same is true of all of Günther's verse addressed to different women. All who aroused his passion stand out as definite personalities, as women first and objects of desire second. They are desired because they are themselves. Thus Günther's erotic verse is never merely lustful and the theme of lust and its slavery is foreign to him. The outstanding characteristic of his love poetry is the *union* of the physical and spiritual. Günther's love is "modern love" in the sense of being multidimensional and problematic. It is also modern in its attempt to inform the erotic relationship, through the ideal of faithfulness, with metaphysical meaning. But, and this is the distinctive feature, its metaphysical meaning is intimately bound up with its physical basis. It does not

211

skip the here and now nor does it see the physical merely in terms of an emblematic "sign." By the same token it does not degrade the physical to pure lust. Since Petrarch, and even before (but not of course in the case of Petrarch himself), the problem of love had, with fairly rare exceptions, been treated in European poetry in a strikingly unproblematic fashion: convention determined all. With Günther, love as an ever new individual revelation and as an ever new individual problem comes into its own.

To a degree, this attitude toward love reflects the attitude of the dawning Enlightenment toward "nature." Men were beginning to turn to the world about them and were trying to formulate theories and explanations of reality on the basis of the phenomena themselves, rather than solely on the basis of religious dogma and ancient authority. With this turning away from the one sure source of truth—revealed religion—to the realm of nature, the world and with it love itself was bound to become problematical. This same about-face naturally brought with it the decline of the emblematic mode in poetry, which dominates the Baroque. It was becoming difficult to posit a perfect relationship between the phenomenal and the noumenal. (Finally of course this was to lead to the rise of the symbolic mode and the reintroduction of the metaphysical by the back door—via the physical.) It should go without saying that this change did not take place overnight. There is much overlap, considerable uncertainty and confusion of poetic modes, frequent "backsliding," if one will, into the older dogmatic, and fundamentally medieval, view of the nature of things and their meaning as pure emblems.

Could we be sure of arranging them in their proper sequence with no important links missing, the poems to Leonore Jachmann would no doubt form the autobiography of a heart. Even in their rather fragmentary state they form such a book, though with tantalizing lacunae and puzzling turns. The first group contains 56 poems, some as short as four lines, the longest 126 lines, and averaging perhaps around 50 lines. They begin with a poem on the theme of fateful love at first sight, tell of the torments of secret passion, then of its declaration, continue with an important sub-group on the spiritual meaning of the physical, turn then to love's majesty as embodied in the beloved, fervently plead the lover's cause in an internalization of the carpe diem theme, tell in a sonnet of the lovers' secret engagement, sing of faithfulness as that which can give love eternal meaning, speaking then of unfaithfulness and jealousy, and conclude with a group of very moving poems on the theme of parting. These are followed by a kind of epilogue consisting of poems written after the lovers' separation. They speak of keeping the faith, of his longing (the most important theme), and end with a letter in which he defends himself against the charge of unfaithfulness and paints a picture of their future happiness. This account follows the arrangement given in Krämer, who tries to stick to a strict chronological sequence. In other words, life itself as reflected in these poems arranges them into a kind of cycle. They form, as Goethe puts it in speaking of Günther's work as a whole, "im Leben ein zweites Leben durch Poesie." We cannot know just what order the poet himself would have given them, had he lived to publish an edition of his own work, but one can speculate with some basis in psychological likelihood that his fanatic "sincerity" would have caused him to follow a similar scheme, though no doubt a less fragmentary one.

These earlier poems to Leonore still show many traces of exteriorized metaphoric usage in the conventional baroque manner. For example (I, 26):

*Gewis, die Lippe führt ein reiches Kaufmannsgut,*
*Und das Gesichte zeigt ein Meer voll Milch und Blut,*
*Allwo die Gratien am Ufer deiner Wangen*
*So Perlen suchen gehn als Purpurschnecken fangen.*

213

Though there is an ingratiating playfulness that bends us to consent, we may still find it a bit difficult to imagine the Graces catching snails on the shores of cheeks full of milk and blood. The aim of this kind of imagery is purely decorative; the images are not meant to be *vollzogen*, translated into actuality. To us, it may hardly seem possible that the poet means this as "serious" poetry. But there is no good reason for thinking that he didn't. The startling thing is that such a passage stands in the vicinity of such delightfully direct and vivid verses as the following (I, 47), in which the lover roughishly begs forgiveness for having taken certain liberties (a frequent motif):

> *Schau nur selbst, die zarten Brüste*
> *Blicken mich so liebreich an,*
> *Dass ich nach der Milch gelüste*
> *Und mich kaum enthalten kan,*
> *Bey so wohlbestellten Sachen*
> *Dich noch einmal rot zu machen.*

Or consider this stanza from one of the most fervent and most internalized of Günther's carpe diem poems (I, 52):

> *Eröfne mir das Feld der Brüste,*
> *Entschleus die wollustschwangre Schoos,*
> *Gieb mir die schönen Lenden blos,*
> *Bis sich des Monden Neid entrüste!*
> *Die Nacht ist unsrer Lust bequem, [geneigt]*
> *Die Sternen schimmern angenehem*
> *Und buhlen uns nur zum Exempel;*
> *Drum gieb mir der Verliebten Kost,*
> *Ich schencke dir der Wollust Most*
> *Zum Opfer in der Keuschheit Tempel.*

At first blush, one might take these lines for a direct imitation of Hofmanswaldau. The image of sacrifice in the last two

214

verses is especially reminiscent of the great eroticist and a turn like "der Wollust Most" (for semen) very typical. But one soon becomes aware that there is an element present here that is foreign to carpe diem poems before Günther. This is the concept of *reciprocity*. The impetuous imperatives demanding submission are balanced by the idea of giving in return ("Ich schencke dir . . ."). Reciprocity is also stressed in the adjective *wollustschwanger*, which for compression of meaning is fully worthy of Goethe: "Entschleus [entschliess] die wollustschwangre Schoos." His desire and its fulfillment are also seen in terms of hers. It is this that makes the act of love *keusch* and the "Schoos" (here of course *sexus, pudendum*) "der Keuschheit Tempel." The lover's argument is raised above the specious faunal logic of the slave of lust and becomes an expression of dedication to true love. It is not without justification that the poem ends with the motif of faithfulness unto death. It is notable that there is no purely decorative imagery in these lines. The striking metaphor "das *Feld* der Brüste" one could almost term "organic"—on this "field" Günther lets shine the envious moon; the beloved becomes part of the cosmos and the act of love itself a fitting rite that follows the example of the shimmering stars.

Günther, as anyone who occupies himself with his work soon realizes, has a deeply religious nature. Love he also endows with religious meaning, though it would be wrong to say that he makes a religion of love. Faithfulness, this is Günther's conviction, can give temporal love eternal meaning. This theme forms the dominant ethical note in this group of poems. This is both modern and problematic. It is modern because of the seriousness with which it takes the temporal and transient; it is problematic because of man's very nature: "Der Menschen Herz verändert wunderlich." Günther keeps recurring to faithfulness as an ideal and as the basic problem of the love relationship (I, 56, emphasis added; and I, 58):

*Mein Kind, was zweifelstu an meiner Redligkeit,*
*Die ihres gleichen doch in deiner Brust verspüret?*

. . . . . . . . . . . . . . . .

*Mein Sinnbild ist ein Ring, der Denckspruch: Sonder*
*Ende;*
Denn wer nicht ewig liebt, der liebet nimmermehr

*Drum liebe nur getrost; denn die Beständigkeit*
*Würckt mir den Hochzeitrock und auch das*
*Leichenkleid.*

Faithfulness is an aspect of *sincerity*, here as always Günther's prime ethical value. The same ideal that, if it could be realized, would eternalize temporal love is also the ideal that makes him a new kind of poet, for in the last analysis his turning away from the rhetorical exteriorization of the Baroque to a more direct and "organic" kind of poetry springs from the same root (I, 82):

*Weine nicht, mein Kind, ich bleibe*
*Dir bis in den Tod getreu.*
*Glaube, was ich denck und schreibe,*
*Ist und heist doch einerley,*
*Weil die Redligkeit zum Lieben*
*Mir Geseze vorgeschrieben.*

The poem "Als er sie seiner beständigen Liebe versicherte" (I, 59) might be called the programmatic piece on the theme of "secularized eternity." The key stanza is the second:

*Glück und Zeit*
*Hasset die Beständigkeit;*
*Doch das Feuer, so ich fühle,*
*Hat die Ewigkeit zum Ziele*
*Und verblendet selbst den Neid.*

The companion piece to this poem, using the same stanza form,[17] is the well known "Abschied von seiner ungetreuen

Liebsten" (I, 70). The exploitation of the same form for both poems points up the problematic nature of the ideal:

> *Wie gedacht,*
> *Vor geliebt, jezt ausgelacht.*
> *Gestern in die Schoos gerissen*
> *Heute von der Brust geschmissen,*
> *Morgen in die Gruft gebracht.*
> *Wie gedacht,*
> *Vor geliebt, jezt ausgelacht.*

For pure lyric quality one of the best poems in the first group of poems to Leonore is this lovely madrigal (I, 36). It too is on the theme of secularized eternity or heaven now:

> *O Liebe,*
> *Was vor innig-süsse Triebe*
> *Hegstu nicht in deiner Brust!*
> *Würden doch nur die Verächter*
> *Einmahl unsrer Wollust Wächter,*
> *Schwör ich bey Amoenens [der Muse] Gunst,*
> *Dass sie erstlich selbst nicht wüsten,*
> *Ob der Himmel zeitlich sey,*
> *Und darnach vor Scham und Reu*
> *Nur vom Zusehn sterben müsten.*
> *Das thäten sie,*
> *Das thäten deine Triebe,*
> *O Liebe!*

Such lines may well remind an English ear of the Elizabethan and Jacobean lyricists and the combination of banter and fervency so typical of their verse. A German ear will probably be reminded of the early Goethe. The conviction and fervency conveyed here is rare in secular German poetry before Günther. For succeeding generations it was to become the touchstone of "genuineness."

One of Günther's best known poems marks the close of

217

the cycle proper—if one may call it that—as it also marks the poet's departure from Schweidnitz. It is the so-called "Abschiedsaria" (I, 84—the title seems not to stem from Günther himself). The stanza structure is simple but effective: five lines of iambic pentameter plus a two-beat "echo" verse that re-enforces the sense of tragic inevitability in the first half of the poem and the sense of sure comfort in the second. (Günther was to use this same stanza form again and even more effectively in another poem of parting, "An Leonoren bey dem anderen Abschiede," I, p. 201.)[18] The first stanza of the "Abschiedsaria":

> *Schweig du doch nur, du Hälfte meiner Brust;*
> *Denn was du weinst, ist Blut aus meinem Hertzen.*[19]
> *Ich taumle so und hab an nichts mehr Lust*
> *Als an der Angst und den getreuen Schmerzen,*
> *Womit der Stern, der unsre Liebe trennt,*
> > *Die Augen brennt.*

How can two who are rightfully and even divinely one (their union is "des Himmels Schluss") survive the anguish of separateness? This is the theme of the poem and the overall structure reflects it exactly. Stanzas 1–5 speak of the pain of parting and ask how it can be overcome:

> *Welch Pflaster kan den tiefen Riss verbinden,*
> *Den tiefen Riss, der mich und dich zulezt*
> > *In Kummer sezt?*

Stanzas 6–10 speak of union even in separation—the "Pflaster" to heal the wound is found. The primary remedy is faithfulness, what else?

> *Wohin ich geh, begleitet mich dein Bild,*
> *Kein fremder Zug wird mir den Schaz entreissen . . .*
> . . . . . . . . . . . . . . .
> *Erinnre dich zum öftern meiner Huld*
> *Und nähre sie mit süssem Angedencken! . . .*

But most interesting in this connection is Stanza 7:

> *Genung! Ich muss; die Marterglocke schlägt.*
> *Hier liegt mein Herz, da nimm es aus dem Munde*
> *Und heb es auf, die Früchte, so es trägt,*
> *Sind Ruh und Trost bey mancher bösen Stunde,*
> *Und lis, so oft dein Gram die Leute flieht,*
> *Mein Abschiedslied.*

The memory of past oneness, the theme of the stanza immediately preceding, is cut through by the inexorable present: "die Marterglocke schlägt. "The "Riss" gapes open. And now a remedy is found in that which he gives the beloved as the most precious part of himself: his poetry. She can always find comfort in reading his "heart," the song of parting itself: "Hier liegt mein Herz, da nimm es aus dem Munde . . ." The metaphor is bold but apt, and startling in its union of the physical and spiritual. This heart will bear fruits of comfort; the pain of parting will be alleviated by the very words that memorialize it. A view of the nature of poetry is subsumed in these lines that will hardly be found in German before Günther. Such faith in the power of poetry is possible only on the basis of the ethic of sincerity.

In spite of its excellencies, however, "Abschiedsaria" is bound to strike the modern reader as only qualifiedly successful. He will be thrown off and puzzled or, what is worse, amused, by such an emblematic figure as

> *Es [dein Bild] macht mich treu und ist ein*
> *Hofnungsschild,*
> *Wenn Neid und Noth Verfolgungssteine schmeissen . . .*

If he is familiar with the tradition, he will recognize such a turn as this as a cliché:

> *So viel bisher dein Antlitz Sonnen wies,*
> *So mancher Blitz wird jezt mein Schröcken bleiben. . . .*

219

And he will find the concatenation of images in the following lines disharmonious, to say the least:

> *Die Zärtligkeit der innerlichen Qual*
> *Erlaubt mir kaum, ein ganzes Wort zu machen.*
> *Was dem geschieht, um welchen Keil und Strahl*
> *Bey heisser Luft in weitem Felde krachen,*
> *Geschieht auch mir durch dieses Donnerwort:*
> *Nun muss ich fort.*

We have to remember that these are still the verses of a schoolboy, a schoolboy of genius to be sure, but one who had not yet (how could he have?) become fully aware of the kind of poetry his own convictions demanded. It may not be wholly unfair to say that the successful lines in Günther's early poems are hardly more than lucky hits, though they prove his genius and indicate the direction toward which he was dimly striving. We will search in vain for similar lucky hits in the verse of most of his contemporaries.

Between the two groups of poems to Leonora fall the poems composed in Leipzig and addressed to "Rosette," "Flavia," and the "Leipzig Leonore." To this period also belong the student songs, including the famous Güntherian version of "Gaudeamus igitur" ("Brüder, lasst uns lustig sein"), and the eminently successful ode to Prince Eugene.[20] The Leipzig erotica and goliardic songs we must neglect. Interesting as they are in themselves, they are by no means as central as the Leonore poems. Only one poem from this group (I, 109) cannot be passed over in silence. Krämer places it among the Rosette poems, with which it seems to have little connection except through the motif of longing for love itself which runs through this group.

> *Was war das vor ein göttlich Paar?*
> *Wo hat die Welt dergleichen Lüste?*
> *So lacht' ihr Mund, so flog das Haar,*
> *So hüpften die gefüllten Brüste.*

*Die Sehnsucht schilt den leeren Raum,*
*Ich weis nicht, was ich selbst begehre.*
*Der Menschen Leben heist ein Traum,*
*O wenn doch meins ein solcher wäre!*

The metrical and rhyme schemes are quite simple: eight lines in iambic tetrameter with alternating rhyme, odd lines are masculine, or even feminine. Simple is also the syntax, which in no way contravenes normal prose order. Descriptive adjectives are used sparingly but tellingly: *göttlich* in line 1 immediately contrasts with *Welt* in line 2; the "*gefüllten* Brüste" in line 4 make the "*leeren* Raum" in line 5 even emptier. This contrastive scheme reflects the basic structure of the poem: the first four lines contain the enrapturing vision, the last four the bald reality: fullness versus emptiness, past versus present. What was the vision the speaker glimpsed? What was the "göttlich Paar"? It is not easy to be sure. Was it a human pair, a blessedly happy couple that passed the poet's lonely window? Or was it rather the "gefüllten Brüste" of some female figure that ran through his dreams? Perhaps it makes little difference. The last two lines would seem to favor the first interpretation, since his dream could not well be to become a pair of breasts, but rather to fill the place of the male in an Adam and Eve situation.[21] Rhythmically, the poem is a small masterpiece. In this respect also there is a distinct contrast between the first half and the second, as is seen most easily in the animation of lines 3-4 and their contrast with line 5:

3) x x́̈ x x́ x x́̈ x x́
4) x x́̈ x x̀ x x́ x x́ x
5) x x́ x̀ x́ x x́ x x́

Taken as a whole, the poem could well be read as a symbol of Günther's existential situation, that of the man outside. I have already indicated that the realization of this situation seems to call forth his best poetry. There is nothing about this poem one could call "baroque," unless it might be the personification of "Sehnsucht." It is a perfect exteriorization of an inner state, and certainly as "modern" as anything written in the eighteenth century. It is highly unlikely that anyone hearing the poem without knowing the author would be able to place it historically, especially if *für* were substituted for *vor*. It is not, however, truly typical of Günther's work, either at this period or later. It remains, like certain passages in his longer poems, a lucky hit.

The second group of poems to Leonore Jachmann, which Krämer dates August, 1719–Autumn, 1720, constitutes the heart of Günther's erotic verse and his most outstanding accomplishment as a poet of love. Günther returned to Silesia, we recall, a defeated man, though a fairly well known poet. His Leipzig Leonore had married another, he had failed to obtain a post as court poet at Dresden, his medical studies were still uncompleted, he had no sure source of income and was largely dependent on charity, he was at loggerheads with his father as well as with a large and influential part of society which regarded him as a drunken wastrel with a caustic pen. His poetic fame, particularly the fame of his brilliant ode to Prince Eugene, could not outweigh all this. Besides, the court at Vienna had ignored him and his ode. But the harsher the blows rained upon him by fate, the better a poet he became. His spiritual exile in Tomi gave rise to his most moving *Tristia*.

The second group of poems to Leonore begins with an *Auftakt* or anacrusis written some time before Günther's actual return to his homeland, but after his break with the Leipzig Leonore. Called "Ode an sein Lenchen" (I, 167), it speaks of his loneliness and longing for love (never was there a man more in love with love!) and of his sense of guilt because of his unfaithfulness to the "true" Leonore, to whom he now yearns to return:

*Ja, ja, ich fühle schon die Rückkunft erster Triebe,*
*Mein Blut erinnert sich der damahls reinen Treu . . .*

But does she still love him? It is impossible that she shouldn't:

*Die Neigung gleicher Art verband uns gar zu scharf.*

The "cycle" proper then begins with his return. An overview of the thematic material of this group of poems (following Krämer's arrangement) results in a scheme something like this:

Return to Silesia—his hopes, preparation for reunion.

Schweidnitz revisited—Leonore gone; faithfulness supreme virtue and basis of hope.

Reunion—a poem of only six lines!

Reunion recollected—marriage in poetry.

Elegiac plaints—how to be one though parted; poem of parting; poem of comfort through remembrance.

"An Leonoren bey dem andern Abschiede"—oneness in separateness, the overriding theme of this group.

Leonore freed of all promises; her refusal of such freedom.

Past in present—the life of memory.

Bitter farewell—reproaches of infidelity.

Bitterness overcome—faithfulness in and through remembrance, possession of the beloved in the spirit.

This schematic outline makes it fairly clear that the "problem" of these poems is the fundamental elegiac problem: how to find positive meaning in a negative situation, how to inwardly overcome a bitter fate. Günther's ethical solution rests on a mystique of faithfulness, his solution as an artist lies in the poetry itself, i.e., in making poetry out of his sorrow, in *saying* what he suffers. To a much more pronounced degree than in the first group of Leonore poems, the second group involves larger social aspects. What actually happens is that a spiritualized solution (but how physically oriented!)

is accepted as a last resource, a *pis-aller*, but there is never any doubt that what is longed for is a bourgeois solution, marriage and acceptance into society. This is the bitter counterpoint, the plural melody, that runs through this whole group. There is nothing here that resembles a romantic idealization of "free" love. Neither is there spiritualization in the Dante-Petrarchan sense.

In comparison with the first group of poems to Leonore the second shows greater poetic maturity, which is certainly not surprizing, considering that Günther had now "cured his Phoebus" and thought long and hard about the nature of poetry. The impression of greater maturity, however, is not solely, or even primarily, due to the rejection of purely decorative metaphor. Rather, the rejection of such metaphor is a sign of something else: Günther has found, at least he is finding to an ever greater degree, his own voice. That is, he is learning to write in consonance with his constantly reiterated ethic of "sincerity."[22] Thus, instead of an occasional poem or an occasional stanza that seems worthy of special study, we are confronted with an embarrassment of choices. The lyrical density of these poems, however, is not usually great, particularly if we measure them against Klopstock, Goethe, Mörike, although it is obvious from such a poem as "Was war das vor ein göttlich Paar?" that Günther is capable of true lyrical density. Why then, since he seems not to be lacking in the quality of feeling necessary to transform the outward into a correlative of the inward, does his poetry not infrequently fail in this regard? The reason, I am inclined to think, is that his most typical poetry is largely autobiographical (this, too, is an aspect of "sincerity") and thus tends to include more external detail than it can successfully transform. The detail sometimes remains suspended in his verse instead of dissolving in a lyrical solution. Or, to change the figure slightly, the solution is oversaturated.

Günther's aim, and it seems to have been a conscious one,

was to make poetry out of the events, both inward and outward, of his own life. Nothing could be more unbaroque,
nothing more indicative of his new concept of the office of
poetry. Nonetheless, he remains the poet "in between," no
matter how we set the termini. He can compose with perfect
mastery an oratorical lyric in the emblematic mode, such as
the one entitled "An Leonore, die immer grünende Hofnung"
(I, 189), the first stanza of which runs:

> Stürmt, reisst und rast, ihr Unglückswinde,
> Zeigt eure ganze Tyranney!
> Verdreht, zerschlizt so Zweig als Rinde
> Und brecht den Hofnungsbaum entzwey!
>> Das Hagelwetter
>> Trift Stamm und Blätter,
>> Die Wurzel bleibt,
>> Bis Sturm und Regen
>> Ihr Wüten legen,
> Da sie von neuem grünt und Äste treibt.

But when one turns to those poems that constitute his peculiar
contribution to German poetry, that is, those which make
poetry out of personal experience without first transforming
it emblematically, one becomes aware that he is a pathfinder
who is still exploring, lyrically speaking, *terra incognita*. It
goes without saying that poems of the latter type, whatever
their imperfections, are the more important. Here Günther is
truly a *Neutöner*.

One of the more successful poems in the autobiographical
manner, one in which the transformation of the external
world into formed feeling (i.e., into poetry) is very nearly
completely achieved, is "Als er 1719. D. 25. September wieder
nach Schweidniz kam" (I, 188). Underlying the seeming
modernity of this poem one detects the convention of the
pastoral, especially in the lines in which the things of nature
are addressed directly and adjured as witnesses of past bliss.

225

But the pastoral too has been transformed; the tone of Günther's verses will not admit of our taking them in the play-acting spirit of the true pastoral: life may be reflected in the virtuality of art but it is still "real." Though even here one may feel that there is some slight residue of untransformed externality, much is redeemed by the vision of Schweidnitz in the last stanza as a place safe from transciency, a heavenly-earthly Jerusalem. The final image spiritualizes all the topographical references that have preceded. The contrasting four-beat line at the close of each stanza, symbolizing the destruction of the dream and time's ineluctable direction, is used with superb effect. It comes to say in purport: only the memory is left—what can be made of it?

Typical in almost every respect of the new kind of poetry Günther was striving to produce is his "Schreiben an seine Leonore. Von Bresslau A. 1719. den 22. Decembr." (I, 193). Written shortly after his brief reunion with Lenore, it celebrates in the virtuality of art a poet's marriage. But it celebrates it only virtually. Precious as their unconventional union may be, it lacks final perfection and remains only on the level of "as if" as long as it lacks social recognition. It is this very insight that gives rise to the poem and lends it its intensity, for the poem is in effect an attempt to substitute the virtual for the real. The poet strives to raise their fleeting union to a higher, more permanent plane through poetry and to make it paradigmatic for future lovers, just as he sees in their own love a repetition of, or, as one might better say, a quotation from, famous love affairs of the past:

*Ich thu, so viel ich kan, dein Denckmahl auszubreiten,*
*Um bey der späten Welt durch deinen Ruhm zu blühn;*
*Wie mancher wird noch Trost aus meinen Liedern ziehn,*
*Wie manchen wird mein Vers zur süssen Regung leiten!*
*So merck ich, wenn mein Mund der Alten Arbeit list,*
*Dass unsre Liebe schon vordem gewesen ist.*

But in the next and final stanza Günther tips his hand—virtuality is not enough (emphasis added):

> *Was hat wohl unser Wuntsch mehr auf der Welt zu*
>   *suchen,*
> *Und welches Glück ist noch wohl unsers Neides werth?*
> Wenn mir des Himmels Huld dich vollends ganz
>   gewährt,
> So *wüte Feind und Groll,* so *mag der Spötter fluchen;*
> *Drey Dinge sind mein Trost: Gott, Wissenschaft und du;*
> *Bey diesen seh ich stets den Stürmen ruhig zu.*

If virtuality is not enough, and if the societal solution is denied, then nothing is left but the memory. Günther tries to accept the Petrarchan solution, the transformation and adoration of the memory of the beloved as a substitute for possession, but he does it only *contre cœur*. The attempt to accept it nonetheless gives rise to his most poignant and tragic erotic verse.

"An Leonoren bey dem andern Abschiede" (I, 201), like the first "Abschiedsaria" and like the three poems that immediately precede it and the two immediately following, treats the theme of oneness in separation:

> *Die lange Noth ist dennoch nicht so starck,*
> *Uns, werther Schaz, dem Geiste nach zu trennen.*

Though keyed to the theme of "dennoch," this is a more pessimistic poem than any that have gone before. The first and last words are "Du daurest mich"; the first are addressed to her, the last to him. The tone of the whole is one of desperation. It is a poem written from the very center of Günther's existential situation. Once more the ever-recurrent pattern of his life has become evident in all its cruelty, once more he has been refused entrance to the world of normal social rites. The central insight is formulated in the lines:

227

*Viel auszustehn und gleichwohl frey zu seyn,*
*Vermag kein Geist, den Lieb und Ruhm nicht stärcken.*

This is his farewell to the beloved. Fame is highly uncertain. The only recourse left is the cultivation of the memory of their love and the hope that fame may finally be won:

*Wohin mich auch mein hart Verhängnis jagt,*
*Da bleibest du ein Trostbild der Gedancken ...*

And:

*Mein Vaterland versagt mir Glück und Stern,*
*Dies blüht vielleicht in unbekandten Ländern.*

From this point on Günther's poems to Leonore are of the memory of their love only. Un-Petrarchan as he is at heart, he is forced to accept the Petrarchan solution (I, 203):

*Nichts ergözt mich mehr auf Erden*
*Als das Weinen in der Nacht,*
*Wenn es unter viel Beschwerden*
*Dein Gedächtnis munter macht.*

Of the poems devoted to making sacred the memory of their love the most powerful are "Bey der Wiederkunft der Nacht auf den 2. April. 1720. in Lauban" (I, 205), which celebrates the anniversary of their first night of love, and "Auf die Morgenzeit bey Erinnerung Leonorens. Den 10. Jul. 1720" (I, 218). Both are written from the nadir of Günther's existence, which is at the same time the zenith of his poetic powers. To this same period belong the poignant poem of renunciation "An Leonoren" ("Mein Kummer weint allein um dich") (I, 209), in which he releases the beloved from all obligations of loyalty, and its companion piece, "Leonorens Antwort" (I, 212), in which she refuses the proffered freedom.

I have spoken of "the Petrarchan solution"; perhaps

it would not be amiss to cite some supporting evidence. *Canzoniere* 61–62 may help to indicate the similarity between the two poets as well as the profound difference.

### 61

*Bendetto sia 'l giorno, e 'l mese, e l'anno,*
*e la stagione, e 'l tempo, e l'ora, e 'l punto,*
*e 'l bel paese, e 'l loco ov'io fui giunto*
*da' duo begli occhi, che legato m'hanno;*
*e benedetto il primo dolce affano*
*chi'i' ebbi ad esser con Amor congiunto,*
*e l'arco, e le saette ond'i' fui punto,*
*e le piaghe che 'n fin al cor mi vanno.*

*Bendette le voci tante ch'io*
*chiamando il nome de mia donna ho sparte,*
*e i sospiri, e le lagrime, e il desio;*
*e benedette sian tutte le carte*
*ov'io fama l'acquisto, e 'l pensier mio,*
*ch'è sol di lei, sì ch'altra non v'ha parte.*

[Blessed be the day, and the month, and the year / and the season, and the time, and the hour, and the minute / and the fair land, and the place where I was taken captive / by two lovely eyes, which have bound me; / and blessed be the first sweet anxiety / I felt upon being made one with Love, / and the bow, and the arrows by which I was pierced, / and the wounds that penetrate to my very heart. / Blessed be all the cries I gave / calling out the name of my mistress / and the sighs, and the tears, and the longing; / and blessed be all the writings / in which I sing her fame, and my thoughts, / which are so solely of her that no other can find place there.]

### 62

*Padre del ciel, dopo i perduti giorni,*
*dopo le notti vaneggiando spese,*

*con quel fero desio ch'al cor s'accese,*
*mirando gli atti per mio mal sì adorni,*
*piacciati omai col tuo lume ch'io torni*
*ad altra vita, et a più belle imprese,*
*sì ch'avendo le reti indarno tese,*
*il mio duro adversario se ne scorni.*
*Or volge, Signor mio, l'undecimo anno*
*ch'i' fui sommeso al dispietato giogo,*
*che sopra i più soggetti è più feroce.*
*Miserere del mio non degno affanno;*
*redùci i pensier vaghi a miglior luogo;*
*ramenta lor come oggi fusti in croce.*

[Heavenly Father, after the lost days, / after the nights spent in vain imaginings, / accompanied by that fierce longing that burned in my heart, / gazing (to my sorrow) on those so gentle ways, / may it please Thee at last that by Thy light I turn / to another life, and to fitter enterprises, / so that, having spread his nets in vain, / my bitter adversary (Satan) may reap ignominy. / Now, O Lord, the eleventh year begins / that I have been subjected to the tyrannous yoke, / which is most tyrannous for those who are most submissive. / Take pity on suffering unworthy of man, / lead my wandering thoughts back to a better place, / remind them how Thou wert crucified this day.]

Signally missing from Günther's erotic poetry in comparison with that of Petrarch is the dialectic of guilt, so clearly illustrated in the sonnets quoted. This is the first thing to strike the attention. The second is that Petrarch's love is from the beginning a cult of memory. It does not strive for fulfillment; indeed, fulfillment would mean its end; impossibility of fulfillment is its condition. Günther's case is quite different. He passionately desires fulfillment in every sense: physical, social, spiritual. Only when such satisfaction is

denied him does he turn to "the Petrarchan solution," the cult
of memory, which is for him strictly a *pis-aller*. Unlike Petrarch, he strives to make the memory life-giving, to fill it
with future meaning. For the Italian poet this is not possible,
since he regards his love as sinful. A case in point is the poem
on the anniversary of the night of April 2, when Leonore
first gave herself to him, for Günther only less sacred than
the night of the Saviour's birth. He would establish this night
in the hearts of *all* lovers as the beginning ("April" means
"opener") of a new year of the soul, that its significance may
be universalized and a new religion of love founded in its
name. The whole poem (I, 206 f.), from which I quote only
twenty lines out of eighty, is a striking example of the union
of the physical and the spiritual that is the mark of Günther's
erotic poetry. The reference to the Incarnation is not meant
blasphemously (as would be the case with Hofmanswaldau),
but as the supreme symbol of the union sought. It throws sudden light on the depth of the poet's adoration and the seriousness of his intention.

> *O seegensvolle Nacht, nun zieh ich dir zu Ehren*
> *Den Mond der Sonne vor, so blass er immer scheint;*
> *Dein Schatten müsse nichts von Mord und Schröcken*
>     *hören,*
> *Und was gebohren wird, das sey dem Glück vereint!*
>
> *Dein helles Abendroth begleit' ein froher Morgen,*
> *Dein Thau sey Engelbrodt, dein Einfluss Fruchtbarkeit;*
> *Es schände dich kein Geiz mit ungerechten Sorgen,*
> *Dein Denckmahl dringe sich durch aller Zeiten Zeit!*
>
> *Dein freundlicher April sey Herr von seines gleichen!*
> *Verliebte, zehlt von ihm des Jahres Circkellauf!*
> *Er las ihm Herbst und Lenz Geschmack und Farben*
>     *reichen*
> *Und thu dem Namen nach des Jahres Vorrath auf!*

231

*Nach jener, die vordem das Licht der Welt gegeben,*
*Bist du mir allemahl die schönste Finsternüss;*
*O warum fing ich doch in dir nicht an zu leben!*
*Es war ein kurzer Raum, der diesen Wuntsch zerriss.*[23]

*Ich feyre Jahr vor Jahr in dir das Fest des Bundes*
*Und opfre, was und wie Gelübd und Recht versprach,*
*Mit Bechern auf das Heil des allerliebsten Mundes,*
*Aus dem das freye Ja mit keuschem Zittern brach.*

More desperate in tone and more poignant is "Auf die Morgenzeit bey Erinnerung Leonorens," which also seeks to draw consolation from remembrance. Here the memory of past happiness in present sorrow is too sharp to be borne and the poet must finally plead for the memories, which he seeks to deactivate by calling "pleasant whims," to disperse (I, 219):

*Verliert euch nur, ihr angenehmen Grillen,*
*Verliert euch, bis mir einst ein bessrer Glückstern*
*scheint.*

Throughout most of this poem there is true transformation of experience into form. Traces of baroque metaphoric usage are not infrequent, but are largely absorbed in the more direct language of the heart, as in these lines from Stanza 1 (I, 218):

*Denn wenn bey deinem [des Morgens] Blick mir ins*
*Gedächtnüss fällt,*
*Wie oft dein holder Stern auf Leonorens Wangen*
*Durch seinen Widerschein mir doppelt aufgegangen,*
*So fühl ich einen Trost, der Noth und Kummer hält.*

The baroque compliment, that the star of love (Venus is the *Morgenstern*) is twice as beautiful when reflected from the cheeks of the beloved, has been "organicized": Leonore is the morning star raised to a higher degree. The stanza structure is symbolic. We find the rhyme scheme abba/cddc and an accentual count of 5445/6666 (Stanza 5 has 5446/6666).

232

The *division* of the stanzas into clear halves reflects the cleft between past and present, the *union* of these halves in one stanza the presence of the past in the present. It is the "not only but also" situation so frequent in poetry. The overall structure of the poem is schematically this:

Stanza 1: The experience of beholding the present morning recalls other mornings experienced with Leonore and temporarily allays present suffering.

Stanzas 2–4: Memories flood back: detailed recollections of mornings in Schweidnitz with the beloved—an island of timeless happiness: "ein Rest der ehmals güldnen Zeiten."

Stanza 5: Plaint for the lost Jerusalem: realization of present situation—the precarious balance attained in Stanza 1, the "Trost, der Noth und Kummer hält" (i.e., allays or counterbalances), is destroyed.

Stanza 6: What is left: only the voluptuousness of despair, which cuts the nerve of resolve and must be dismissed if life is to go on.

The course of the poem shows how determinedly Günther stands on the side of life. Even the memory of his love for Leonore, the dearest thing he possesses, he will strive to sacrifice if it block the way to that which is life-giving. But unlike Petrarch, who also seeks to renounce the memory of his love, Günther does not repudiate love itself. It could never be for him a "dispietato giogo" (despotic yoke) or a net spread by Satan to catch his soul. Even here it is the best and highest and most sincere experience he can hope for. The Middle Ages, still just beneath the surface throughout the seventeenth century, when such an about-face as that we find in Petrarch is almost the rule in erotic poetry, are far behind us here. Life has become meaningful in itself, not merely as an emblem. This is of course the deeper reason why Günther, in contrast to his immediate predecessors, is so committed to personal experience as the theme of his song. But the other

233

side of the coin is that experience, "life," if it must be taken as a value in itself, can also become a source of despair, *because* it cannot be reduced to a mere emblem. This aspect comes through with particular clarity in the fifth stanza, with its intense secularization of religious values (I, 219):

> *Ach, Schweidniz, ach du Bild von Salems Thoren,*
> *Du Lustplaz meiner jungen Zeit,*
> *Die sich den Musen ganz geweiht,*
> *Was hab ich nicht mit dir vor Fried und Heil verloren!*
> *Ich seh durch Thrän und Angst, und sieh, du bist*
> > *nicht da,*
> *Des Tages tausendmahl mit grössrer Angst zurücke*
> *Als jen gefangnes Volck, das mit betrübtem Blicke*
> *Die Gegend Canaans aus Babels Fenstern sah.*

Schubert, it has been said, could set a signpost to music. Günther is a genius of a similar order. The very type of a *Gelegenheitsdichter*, he can make poetry out of any experience. Nonetheless, the quality of the experience seems to stand in direct relationship to the quality, certainly to the intensity, of the poetry that celebrates it. The poems to "Phillis," the sensible and sophisticated daughter of a country parson, to whose arms Günther flew as a final refuge, are a case in point. Comparatively speaking, they are more important for the light they shed on Günther's intense longing to be allowed to enter the social order and become "ein nüzlich Glied der Republic" (I, 244) than as poems in their own right. These poems lack the transforming fire that characterizes the poems to Leonore. It would seem to be one more indication of the fundamental role of "sincerity" in Günther's work. "Sincerity" relates for him not only to truthfulness and the ideal of faithfulness but also to verisimilitude. This quality again sets him apart from the Baroque. Were he a typical baroque poet, it is doubtful that one could even distinguish outwardly between his loves (except perhaps by the color of their hair), much less detect a distinct difference in tone in the poems addressed to them. Even Fleming could switch from Elsabe to Anna without perceptibly changing pitch! Günther's loves are unmistakably individualized.

Taken as a whole, Günther's lamentations (*Klagelieder*) form the most gripping body of German poetry between Greiffenberg and Klopstock. In fact, in their power to directly involve the mind and heart they probably surpass for the modern reader anything in Klopstock. Günther criticism, to its detriment, has not yet explored these poems thoroughly and sympathetically. Nor can it here be my task to investigate them in depth.

Like the poems to Leonore, the lamentations form a kind of cycle. They trace the course of Günther's religious experience. "Drey Dinge sind mein Trost: Gott, Wissenschaft und du . . ." "Du" is love, the thou-relationship, and the union of the spiritual and the physical. "Wissenschaft" is learning, for Günther primarily philosophy and medicine, but also poetry, the "science" of the word. "Gott" is for him above all the experience of the father-son relationship in terms of man's relationship to the divine.

Günther's religious experience bears all the marks of an acute crisis. It is a conversion experience arising out of suffering. The problem of the lamentations is to find the meaning of suffering, or, more precisely, to find the meaning of Günther's personal suffering. A second Job, he defies God to explain Himself. The solution is as old as the problem: through suffering man becomes aware of God and His love. It is one of His ways of communicating with man. The insistence on the particular, on the personal conversion, and the rejection of ready-made answers might be interpreted

235

as a pietistic trait, but it can probably just as well be seen as Lutheranism of the older school.

Leading practitioners of Günther criticism have either been unwilling to see or have attempted to discount the centrality of religion in Günther's work. Krämer (preface, *Werke*, II), in an excess of critical blindness that is enough to make one doubt that he understands the poet at all, writes off Günther's religiosity as conventional piety. For Krämer (II, xi), the philosophy of Leibniz and Wolff is "der Sinn seines [G.s] Lebens" and Günther is "der dichterische Verkünder des Leibniz-Wolffschen Weltbildes" (II, xx). Dahlke's view is almost as distorted and in its rather cynical deprecation of the seriousness of Günther's religious experience perhaps even more misleading. For Dahlke, the poet, having undergone the positive influence of the Enlightenment, "lapses" under the stress of his suffering back into Lutheranism, which is of course a great shame (*Entwicklung*, p. 155 *et passim*). Delbono's discussion of Günther's religiosity (*Umanità*, pp. 158 ff.), while not giving such a distorted picture, does not follow the poet's crisis to the end, but leaves him, like the theodicy he rejects, "with his legs in the air" (p. 159). These positions, it should be pointed out, have not gone unchallenged. Krämer's position, in fact, has been thoroughly discredited by Israel Stamm in one of the best pieces of Günther criticism that has yet appeared.[24] Dahlke's hand is called by Winkler in his Princeton thesis (p. 54).

It is not easy to give an overview of the lamentations. Since they follow the poet's actual experience, there is a tendency to switch from one position to another, to try this solution and then that in a desperate attempt to find meaning. Nonetheless, the lamentations do come to a climax, and this climax can best be described as a conversion. Once he has gained this higher ground, Günther, so far as I can see, never wholly retreats. From now on he views experience, especially the key experience of suffering, in a new light.

236

There is a distinct dialectic in these poems. We may perhaps call it the dialectic of the Enlightenment versus revealed religion, but with this caveat: the validity of revealed religion is not accepted merely on the basis of authority; rather, its standpoint is arrived at existentially, through personal suffering. This dialectic, though not yet in intense form, is already evident in "Lezte Gedancken" (II, 35), a thematically important poem from the Leipzig period (1718), written from what Günther believed might well prove to be his deathbed. At the beginning of the poem, the poet seems determined to accept death with enlightened stoicism; there is no hint of "Christian" dying:

*Also schlies ich meinen Tod aus den innerlichen Zeichen*
*Und so mach ich mich gefast, ihm getrost die Hand zu*
*reichen,*
*Nicht aus Ungedult und Jammer, sondern mit*
*Gelassenheit,*
*Weil mich dies die Weissheit lehret, jenes die Vernunft*
*verbeut.*

. . . . . . . . . . . . . . . . . . . .

*Und das alte Muss erklingt, nehm ich unter Scherz und*
*Lachen*
*Meinen Abschied von der Erde, wie ein Gast zu später*
*Zeit*
*Lustig von dem Schmause wandert und noch mancher*
*[sic] Jauchzer schreyt.*

One can hardly speak of a struggle in this poem. There is no real confrontation with the deity, no bitter questioning of the meaning of suffering, which, if anything, is seen as meaningless divine cruelty (II, 37):

*Was mein Herz und Leib gelidten, ist nur jenem recht*
*bekand,*
*Der mich etwa nur zur Plage in dies Marterhaus gesand.*

237

Gratitude at release from suffering, not the meaning of suffering itself, is the predominant motif:

> *... da die Menge der Beschwerden*
> *Mit der morschen Hütte sincket, den gefangnen*
> *Geist erlöst*
> *Und ihn aus dem Sclavenhause in das Land der Freyheit*
> *stösst.*

Toward the end (the poem is 228 lines long), when it comes to taking leave of his beloved—"O was braucht es, dich zu lassen, vor so grosse Sterbekunst!"—he first promises to meet her in the Elysian Fields in the company of Petrarch and Laura (Petrarch, it seems, has suddenly become a pagan!), then, dismissing this as "bethörtes Fabelwerck," among the blessed "vor des Lammes Gnadenstuhle." This leads to a passage questioning the nature of the soul (II, 42):

> *Seele, fort, du hast nun Zeit, deinen Frieden zu*
> *bedencken;*
> *Aber welch ein Zweifelmuth mehrt dein innerliches*
> *Kräncken?*
> *Wirstu durch dies Ganze wandern? Bistu etwas oder*
> *nichts?*
> *Oder ein getrennter Funcke von dem Wesen jenes*
> *Lichts?*

In the end, he accepts the promise of revealed religion:

> *Du, mein gütiger Erlöser, Heil der Welt und Lebensfürst,*
> . . . . . . . . . . . . . . . . . . . . . .
> *Ich ergreife dein Verdienst, ich vertraue deinen Wunden,*
> . . . . . . . . . . . . . . . . . . . . . .
> *Ich gesteh, ich bin ein Sünder, doch du bist auch*
> *Gottes Sohn,*
> *Und verspreche mir das Leben so gewis, als hätt ich's*
> *schon.*

The acceptance of the promise of the Cross, though uttered in tones of true conviction, seems almost an afterthought, or even worse, an acceptance of Christianity in order not to miss any bets. The poem as a whole has a strange indecisiveness about it: Enlightenment, paganism, Christianity; the sweetness of life and the determination not to part from it embittered, gratitude at release from unbearable suffering, acceptance of the divine promise. All these things stand in juxtaposition without really dovetailing into each other. The Christian view, to be sure, has the last word and is accepted as the final answer, but the meaning of suffering, here the equivalent of the meaning of life itself, is not discovered. The Christian answer is not arrived at through interpretation of personal experience. The real struggle to find the meaning of suffering and true confrontation with the deity is yet to come. This struggle reaches its peak in the Lauban poems.

The hymn-like "Als er Gottes Liebe um Barmherzigkeit anflehte" is a powerful cry from the depths to be made aware of divine love now, on this plane (II, 73; emphasis added):

> *Denn ob ich gleich vor Liebe brenne,*
> *So ist doch alles blind gezielt,*
> *Wenn nicht mein eusserstes Verlangen,*
> *Dich zu umfangen,*
> Schon auf der Welt *den Himmel fühlt.*

Tortured by a sense of alienation from the divine, he begs for love as men understand it. But this the heavenly Father was not to vouchsafe him any more than the earthly one. Suffering, not ecstasy, was Günther's lot, and his problem remained how to find God's love in suffering itself. It was almost inevitable that he should turn to Leibniz's theodicy for an answer, and a number of passages in his work are nothing but Leibniz turned into verse, though this is far from making the latter's philosophy "the meaning of his

239

life." In a letter to a young poet, Markhard von Riedenhausen, whom he rather piteously calls "Von meiner Poesie der erstgebohrne Sohn" (II, 89) and for whom he is full of fatherly advice, we find this passage of rhymed theodicy (II, 93):

> *Gott lege, was er will und was mir zukommt auf.*
> *Er wird und darf auch nicht den wohlbekannten Lauf*
> *Der grossen Creatur [des Makrokosmos] erst mir zu*
> *Liebe stören.*
> *Sein Zweck ist überhaupt des Weltgebäudes Heil:*
> *Wir, ich und mein Creuz, sind davon nur ein Theil*
> *Und müssen auch den Schmuck der ganzen Ordnung*
> *mehren.*

These lines, too, were written from Lauban, in the midst of deepest privation and physical suffering, when he felt deserted by all; truly a *Grenzsituation* (II, 93):

> *Kein Freund, kein Mensch, kein Hund erfährt mein*
> *Ungemach;*
> *Dies kan ich auch sogar im Schlafe nicht vergessen.*

There seems no reason to doubt that Günther hoped that philosophical comfort would see him through. But the event proved otherwise. Such comfort was too cold for one who longed for the embrace of divine love "schon auf der Welt." The poems immediately following the letter to Riedenhausen are face-to-face confrontations with the deity. They speak of his conversion.

Though one can hardly maintain that the Leibnizian explanation of the meaning of (apparent) evil and (real) suffering in creation excludes the strictly Christian interpretation, still the difference for the suffering individual is tremendous. One is wholly impersonal, the other wholly personal; one has to do with the maintenance of the best of all possible worlds, the other with the salvation of the individual soul. The turn

240

from philosophy to religion is seen in such poems as "Um Beständigkeit" (II, 95), "Dancksagung vor göttliche Züchtigung und Langmuth" (II, 97), and "Als er sein festes Vertrauen auf Gott sezte" (II, 99). The meaning of suffering is now sought and found not "in des Weltgebäudes Heil" but in the salvation of Johann Christian Günther. In "Um Beständigkeit" Satan's most subtle temptation, the temptation of despair, is overcome and in "Dancksagung vor göttliche Züchtigung . . ." the negative rendered positive (II, 97):

*Ich dancke dir vor meine Zähren*
*Und vor der Seelen Angst und Leid,*
*Ihr Ernst entdecket mein Bekehren*
*Und würcket mir zur Seeligkeit.*
*Verschonen war die gröste Strafe,*
*Ich hätte bei dem Lasterschlafe*
*Gewis den lezten Tod erlebt.*
*Die Noth erscheint zur rechten Stunde*
*So wie ein Arzt durch Blut und Wunde*
*Die eusserste Gefahr mit kleinen Schmerzen hebt.*

This victory is not without its price. It is undeniable that the conversion experience brings with it, at least temporarily, a certain *contemptus mundi*, which we may perhaps interpret as self-administered psychological reinforcement of the new position. In any event, lines such as the following sound more like Gryphius than Günther (II, 99 f.):

*Wie können doch die eitlen Sachen,*
*Die wilde Lust, die Pracht der Welt,*
*Dich gar so blind und hizig machen,*
*Da doch ihr Schein wie Glas zerfällt!*
*Der Eckel kommt von geilen Küssen,*
*Die Ehrsucht füllt ihr weit Gewissen*
*Mit später Reu, die Hand mit Wind . . .*

Günther does not stop with his own conversion but sets about to convert his contemporaries, generalizing, it would seem,

241

on the basis of his own experience. "Bussgedancken über den Zustand der Welt. Den 9. April. 1720." (II, 103–4), is a fiery jeremiad, a *Zeitgedicht* of great power excoriating contemporary society and preaching the message of repentance and acceptance of the Saviour:

> *O Mensch, so gieb doch Gott die Ehre*
> *Und hör einmahl sein Wort aus mir;*
> *Damit er dich auch wieder höre,*
> *Steht jezt die Rache vor der Thür.*
> *Dein Vorwiz dürfte fragen müssen:*
> *Du laufst, wer schickt dich? Mein Gewissen,*
> *Das andre gern ermahnen soll.*
> *Ich bessre die verfluchten Triebe*
> *Und werd auch jezo dir zu Liebe*
> *Aus hoher Gnade gnadenvoll.*

Higher ground has been gained, now begins the struggle to keep it. It is these poems of intense struggle that have received most critical attention, and not without reason, but we would do well to remember their *place* in Günther's religious development, namely, that they come *after* the conversion experience and are in the nature of holding actions. As such, they are finally successful. It is absurd and critically irresponsible to discount these poems, which, besides being central to our understanding of Günther, are among the most gripping in the German language, as conventional piety or weak-willed "lapsing" into Lutheranism. If there was any "lapsing" it came before these poems. The most famous is of course "Als er durch innerlichen Trost bey der Ungedult gestärcket wurde" ("Gedult, Gelassenheit . . .") (II, 123).

"Gedult, Gelassenheit . . ." represents the peak (or nadir) of Günther's extensive poetry of lamentation, but it does not represent his final religious position. The seven ten–line stanzas with the rhyme scheme ababccdeed are thematically disposed as follows:

242

1–3: There is indeed a God, but He is a malicious being who tortures His own creatures; it is therefore insane to practice virtues predicated on a benevolent deity.

4–6: God Himself, according to whose highest laws (as I was given to understand them) I have attempted to govern my life, is to blame for my misfortunes and afflictions; consequently I deny utterly the worth of the life He has given me.

7: The curse is broken at its height; the speaker suddenly feels the divine presence and realizes that his despair is the sin of sins; he sinks exhausted into the arms of the Redeemer.

The poem is an attempt to substitute the anti-values of nihilism for the values of Christianity and the Enlightenment. The attempt fails. It fails because the "I" of the poem even in its deepest despair cannot escape the still, small voice of God's love. Even as it rants this voice seems to be whispering in its ear words at cross-purposes to the tirade. This comes out, as will be shown, in the peculiar self-contradictory nature of the argument. The stance of the "I" is not, however, atheistic nor ever in danger of becoming so. It *is* blasphemous. But blasphemy is the way in which the damned keep in touch with the divine. Such a relationship is impossible without belief.[25]

The nihilism preached in this poem is extreme, the blasphemy shocking. The determination to explore the gulf of nothingness seems to know no bounds. The Christian virtues —and those of the Enlightenment—are repudiated; God does not (perhaps He cannot) fulfill His promise; He Himself leads me astray; men are to Him "as flies to wanton boys," He kills them for His sport; those who claim to follow Him are hypocrites who laugh at an honest man and cast him out of their houses; life itself is an anti-value, it would have been better never to have been born. In short, to try to live according to the Christian virtues means to suffer unendurably. Yet even as he rages, Günther (or, to be more exact, the voice of the poem) constantly implies the supreme value of all that is rejected. This shows itself in the strange logic of the argu-

243

ment, particularly in Stanzas 1, 3, and 5. Note the wording
here (II, 123):

> *Gedult, Gelassenheit, treu fromm und redlich seyn,*
> *Und wie ihr Tugenden euch sonst noch alle nennet,*
> *Verzeiht es, doch nicht mir, nein, sondern meiner*
> *  Pein,*
> *Die unaufhörlich tobt und bis zum Marcke brennet,*
> *Ich geb euch mit Vernunft und reifem Wohlbedacht,*
> *Merckt dieses Wort nur wohl, von nun an gute Nacht;*
> *Und dass ich euch gedient, das nenn ich eine Sünde...*

The virtues are repudiated, but in the same breath are asked
to forgive—not him who repudiates them but his torment.
Nonetheless it is claimed that they are denied "mit Vernunft
und Wohlbedacht"—a well considered decision arrived at
under torture! To have served such virtues is now called a
sin. A sin against what? Against hedonism? All values seem
to be reversed, yet there is no footing upon which counter-
values can rest. In Stanza 3, God is accused of making him
resist the good, "damit die frömmste Welt das Ärgste von mir
meine" and out of this (Stanza 4) spring all his afflictions.
This borders on paranoia. And what good was he resisting, if
the good does not consist in following the virtues just repudiated? In Stanza 5, the characteristic pose of the blasphemer
is assumed: I know that I am just and humane and love my
neighbor, may all evil spirits—which are nothing but Christian lies!—seize me if this isn't so. "Was wird mir nun davor?
Ein Leben voller Noth." Therefore nothingness would be
preferable (II, 124):

> *O dass doch nicht das Ey, in dem mein Bildnüss hing,*
> *Durch Fäulung oder Brand der Mutter Schoos*
> *  entgieng,*
> *Bevor mein armer Geist dies Angsthaus eingenommen!*
> *Jezt läg ich in der Ruh bey denen, die nicht sind...*

244

As a cry of despair the poem is piteous and moving. This mad, unreasonable ranting reflects with great verisimilitude the agony of a man tortured beyond endurance. As "philosophy" it is childish, unless we interpret it in existentialistic terms as awareness of crisis, insight into the inevitability of "Scheitern."

In Stanza 2 (II, 123), in a passage of bitter blasphemy, the "I" asks:

*Wo steckt denn nun der Gott, der helfen will und kan?*
*Er nimmt ja, wie ihr sprecht, die gröbsten Sünder an:*
*Ich will der gröbste seyn, ich warthe, schrey und leide;*
*Wo bleibt denn auch sein Sohn? Wo ist der Geist*
  *der Ruh?*
*Langt jenes Unschuldskleid und dieses Kraft nicht zu,*
*Dass beider Liebe mich vor Gottes Zorn bekleide?*

In the final stanza (II, 124), the love of this triune God evinces itself in its forbearance. The turn from rebellion and blasphemy to submission and repentance is sudden and basically inexplicable. It is a gift of grace, unmerited, given of God's free will, quite according to Luther:

*Verflucht sey Stell und Licht! — Ach ewige Gedult,*
*Was war das vor ein Ruck von deinem Liebesschlage!*
*Ach, fahre weiter fort, damit die grosse Schuld*
*Verzweiflungsvoller Angst mich nicht zu Boden schlage.*

The patience of the Eternal has not taken him at his word but understood his blasphemy as we are also meant to understand it and as the illogicalness of his argument implied: as an expression of suffering, of longing for a world in which God's laws are followed and in which "Geduld, Gelassenheit, treu, fromm und redlich seyn" are virtues that are indeed rewarded. Of such a world the "I" of this poem has no hope, nor does the later Günther. It seems doubtful that he ever attains to the insight contained in Matthew 6, that those who trumpet forth their good deeds already "have their reward." Nonetheless, the "Liebesschlag" is the reward of the Father "who sees in secret."

In the last six lines, the poet turns to Jesus, identifying his suffering with His. Suffering leads to the Cross, at once the sign of all suffering and its overcoming. For Dahlke (*Entwicklung*, p. 170), this is a "Rückfall in die Theologie des 17. Jahrhunderts." For Günther, it is a way, and finally the only way, of finding meaning in suffering. Death is the only release, but death is the gate to eternal life: "Die Rettung ist allein mein Tod *und* dein Erbarmen." It may be argued that the meaning of suffering is not as clearly enunciated here as in the earlier poem "Dancksagung vor göttliche Züchtigung . . ." discussed above. It is true that its meaning is only implied, yet the implication is clear enough. The anti-value of nihilism cannot finally displace the values predicated on a God of love, and suffering proves to be the rock on which faith rather than disbelief is founded. The whole Christian experience points in the same direction, not merely "the theology of the 17th century."

In the poems immediately following "Gedult, Gelassenheit . . ." the dubious battle is still fiercely waged, though there is no renewed attempt to assume the position of nihilism. "Er klaget in der Einsamkeit" (II, 130) reviews once more his desperate plight and ends with a plea to the heavenly Father to work a miracle in his behalf. The next poem "An Gott" (II, 133–34) continues this theme. Firm ground is now gained again, though no outward miracle has yet been wrought. An inner one, however, has come to pass: he has learned to say "Thy will be done":

> *Getrost, mein Herz, so muss es seyn,*
> *Wir sollen blos den Höchsten loben.*

Finally, in "Die Zuversicht des Geistes zu Gott" (II, 136), the "I" of the lamentations has come full circle and the im-

246

plication of "Gedult, Gelassenheit . . ." is made explicit. I quote the whole poem:

> Es kommt mir sauer an, ich zitter wie ein Rohr
> Und bin mehr Schein als Mensch. Allein wer kan davor?
> Du, Herr, verstellst dich mir und magst dich auch
>     verstellen.
> Ich ehre deinen Grimm bey noch so schweren Fällen;
> Vermehr auch Schlag und Zorn, du strafst mich nie zu
>     hart,
> Ich seh gleichwohl daraus des Vaters Gegenwart,
> Des Vaters, der mich nicht aus blindem Eifer schläget,
> Nein, sondern nur dadurch zu Reu und Leid beweget.
> Wer weis, zu was es dient! Ich bitte dich um nichts
> Als dann und wann um Trost des holden Angesichts.
> Sonst gieb mir, was du wilst, ich bin zu blind zum
>     Wehlen;
> Du, Vater, wirst mich doch nicht über Kräfte quälen.
> Spott, Hunger, Fluch und Neid und gar verächtlich
>     seyn
> Geht freylich, wer es fühlt, dem Fleische bitter ein;
> Doch wenn mich auch dein Zorn bis in die Hölle triebe,
> So predigt ich auch dort die Wollust deiner Liebe.

In this cycle God is known almost exclusively through His anger. But this anger, such is the final insight, is a sign of love, a "Liebesschlag." To man lost in sin it is the only way God can reveal Himself.

One may perhaps be allowed to speculate that Günther's basic, and only half-recognized, problem is his inability to confess his sinfulness, i.e., to admit it wholeheartedly to himself. His work bristles with self-defensiveness and is full of excuses for his socially unacceptable conduct. On the societal plane, youthful exuberance and, on a deeper level, "sincerity" may indeed be excuse enough. Certainly, the punishment seems grossly out of proportion to the crime. This is his

247

argument in the poems to his father (cf., e.g., II, 198 ff., lines
45–74). But on a religious plane the same attitude becomes
one of revolt and blindness to sin. Here the poet stylizes himself as a second Job. But is this not a shield against the con-
fession of sin? It seems quite possible that he was faced with
two irreconcilables, one stemming from the new ideal of
"sincerity" and the right of the individual to develop according to his inborn tendencies, and the other from Christian,
especially Lutheran, dogma. Nothing is more difficult for
Günther than to admit his own sinfulness, because such an
admission on a religious plane damages his case on the social
one. His attempt to assume the standpoint of Pelagianism is
finally doomed to defeat. Man, in his fallen state, cannot work
out his salvation alone. Grace must be added. Perhaps one
may see in this struggle another instance of Günther's "in-
betweenness"—between Pascal and Gryphius on the one hand
and Goethe on the other. His final position is nearer the
former than the latter. This whole complex in Günther's
work still awaits investigation.

Günther's religious development does not end with the
last poem quoted above, but we cannot follow it in further
detail here. It must suffice to say that the Günther who has
passed through the crucible of suffering and conversion attains approximately the standpoint of Hamann after his conversion experience, namely, that of "*Est*, ergo cogito," God
is, therefore I (am able to) think, or simply: He is, therefore
I am. God's all-presence and love is revealed to Günther above
all through his suffering. But it was also revealed, so he believed, in his release from suffering, which he regarded as a
veritable miracle (II, 143 f.—points of suspension in lines 3–4
in poem as printed):

> *Gott zürnt und bleibt doch Gott, das ist voll Lieb und
> Treu,*
>
> . . . . . . . . . . . . . . . . . .
> . . . . . . . . . . . . . . . . .

. . . . . . . . . . . . . . . . . . . .

*Drum spreche doch kein Mensch: Nun bin ich*
   *hingebracht . . .*

. . . . . . . . . . . . . . . . . . . .

*Ich war schon im Begriff und wollte— —[mich*
   *umbringen]*
[here follows a veiled reference to his rescue]

. . . . . . . . . . . . . . . . . . . .

*Man meint, es hätten längst die Wunder aufgehört;*
*Ihr Thoren böser Art, wie seichte steht der Glauben!*

. . . . . . . . . . . . . . . . . . . .

*Durchgeht den Lebenslauf bald von den ersten Jahren:*
*Je mehr ihr Stunden zehlt, je mehr ich Wunder seh,*
*Die ihr so gut als ich von Gottes Huld erfahren.*

. . . . . . . . . . . . . . . . . . . .

*Ich wende kaum die Hand, so folgt ein besser Ende . . .*

Divine Providence is everywhere, all that happens is God's
will, which is absolutely good. Leibniz again? Much rather
Matthew 10, 29 ff.: "Are not two sparrows sold for a penny?
And not one of them will fall to the ground without your
Father's will. But even the hairs of your head are numbered.
Fear not therefore . . ." In short, *everything* is a "miracle,"
evidence of God's *personal* will in relation to the individual,
not merely to "des Weltgebäudes Heil." Man must only learn
to say "Thy will be done." In the German Baroque the most
sublime expression of this sense of God's all-presence is found
in the poetry of Catharina Regina von Greiffenberg. Its most
profound formulation in the eighteenth century is found in
the works of Johann Georg Hamann. Between Hamann and
Catharina stands Johann Christian Günther.

    We have devoted an incommensurate amount of space to
Günther. This was in part necessary because the state of
Günther scholarship still cannot provide the literary historian
with ready formulae for the illustration of the poet's develop-

249

ment. In part it was necessary because of the amazing richness of his work, a richness that derives principally from his
new attitude toward the function of poetry as personal con-
fession. Even so, we have discussed only two of his central
themes, and these only in a cursory fashion: love, or man's
relationship to woman, and religion, or man's relationship to
the divine. The important theme of the individual's relationship to society, especially of course the poet's relationship,
we have mentioned only in passing. Basically, Günther still
abides our question.

NOTES
SELECTED BIBLIOGRAPHY
INDEX

NOTES

## CHAPTER ONE

1. The Janus-faced nature of Lutheranism may be seen with particular clarity in the history of Lutheran universities, especially in the gradual displacement of Wittenberg, the scholastically minded defender of "Altluthertum," by Jena, where the New Learning began to gain a firm foothold around the middle of the seventeenth century. Cf. Herbert Schöffler, *Deutscher Osten im deutschen Geist* (Frankfurt a.M., 1940), pp. 156–76: "Jena als Einbruchstor des neuen westeuropäischen Denkens in das Luthertum."

2. For a detailed discussion of this complicated question, see Karl Otto Conrady, *Lateinische Dichtungstradition und die deutsche Lyrik des 17. Jahrhunderts* (Bonn, 1962).

3. Cf. Walter Brauer, "Jakob Regnart, Johann Hermann Schein und die Anfänge der deutschen Barocklyrik," *Deutsche Vierteljahrsschrift*, XVII (1939), 371–404.

4. Collected works: *G. R. Weckherlins Gedichte*, ed. H. Fischer, 3 vols. (Tübingen, 1894–95, 1907). Selections in: *Deutsche Literatur in Entwicklungsreihen, Reihe Barock, Barocklyrik 1*, ed. H. Cysarz (Leipzig, 1937); *Das Zeitalter des Barock, Texte und Zeugnisse*, ed. A. Schöne (München, 1963), and other anthologies.

5. This sonnet has been beautifully explicated by Walter Naumann, *Traum und Tradition in der deutschen Lyrik* (Stuttgart, 1966), pp. 103–9.

6. Born 1597 in Silesia at Bunzlau-on-the-Bober (hence the sobriquet "Boberschwan") of a well-to-do burgher family (his father was a butcher). While still a student at the gymnasium in Breslau, published a "defense" of the German language, *Aristarchus sive de contemptu linguae teutonicae* (1617). As a student at Heidelberg in 1618 associated with young humanists interested in language

reform. In 1619–21 in Holland, then Denmark. Especially influenced by the Dutch poet and scholar Daniel Heinsius. In 1622 professor at a newly founded gymnasium at Weissenburg in Transylvania, where he studied ancient Roman remains on the side. Returning to Silesia, he wrote (in five days) his *Buch von der Deutschen Poeterey* (1624) and published in the next year a corrected edition of his *Teutsche Poemata*, which had already been brought out the year before by his Heidelberg friend Wilhelm Zincgref without O.'s express consent. Crowned *poeta laureatus* by Emperor Ferdinand II. Though a Protestant, O. served (1626–32) as secretary to the all too energetic counter-reformer Karl Hannibal von Dohna, president of the imperial chamber in Breslau. Ennobled in 1629. Secret mission to Paris in 1630. After the expulsion of Dohna, O. entered the service of the Protestant dukes of Silesia. When imperial troops re-entered Silesia in 1634, O. fled to Thorn in West Prussia, finally settling in Danzig, where he was appointed historiographer by the Polish monarch Vladislav IV in 1637. Died of the plague in Danzig, Aug. 20, 1639.

A modern critical edition of O.'s works is in the process of publication. Presently available are *Teutsche Poemata* (1624), ed. G. Witkowski (Halle, 1902—*Neudrucke deutscher Literaturwerke des 16. u. 17. Jahrhunderts*, no. 189–92); *Buch von der deutschen Poeterei*, ed. W. Braune (Halle 1882—*Neudr.* No. 1); *Geistliche Poemata* (1638), ed. E. Trunz (Tübingen, 1966—*Deutsche Neudrucke, Reihe Barock* 1); *Weltliche Poemata* (1644, 1. Teil), ed. E. Trunz (Tübingen, 1967—*Deutsche Neudrucke, Reihe Barock* 2); *Weltliche und Geistliche Poemata*, ed. H. Oesterley (Berlin and Stuttgart, n.d.—Kürschner's *Deutsche National-Litteratur*, Bd. 27): selections in: *Deutsche Literatur in Entwicklungsreihen, Reihe Barock, Barocklyrik* 1, ed. H. Cysarz (Leipzig, 1937); *Das Zeitalter des Barock, Texte und Zeugnisse*, ed. A. Schöne (München, 1963), and other anthologies.

7. Bruno Markwardt, *Geschichte der deutschen Poetik*, Bd. 1 (Berlin and Leipzig, 1937), gives exhaustive information.
8. Cf. Paul Böckmann, *Formgeschichte der deutschen Dichtung* Bd. I (Hamburg, 1949), pp. 318 ff.
9. See Joachim Dyck, *Ticht-Kunst: Deutsche Barocklyrik und rhetorische Tradition* (Bad Homburg von der Höhe, etc., 1966), on whom I am largely dependent, for a detailed discussion.
10. Günther Müller, *Geschichte des deutschen Liedes* (München, 1925—reprint Bad Homburg v. d. H., 1959).
11. As, e.g., Günther Weydt, "Nachahmung und Schöpfung bei Opitz: Die frühen Sonette und das Werk der Veronica Gambara," *Euphorion*, L (1956), 1–26.
12. Müller, *Lied*, pp. 52 ff. Gundolf, in *Deutsche Barockforschung: Dokumentation einer Epoche*, ed. R. Alewyn (Köln and Berlin, 2. Aufl., 1966), pp. 133 ff. (Gundolf's essay first appeared in 1923.)

13. Martin Opitz, *Teutsche Poemata*, ed. G. Witkowski (Halle, 1902),
    p. 8.
14. *Ibid.*, pp. 7 f. My emphasis. "... im Heldenbuch und sonsten
    dergleichen" refers to medieval German poetry.
15. Born 1609 at Hartenstein in the Erzgebirge (Saxony), the son of
    a well-to-do Lutheran pastor. Educated at the famous Thomas-
    schule in Leipzig, where the poet-musician Johann Hermann Schein
    was one of his teachers (F. was very musical), later at the Uni-
    versity of Leipzig, where he studied medicine and belonged to a
    group of student-poets who introduced him to the new poetry as
    promulgated by Opitz. O. remained F.'s ideal mentor for the rest
    of his life. Earlier verse in Latin. In 1633, F. joined an expedition
    being sent by Frederick III, Duke of Holstein-Gottorp, to the
    Czar of Russia for the purpose of stimulating trade. Out of this
    venture arose a second and much more hazardous one in the form
    of an expedition to Ispahan to interview the Shah of Persia. Be-
    tween expeditions, F. and a number of his companions were de-
    tained in Reval on the Baltic. Here the poet fell in love with Elsabe
    Niehus, the daughter of a rich merchant, and became (not quite
    officially, it seems,) engaged to her. Much against Elsabe's wishes,
    F. insisted on participating in the expedition to Persia. Thus he
    spent altogether some six years of his life in distant lands, cut off
    from family and fiancée except for an occasional letter. Much of his
    poetry arises out of this situation. Returning to the West in 1639
    (Elsabe had meanwhile married another man and F. had decided
    he was in love with her sister), he completed his medical studies
    in Leiden and was just settling down to practice in Hamburg
    when he died of a sudden illness. His *Teutsche Poemata* appeared
    posthumously in 1642. Modern edition: *Paul Flemings Deutsche
    Gedichte*, ed. J. M. Lappenberg, 2 vols. (Stuttgart, 1865—reprint
    Darmstadt, 1965); selections in all anthologies; extensive selection
    in Kürschner's *Deutsche National-Litteratur*, Bd. 28.
16. *Gedichte*, ed. Lappenberg, p. 460. For the substance of my re-
    marks on this sonnet I am much indebted to Naumann, *Traum
    und Tradition*, pp. 110–18.
17. For Fleming and the Petrarchan tradition, see Hans Pyritz, *Paul
    Flemings deutsche Liebeslyrik* (Leipzig, 1932).
18. Pyritz, *Liebeslyrik*, pp. 208 ff.
19. Collected works: *Simon Dach, Gedichte*, ed. W. Ziesemer, 4 vols.
    (Halle, 1936–38); extensive selection: *Gedichte von Simon Dach*,
    ed. H. Oesterley (Leipzig, 1876—*Deutsche Dichter des 17. Jahr-
    hunderts*, Bd. 9); characteristic pieces in Schöne, *Barock*, and
    Cysarz, *Entwicklungsreihen*.
20. Kaspar Stieler, *Teutsche Sekretariat-Kunst* ... (Nürnberg, 1673).
    Quoted after Dyck, *Ticht-Kunst*, p. 97.
21. Cf. Ivar Ljungerud, "Ehren-Rettung M. Simonis Dachii," *Eupho-
    rion*, LXI (1967), 36–83.

22. Characteristic selection: *Dichtungen von Johann Rist,* ed. K. Goedeke and E. Goetze (Leipzig, 1885—*Deutsche Dichter des 17. Jahrhunderts,* Bd. 15).

23. A generous selection from Logau's work is contained in *Sinngedichte von Friedrich von Logau,* ed. G. Eitner (Leipzig, 1870—*Deutsche Dichter des 17. Jahrhunderts,* Bd. 3).

## CHAPTER TWO

1. The discussion of the hymn is especially indebted to the following sources: Waltraut-Ingeborg Geppert, "Kirchenlied," in Merker-Stammler, *Reallexikon der deutschen Literarturgeschichte,* 2. Aufl. (Berlin, 1958); Hermann Hering, "Kirchenlied, III, deutsche," *Realencyklopädie für protestantische Theologie und Kirche,* ed. A. Hauck, 3. Aufl., vol. 10 (Leipzig, 1901); *A Dictionary of Hymnology,* ed. John Julian (New York, 1892); G. Pfannmüller, "Einleitung," *Lied- Spruch- und Fabeldichtung im Dienste der Reformation* (Leipzig, 1938—*Entwicklungsreihen, Reihe Reformation,* Bd. 4); Martin Schmidt, "Evangelische Kirchengeschichte Deutschlands von der Reformation bis zur Gegenwart," *Deutsche Philologie im Aufriss,* ed. W. Stammler, Bd. III (Berlin, 1957).

Standard collections of German hymns are: *Das deutsche Kirchenlied von der ältesten Zeit bis zu Anfang des 17. Jahrhunderts,* ed. Philipp Wackernagel, 5 vols. (Leipzig, 1864-77); *Das deutsche evangelische Kirchenlied des 17. Jahrhunderts,* ed. Albert Fischer and W. Tümpel, 6 vols. (Gütersloh, 1904-16). Useful and widely available are: *Das deutsche Kirchenl. des 16. u. 17. Jahrhunderts,* ed. Eugen Wolff (Stuttgart [1894]—Kürschner's *Deutsche National-Litteratur,* vol. 31); the volume in the *Entwicklungsreihen* noted above; the three volumes of "Barocklyrik" edited by H. Cysarz in the same series, esp. Bd. 3; any *Gesangbuch der Evangelischen Kirche.*

2. The son of a burgomaster in Gräfenhaynichen, near Wittenberg, G. seems to have attended this seat of Lutheran learning for an unusual number of years. He matriculated in 1628 and was still listed as "studiosus" in 1641. Upon leaving Wittenberg (1642-43), he went to Berlin, where he both tutored and preached. As pastor of the Nikolaikirche he became involved in the struggle between the Lutheran clergy and Friedrich Wilhelm, the Great Elector, who, being of the Reformed Church (Calvinist), demanded that the Lutheran pastors sign an agreement not to attack this church from the pulpit. Gerhardt, who regarded this as an infringement of his right to teach and preach, refused to sign and was accordingly removed from office. He later found a post at Lübben, in the Spreewald, where he remained until his death. The outward circumstances of his life were mostly gloomy. His youth coincided

with the horrors of the Thirty Years War, he obtained a settled position only at forty-four years of age and was not able to marry until he was forty-eight. His wife died young. Only one of his five children survived childhood. The people among whom he spent his last years were crude and unfriendly. The motto on one of his portraits reads: "Theologus in cribro Satanae versatus," a theologian shaken in Satan's sieve. No collection of G.'s hymns was published until 1667. Their inward glow is in strong contrast to the dismal circumstances of his outward life.

3. Wilhelm Wackernagel, *Geschichte der deutschen Literatur*, 2. Aufl. (Basel, 1894), p. 241.

4. *Deutsche Gegenreformation und deutsches Barock* (Stuttgart, 1935), p. 257.

5. Friederich Spee (von Langenfeld) was born at Kaiserswerth, near Düsseldorf, of an old Rhenish noble family and educated at a Jesuit gymnasium in Cologne. In 1610, he entered the Jesuit order and after earning his *magister artium* in Würzburg was sent as a teacher to various towns in the Rhineland. When the General of his order refused his request to be sent as a missionary to India (Spee longed to emulate St. Francis Xavier), he pursued a four-year course in theology at Mainz and afterwards served at various Jesuit schools and universities as a professor. He was ordained in 1622. Around 1627 he wrote one of the most courageous books of the century, the *Cautio criminalis*, or Warning to Criminalists (i.e. judges, inquisitors, etc.), published anonymously in 1630. Spee's authorship soon became known and at once made him a storm center. This epoch-making work, the *Uncle Tom's Cabin* of its day, was directed against one of the most widespread and most pernicious evils of the seventeenth century, the trial and condemnation of persons of all ages and conditions for witchcraft. Spee's publicizing of the inhuman practices connected with these judicial murders helped to bring them to a stop. The frequently repeated legend that Spee himself personally accompanied "over 200" victims to the stake appears to have no basis in fact, though he did upon occasion serve as confessor to persons accused of witchcraft. In 1629, while acting as missionary to the Protestant enclave of Peine, near Hildesheim, Spee almost met his death at the hands of a would-be murderer. Tradition has it that he composed much of his principal poetic work, *Trutznachtigall*, while recuperating from his wounds in a rural retreat. The last act of Spee's life took place in Trier, where he finished *Trutznachtigall* and prepared a beautiful manuscript for the inspection of the censor. The vicissitudes of war kept the work from appearing until many years later. In March, 1635, the town of Trier, then in the hands of the French, was captured by imperial troops. In his tireless efforts to succor the sick and wounded, Spee contracted a pestilent fever and died in August of the same year. As

a personality, there is no more attractive figure in seventeenth-century Germany than this compassionate Jesuit priest. The standard critical edition of *Trutznachtigall* is by Gustave O. Arlt (Halle, 1936—*Neudrucke deutscher Literaturwerke des 16. und 17. Jahrhunderts*, no. 292–301). Also very useful, especially for its glosses, is *Trutz-Nachtigal von Friedrich Spe*, ed. Gustav Balke (Leipzig, 1879—*Deutsche Dichter des 17. Jahrhunderts*, Bd. 13). Spee's life and works have been treated extensively by Emmy Rosenfeld, *Friedrich Spee von Langenfeld: Eine Stimme in der Wüste* (Berlin, 1958); her work is particularly valuable for its picture of the times. A new critical edition of Spee's works is presently (1971) in the process of publication.

6. Eichendorff, *Werke und Schriften*, ed. G. Baumann and S. Grosse, vol. 4 (Darmstadt, 1959), p. 477.

7. The question of the influence of Loyola's *Exercitia spiritualia* on Spee's work has been discussed by Warren R. Maurer, "Spee, Southwell, and the Poetry of Meditation," *Comparative Literature*, xv (1963), 15–22. Those familiar with the "meditation upon hell" in Chap. III of James Joyce's *Portrait of the Artist* will know what is meant by a Jesuit "composition," though this, Loyola's fifth exercise, plays no role in *TN*.

8. Eric Jacobsen, *Die Metamorphosen der Liebe und Friedrich Spees "Trutznachtigall"* (Copenhagen, 1954), p. 158. Jacobsen's monograph is an elaborately erudite investigation of *TN* as a parody of secular amatory poetry.

9. For more detailed discussion and proof of this as well as a number of other points mentioned below, see Robert M. Browning, "On the Numerical Composition of Friedrich Spee's *TN*," in *Festschrift für Detlev W. Schumann* (München, 1970), pp. 28–39.

10. The critical edition by G. O. Arlt, a reprint of the editio princeps of 1649, contains fifty-two poems, but the fifty-second is not found in any of the three extant manuscripts. It is definitely inorganic to the structure of the cycle.

11. The distinction between the two kinds of love, which plays a considerable role in the structure of *TN*, is developed by Spee in his *Güldenes Tugendbuch*, especially in the introduction. For discussion, see F. W. C. Lieder, "Friedrich Spee and the *Théodicée* of Leibniz," *Journal of English and Germanic Philology*, xi (1912), 146–72; 321–54; also Browning, pp. 35–37.

12. Born December 1624 in Breslau, the son of a Polish nobleman of German culture and Lutheran faith and a German mother thirty-eight years younger than her husband, Scheffler was left an orphan at fourteen. He attended the famous Elizabeth-Gymnasium in his native city, where one of his teachers was Christoph Köler, the first biographer of Opitz and an enthusiastic proponent of the new poetry. In 1643 S. went to Strassburg to study medicine, then in the summer of 1644 to Leiden. Holland was the haven of

258

those persecuted for religious reasons, and the country was full of various religious sects. Scheffler was later accused of having associated with the Anabaptists, a serious fault in the eyes of both Lutherans and Catholics. In September 1647 he matriculated at the University of Padua, a famous medical center, and received a degree in philosophy and medicine in 1648. In 1649 S. was appointed court physician to the Protestant court of Oels in Silesia, where he came under the influence of Abraham von Frankenberg, an erudite follower of Jakob Böhme (1575–1624), the great Silesian mystic. Upon his death in 1652, Frankenberg willed at least part of his collection of mystical and occult writings to Scheffler, who composed a funeral elegy for his benefactor. Through Frankenberg, Scheffler seems to have become acquainted with the writings of a man who was to strongly influence the form and content of his own work: the mystic Daniel Czepko von Reigersfeld (1605–60). Shortly after Frankenberg's death, Scheffler got into difficulties with the Lutheran establishment over the attempted publication of a collection of mystical prayers. In 1653, he was converted to Catholicism, having left the court of Oels some time before. Under the influence and patronage of Sebastian of Rostock, chief agent of the Counter Reformation in Breslau, Scheffler himself soon became a fanatic counter-reformer. In 1657 his two most important poetical works appeared under the name "Angelus Silesius": *Cherubinischer Wandersmann* and *Heilige Seelenlust*. Beyond the fact that they must have been written between 1651 and 1657, their genesis is not known.

Ordained a priest in 1661, Scheffler did not enter orders, though he had close connections with both the Franciscans and the Jesuits. From 1663 onward, he engaged in polemical pamphleteering of the most fanatical kind—he claimed to have written fifty-five tracts between 1663 and 1675. Thirty-nine of these were collected under the title of *Ecclesologia*, an energetic defense of the Catholic Church. In 1674, the once great poet of the mystical way published a longish, Breughelesque poem called *Sinnliche Beschreibung der vier letzten Dinge*, full of hellfire and damnation eschatology. He died, a lonely and disappointed man, in the hospital of St. Matthias in Breslau, the church in which he had been converted. A Jesuit delivered his funeral oration.

Standard editions: Angelus Silesius. *Sämtliche poetische Werke und eine Auswahl aus seinen Streitschriften*, ed. G. Ellinger (Berlin, 1923), 2 vols.; of this edition, *Heilige Seelenlust* and *Cherubinischer Wandersmann* also appear in *Neudrucke des 16. und 17. Jahrhunderts* as nos. 177–81 and 135–38 respectively; *Sämtliche poetische Werke*, ed. H. L. Held (München, 1952), 3 vols. (with extensive introduction and thorough documentation; normalized text). *CW* is also available in *Sammlung Dietrich*, Bd. 64, ed. W.-E. Peuckert, whose commentary stresses the influence of Böhme and pansophic thought. Best introduction for the English speaking reader is Jeffrey L. Sammons, *Angelus Silesius* (New York, 1967).

13. For detailed discussion of Scheffler's handling of this form, see Benno von Wiese, "Die Antithetik in den Alexandrinern des Angelus Silesius," *Euphorion*, XXIX (1928), 503–22; reprinted in *Deutsche Barockforschung*, ed. Alewyn (Köln/Berlin, 1966).

14. See Ellinger's edition of *HS, Neudrucke* no. 177–81 (Halle, 1901), pp. xx ff.

15. Hans-Joachim Frank, *Catharina Regina von Greiffenberg: Leben und Welt der barocken Dichterin* (Göttingen, 1967), p. 133 (emphasis added).

The poetess was born September 7, 1633, in Lower Austria at Castle Seisenegg near Amstetten on the Ybbs. The family's nobility was of recent date; Catharina's grandfather was a burgher ennobled by Emperor Rudolph II for distinguished service to the crown. Like most of the Austrian "ständischen Adel"—in distinction to the much older landed nobility—the family was Lutheran. The death of the father in 1641 left the mother and two daughters in straitened circumstances. Catharina's paternal uncle, Hans Rudolph, took over the management of the estate and the education of his nieces. Catharina received excellent instruction and became quite learned even by the high standards of her day. She seems to have had a special liking for Latin and Italian authors and for French Renaissance poetry (she later translated Du Bartas) and she was an avid reader of religious works. In 1629, the *Restitutionsedikt* issued by Emperor Ferdinand II, which forced all Protestant clergy and teachers to leave Austria, left the Lutherans of that country without an organized church. Many emigrated to Bavaria, some were converted to Catholicism. By the end of the century there was no Lutheran nobility left in Austria—the Counter Reformation was a success. According to Catharina's modern biographer, H.-J. Frank, the poetess' religious breakthrough occurred when she was eighteen, at the death of her younger sister. From this time on her life was governed by the "Deogloria" concept, by which she means returning praise to the Creator for His blessings, giving back to God, through her poetry, what He has given us. By the time she was twenty-six, Catharina had so far perfected herself in poetic expression that her mentor *in poeticis*, Johann Wilhelm von Stubenberg (a hymnist and translator, especially from Spanish), felt justified in submitting a sample of her work to Sigmund von Birken, the head of the very active Nürnberg circle of poets. Birken was amazed and delighted. Through his offices a publisher was found for her *Geistliche Sonette, Lieder und Gedichte* (Nürnberg, 1662). Birken himself contributed a "Vor-Ansprache."

In 1663, Catharina fled to Bavaria (Nürnberg) to escape the imminent danger of a Turkish invasion. Meanwhile, her uncle and protector, Hans Rudolph, who was some thirty years her senior,

had proposed marriage, much to Catharina's distress and embarrassment. She did, however, marry him after permission had been obtained from the Protestant margrave of Brandenburg-Bayreuth.
This marriage to one of such near kin was a source of many of her
later troubles and humiliations.

In exile, Catharina completed her long and erudite "Helden-
Gedicht" in over 7,000 alexandrines called *Sieges-Seule der Busse
und Glaubens / wider den Erbfeind* [i.e. Islam] *Christlichen Na-
mens*, which tells the story of Islam's quarrel with Christianity. For
Catharina, it is the struggle of the principle of evil with the good.
Mohammed is seen as a scourge sent by God to bring the Christians
to their senses. It is dedicated to "mein werthes Teutsches Vaterland." Its message is ecumenical: a challenge to all Christians to
unite in one body under the hegemony of the house of Habsburg
and complete the work of the Crusades by Christianizing the East.
Catharina's most successful work so far as public recognition goes
was *Nichts als Jesus* (1672), a series of twelve meditations, mostly
in prose.

In 1665, Hans Rudolph and his wife returned to Austria to set-
tle their estate. Hans Rudolph was forthwith arrested for marrying
his niece and forbidden to communicate with her. But, apparently
through intercession in high places, he was finally given full freedom and the couple stayed on in Seisenegg for over a decade. Concerning this period (1665-79) we are unusually well informed due
to a series of letters written by Catharina to her fellow poet S. von
Birken. The poetess speaks of her life among the vulgar Lower
Austrian *Krautjunker* and their families as "das unruhigste" and at
the same time "das langweiligste Leben von der Welt." Her main
relaxation was hunting, to which she was passionately devoted. Confessional differences and of course her "peculiar" marriage also
played a part in making her life unhappy. In addition to all this, she
suffered from poor health and failing eyesight. Upon the death of
Hans Rudolph in 1676, she was immediately set upon by greedy
creditors, who managed to cheat her of most of her inheritance.
Longing for surcease of her woes, she returned to Nürnberg in
1680, where she died April 8, 1694.

Through her letters to Birken we catch a glimpse of the "secret
life" of this remarkable woman. She had purposed in her heart—to
convert the Emperor to Lutheranism! This was to be the key to her
utopian scheme for bringing about a union of all Christians under
the house of Habsburg. Never does she seem to have faltered in her
resolve—though there were periods of deep discouragement—and
never does she appear to have considered any alternative. Her attitude toward the ruling house was that of a wise but obedient child
toward a willful and erring parent. She made at least three different
attempts to see the Emperor in person, but never succeeded in getting farther than his confessor (who tried to convert *her*!) and the

261

court librarian. She was of course of far too lowly status to be received officially at court. Her writings contain a number of veiled references to this secret "Vorhaben," on which she spent a great amount of time and energy.

Utopian though this scheme may have been, it was neither unprecedented nor without successors. No less a man than Leibniz was a little later to dream not dissimilar dreams and her older contemporary, Comenius, the great pedagogical reformer, devoted himself to similar irenic strivings. Catharina's religiosity, partly no doubt because she had been cut off from her church in her formative years, was anything but hidebound and doctrinaire. Rather she cultivated a personal, inward kind of fervency, in striking contrast to the ossified Lutheranism of her day. Thus she had herself already taken the first step toward an *oikoumene*, the Kingdom to come. Perhaps she felt that the next step was now up to the Emperor?

At this writing (1969) there is still no critical edition of the works of C. R. v. G. Her most important collection of poetry, *Geistliche Sonette, Lieder und Gedichte* (1662), is available in a photographic reprint issued by the Wissenschaftliche Buchgesellschaft, Darmstadt, 1967; *C. R. v. G. Gedichte*, ausgewählt und mit einem Nachwort herausgegeben von Hubert Gersch (Berlin, 1964), contains fifty-three well-chosen entries in modernized spelling and punctuation. Hans-Joachim Frank (cited above), has written an important work on the life of the poetess; two Zürich dissertations, Leo Villiger, *C. R. v. G. Zu Sprache und Welt der barocken Dichterin* (1952), and Peter Maurice Daly, *Die Metaphorik in den "Sonetten" der C. R. v. G.* (1964), are solid and useful.

16. The title page of *G.S., L.u.G.* might lead one to think that the arrangement of the poems is not by the poetess. It reads in full: "Geistliche Sonnette / Lieder und Gedichte zu Gottseeligem Zeitvertreib erfunden und gesetzet durch Fräulein Catharina Regina / Fräulein von Greiffenberg / geb. Freyherrin von Seyssenegg: Nunmehr Ihr zu Ehren und Gedächtniss / zwar ohne ihr Wissen / zum Druck gefördert durch ihren Vettern [!] Hanns Rudolf von Greiffenberg / Freyherrn zu Seyssenegg." The key word, however, is *gesetzet* "arranged." The structure of the cycle has not yet been examined in detail.

17. This sacrament had such an irresistible appeal for her that she undertook long and arduous journeys to Bavaria and Hungary to take communion in her church. Indeed, she even posed the thorny theological question as to whether she might not administer the Eucharist to herself! (Cf. Daly, p. 146, n.203.)

18. Tithonus, the husband (lover) of Aurora, the dawn.

19. I.e., the wounds of the Savior.

20. Richard Newald, *Vom Späthumanismus zur Empfindsamkeit, 1570–1750* (München, 1961), p. 250.

21. English-speaking readers, when given a chance, seem to have been

quick to appreciate Catharina's qualities. George C. Schoolfield's pathfinding anthology, *The German Lyric of the Baroque in English Translation* (Chapel Hill, N. C., 1961), contains sixteen entries under Greiffenberg; Frank J. Warnke's *European Metaphysical Poetry* (New Haven, Conn., 1961), includes two of her sonnets in polished translation with the German *en face*. To judge by his surname and some of his references, P. M. Daly also seems to belong to the English-speaking world. So attractive do I personally find Catharina's work that I cannot resist the immodest urge to offer a translation of my own:

> *O Wort! dem alle Wort zu wenig, es zu preisen!*
> *O Wort! durch welches ward, das man mit Worten nennt.*
> *Durch dich, o Wesen-Wort! man dessen Selbstheit kennt,*
> *Der seinen Allheit-Glanz, dich zeugend, wollte weisen.*
>
> *O Wort! das auf das Wort des Engels wollte reisen*
> *In keuschen Tugend-Thron! das bleibet ungetrennt*
> *Von seinem Ausspruch-Mund, doch alle Welt durchrennt.*
> *Wort! das mit Worten kan, die voll der Werke, speisen.*
>
> *Wort! das eh als sein Mund und Zunge war geboren!*
> *Ja, Wort! das seinen Mund und Zunge selbst erschuf!*
> *Wort! das zu reden ihm durch Schweigen hat erkoren!*
>
> *Wort! des Unmündigkeit die ganze Welt ausruft,*
> *O Wort! das Gott beredt zum Schaffen und Erlösen,*
> *Wollst Worte dir zu Lob in mir jetzt auserlesen.*
>
> [Gersch, p. 9]
>
> *O Word! for which all words are insufficient praise!*
> *O Word! through which that is that we with words do name.*
> *Through thee, O Word of Words! we know the very same*
> *Who, by creating thee, did show His own true ways.*
>
> *O Word! that on the word of angel took its way*
> *To Virtue's chastest throne! that ever doth remain*
> *In God's own mouth, yet through the world doth reign.*
> *Word! that with effective words our hunger can allay.*
>
> *Word! that was before its mouth and tongue were born!*
> *Yes, Word! that did own mouth and tongue itself create!*
> *Word! that yet for speech to silence is foresworn!*
>
> *Word! whose immaturity the whole world's state doth state!*
> *O Word! persuader to creation and redemption,*
> *Choose now in me the words of praise and contemplation.*

22. Born February 25, 1651 in Breslau, the son of a Lutheran burgher who died a few years after his birth, K. was educated at the Magdalenen-Gymnasium in his native city, a school with an excellent humanistic tradition. He seems to have been a sickly child. A stammerer, he avoided association with his peer group and buried him-

self in the public library. He acquired quite a formidable learning, and published his first volume of verse, a collection of epigrammatic epitaphs ("Grabschriftten") at seventeen. During a serious illness in 1669, when he was eighteen, K. experienced an "illumination" which he later regarded as epoch-making. At nineteen he entered the University of Jena to study law, but seems to have spent most of his time composing poetry and other works rather than in attending lectures. He published extensively while there, bringing out a cycle of fifty sonnets (*Himmlische Libes-Küsse*) and two prose compilations of around 800 pages each, as well as a second edition of his epitaphs. At this period he seems well on the way to becoming a typical baroque polyhistor.

In 1673, K. left Jena for Leiden, the intellectual Mecca of the Silesians. Leiden marks the turning point in his life and thought. Here he first read the works of Jakob Böhme and became converted to chiliasm, the doctrine of the (imminent) end of the present world order and the coming of the Millennium. He renounced all learning as a snare of Satan and devoted himself wholly to religion. The first fruit of his intense preoccupation with Böhme was a remarkable book called *Neubegeisterter Böhme*, or Böhme Newly Inspired (Leiden, 1674), prophesying the coming thousand-year kingdom and calling for a union of all Protestants. K.'s role in the salvational scheme is here already adumbrated. His poetry now becomes wholly subservient to his "mission," the handmaid of his religion. (It was no accident that K.'s chiliasm took such a pronounced form in Holland. The Netherlands were rife with all kinds of "prophets," and Amsterdam, the Los Angeles of the seventeenth century, was the center of *outré* sectarianism.)

From about 1675 on, we find K. now in Amsterdam and other Dutch cities, now in Lübeck, now in or near London, in the Near East, in Paris, Geneva, Berlin, and finally in Moscow, where he was destined to meet his tragic end. He seems a driven man. Though almost constantly in the company of religious enthusiasts, only a few accepted the special brand of chiliasm he called "Kühlmannstum." He lived his life isolated by his monomania, trying to save a world indifferent to his message.

In broad outline K.'s doctrine in its more or less final form was approximately as follows: The end of the present world order is at hand (the exact date varies), the Millennium will be (is being?) ushered in by the reign of Kuhlmann, who is the son of the Son of God, Christ's regent and forerunner. (The paternity of Christ is peculiar to K.'s doctrine; he thus avoids, though barely, the Messianic heresy.) K. sees himself as having been foretold by certain "prophets," among them personal acquaintances, two of them even his wives. The members of the "Cool Kingdom" (Kühlreich) will be those who have accepted K.'s doctrine. The whole concept is based on the idea of the Third Covenant (K. speaks of a "Kühlbund"), or the reign of the Holy Ghost after the dispensations of the Father and the Son have been superseded. It is teaching that goes back at least as far as the Cistercian abbot Joachim of Fiore (died 1201). The reign of the Holy Ghost ("Kühlzeit") with K. as regent will last until the coming of the Millennium proper, when Christ will rule with the saints. Meanwhile there is work to be done: the conversion of all who can be made to listen to the doctrine of Kühlmannstum. Especially singled out for conversion are those in high office, princes and potentates, to whom K. addresses "open letters" (Sendschreiben); the Pope, being the Antichrist, is of course left to stew in his own juice. (K.'s anti-Catholicism is almost his only point of similarity with Luther.) Necessary to the plan of salvation is also the conversion of the Turks (Islam) and the Jews.

In 1677, financed by an English Quaker named Bathurst, K. set out for Constantinople to redeem the Turks. He took with him his first wife, a woman twice his own age, who claimed to be his "spiritual mother," and her three children. K. was unable to interview the Sultan, who was campaigning in foreign parts. The whole venture was a sad fiasco. In spite of this, K. succeeded in persuading himself that the Turks had been converted "in the spirit." This mental trick also served him in good stead later when he was prevented by lack of funds from proceeding to Jerusalem to convert the Jews. This time he got no farther than Geneva, but while there he composed a series of twenty-one "Jerusalemgesänge," interpreting physical defeat in terms of spiritual victory. This was the famous "Geistreise" to Jerusalem, and it was not the last such spiritual journey he planned to undertake. Meanwhile K. had begun to publish the work for which he lives in German literature, the *Kühlpsalter* (Amsterdam, 1684–86). Without this work we might dismiss him as no more than a psychopathic heretic; with it, we must give him consideration as a poet.

The final, catastrophic act of K.'s life took place in Russia, the Russia of the Czars Peter the First and his sister Sophia, where he went in 1689 to convert the world of Greek orthodoxy to Kuhlmannism, Moscow being the "third Rome." Shortly after arriving in Moscow he was arrested and a few months later (October 3, 1689) burned alive, probably on the banks of the Moskva, together with a certain Nordermann, his last disciple. The protocol of the trial clearly shows that it was not on grounds of heresy so much as on grounds of sedition that K. suffered the death penalty. The political element inherent in all Third Covenant plans of salvation was especially important because of conditions then prevailing in Russia. The czars unfortunately took K. seriously.

Though announced since 1962, the edition of the *Kühlpsalter* being prepared by Robert L. Beare for *Neudrucke des 16. und 17. Jahrhunderts* had not appeared at this writing (Fall 1969). The most thorough investigation of K. to date, especially from the standpoint of his doctrine, biography, and historical background, is the 600-page monograph by a critic of the Marxist school, Walter Dietze, *Quirinus Kuhlmann: Ketzer und Poet* (Berlin, 1963). Useful as an introduction is the article by Robert L. Beare, "Quirinus Kuhlmann: The Religious Apprenticeship," *PMLA*, lxvii (Sept. 1953), 828–62. Werner Vordtriede's selection, *Quirinus Kuhlmann: Aus dem Kühlpsalter* (Berlin [1966]), contains an excellent afterword, but the book itself hardly gives an accurate picture of K.'s work, which, being a unit, resists anthologizing. The study by Claus Victor Bock, *Q. Kuhlman als Dichter: Ein Beitrag zur Charakteristik des Ekstatikers* (Bern, 1957), though containing penetrating stylistic observations, tends to be thesis-ridden (K. as a shaman). The best work on K.'s language that has come to my attention is the dissertation by Heinrich Erk, "Offenbarung und heilige Sprache im 'Kühlpsalter' Quirin Kuhlmanns," (Göttingen, 1953—microfilm). (The copy made available to me was so poorly reproduced as to be illegible in many places.) Also valuable in this regard are the following articles: Leonard Forster and A. A. Parker, "Quirinus Kuhlmann and the Poetry of St. John of the Cross," *Bulletin of Hispanic Studies*, xxv (Jan. 1958), 1–23 (on Part I of the 62nd Kühlpsalm); Leonard Forster, "Zu den Quellen des 'Kühlpsalters': Der 5. Kühlpsalm und der Jubilus des Pseudo-Bernhard," *Euphorion*, lii (1958), 256–71.

23. Recent students of the *Kühlpsalter* are agreed on this point. In presentations based on an older view of the nature of K.'s language, however, one can meet such formulations as "sein Sprachgefühl, das ans Expressionistische streift," "Freiheit der Wortbildung, der metaphorischen Verschiebungen," "halb bewusstes Zungenreden," "Zügellosigkeit des Ausdrucks, bei dem der einzige Willenrest der zur Hyperbel ist," etc. (All quotations from Werner Kohlschmidt, *Geschichte der deutschen Literatur vom Barock zur Klassik*—Stuttgart, 1965—ii, 104.)

24. See Dietze, pp. 239 ff., for a detailed discussion of Kuhlmann's explication of his own name.

25. Vordtriede, p. 91, puts it very aptly: "Kuhlmann ist im 'Kühlpsalter' nicht ein Prophet, der auch dichtet; er ist Dichter, weil er Prophet ist. Dichtung hat für ihn kein Eigenrecht als Werk, sie ist ihrem Wesen nach Prophetie . . ."

## CHAPTER THREE

1. Gryphius (the name is a Latinized form of Greif) was born in the year of Shakespeare's death at Glogau in Silesia. His father, a Lutheran pastor, died when Andreas was only four years old. His mother, who remarried, died when he was eleven. Due to the tense religious situation, at that time equivalent to the political situation,

Andreas left Glogau with his stepfather Michael Eder for Driebitz, a small town in Poland, at the age of twelve. After studying on his own for some time, G. was at last able to enter the Gymnasium in Fraustadt (in Poland), where he distinguished himself as a scholar while contributing to his own support by tutoring. He left Fraustadt in 1634, after having published his first known work, a Latin epic on the Slaughter of the Innocents. Like many Silesians of that day, G. now went to the culturally and economically flourishing city of Danzig, which was removed from the tumult of war. Here he obtained a post as tutor in the household of the admiral of the Polish navy, a Scotsman by the name of Seton, and continued to pursue his studies at the local Gymnasium, where he especially came under the influence of the mathematician and astronomer Peter Crüger (who was also professor of poetry!) and of Johann Mochinger, professor of eloquence. Through them, both enthusiastic Opitzians, G. was made aware of the new German poetry and was soon composing German sonnets himself.

In 1636, G. accepted a post as tutor to the children of a wealthy Fraustadt jurist and scholar, Georg Schönborner, of whose excellent library he made extensive use. In 1637, his first volume of German verse, the so-called "Lissaer Sonette" (published in Polish Lissa), appeared. Among them are some of his best known poems. After the death of Schönborner, G., now twenty-two years old, went to Holland with his patron's sons to enter them and himself in the university. He matriculated in Leiden, the favorite university of upper class Silesians of the day, and was soon immersed in the most various studies, ranging from anatomy to jurisprudence. He also lectured on an astonishing number of subjects himself—geography, mathematics, logic, astronomy, chiromancy (!), anatomy. His lectures were very popular. Already a learned man (he mastered nine languages and read their literatures), G. became well acquainted with the leading lights of the Dutch intellectual world, at that time perhaps the most advanced in Europe. He spent six consecutive years in Holland and published there most of his earlier work.

As tutor to the son of a German merchant and in the company of a group of young men, G. undertook in 1644 a journey through France and Italy, stopping for longer periods in Paris, Angers, Florence, Rome, and Venice. When the group disbanded in Strassburg in 1646, G. remained in the Alsatian city for another year, cultivating the company of its learned men and working on his poetry. In the spring of 1647, he set out with his pupil for home, going by way of the Rhineland and Holland. In November, he was again with his stepfather in Fraustadt, having been abroad for nine years. It is interesting to note how much of the Thirty Years War Gryphius missed through his sojourns in Poland, Danzig, Leiden, France, Italy, the Rhineland (Strassburg was neutral!). Actually, it was only for a fairly brief period in his childhood and early youth that

267

he experienced the war at first hand, though he may have often had before his eyes the grim signs of its effects. G. came home a widely known, indeed almost a famous man. His reputation as a scholar and a poet and his many connections in the world of learning brought him offers of professorships from no less than three universities: Frankfurt on Oder, Uppsala, and Heidelberg. He refused them all to enter public life and was elected, in 1650, as syndic (counsellor) of the diet of the principality of Glogau, a post which he held until his death. He married in 1649. Of his seven children, only his eldest son, who was later to edit his father's collected works, survived to maturity. As legal representative of Glogau, G. displayed much skill and energy in defending the rights of the principality against the demands of the Habsburgs. He died of a heart attack in the midst of a committee meeting at the age of 48. His contemporary fame as a man of letters rested as much on his plays, both tragedies and comedies, and on his funeral orations as on his lyric poetry, but it is to the latter that he principally owes his present prominent place in the history of German literature.

Standard edition of G.'s works: *Gesamtausgabe der deutschsprachigen Werke*, ed. Marian Szyrocki (lyric) and Hugh Powell (drama) (Tübingen, 1963 ff.—*Neudrucke deutscher Literaturwerke*, Neue Folge, 9 ff.); also useful, though not always accurate: *Werke*, ed. Hermann Palm (Tübingen, 1884). Palm's edition is based on the edition of 1698 by G.'s son Christian; Szyrocki's follows "the earliest complete printing" of the poem in question. Since he is the most widely studied poet of the German Baroque, the literature on G. is extensive. Especially important studies: Gerhard Fricke, *Die Bildlichkeit in der Dichtung des Andreas Gryphius* (Berlin, 1933); Erich Trunz, "Fünf Sonette des Andreas Gryphius," *Vom Geist der Dichtung* (Festschrift R. Petsch—Hamburg, 1949, pp. 180 ff.); Marian Szyrocki, *Andreas Gryphius: Sein Leben und Werk* (Tübingen, 1964); Dietrich Walter Jöns, *Das "Sinnen-Bild": Studien zur allegorischen Bildlichkeit bei Andreas Gryphius* (Stuttgart, 1966). Eberhard Mannack, *Andreas Gryphius* (Sammlung Metzler —Stuttgart, 1968) which reviews the literature and summarizes its findings, is the best vade mecum for the student.
2. "dem . . . lebt," i.e. the human spirit ("Geist, in den Sinnen behaust").
3. A period in G.'s punctuation is often equivalent to a comma in modern usage.
4. Karl Viëtor, in his *Geschichte der deutschen Ode* (München, 1923), treats G.'s "Pindaric" odes, for which he has high praise, rather fully. V.'s enthusiasm may be due in part to his rare joy at finding respectable odic verse in the context of seventeenth-century German poetry.
5. Cf. Victor Giraud, *Blaise Pascal: Etudes d'histoire morale* (Paris, 1910), p. 314.

6. See Friedrich Ohly, "Vom geistigen Sinn des Wortes im Mittelalter," *Zeitschrift für deutsches Altertum und deutsche Literatur,* vol. 89 (1958/59), pp. 1 ff., for this whole question.
7. Reproduced in Germain Bazin, *The Baroque: Principles, Styles, Modes, Themes* (Greenwich, Conn., 1968), plate 385.
8. The final verse, built on the "summation scheme," is a substitute for the usual envoy, which always incorporates all end-words.
9. See *Der junge Gryphius* (Berlin, 1959), pp. 88 ff.
10. Information drawn from editor's introduction to *Werke,* I, ix ff.
11. Cf. M. Szyrocki, *Leben u. Werk,* p. 48; also introduction to *Werke,* I, p. ix, and *Gryphius: Werke in einem Band* (Weimar, 1963), p. 11.
12. "Sonettenkunst des Barock: Zum Problem der Umarbeitung bei A.G.," *Jahrbuch der deutschen Schillergesellschaft,* IX (1965), 1–32.
13. *Schwert*—planke an der seite des schiffs, bestimmt, dasselbe zu schützen gegen die neigung vor dem winde (H. Palm's note).
14. Cf. Victor Manheimer, *Die Lyrik des Andreas Gryphius* (Berlin, 1904), p. 135. M. Szyrocki, on the other hand, *Leben u. Werke,* p. 62, after demonstrating the principle of numerical composition in the Lissa sonnets, seems to doubt that Books I and II are built on any particular compositional principle and makes no attempt to find one. Szyrocki's observations regarding the Lissa Sonnets have been subjected to critical examination by Hugo Bekker, "Gryphius's Lissa-Sonnets," *Modern Language Review,* vol. 63 (1968), pp. 618–27, though B. casts no doubt on G.'s interest in numerology.
15. Up to now, so far as I can determine, the only sub-cycles in this book that have been subjected to closer scrutiny are the first four sonnets and nos. 46–49, the four sonnets on the Last Things. Cf. A. G. de Capua, "Two Quartets: Sonnet Cycles by A. G.," *Monatshefte,* LIX (1967), 325–29.
16. Cf Wisdom of Sirach, 48, 1 f.: "Then the prophet Elijah arose like fire, And his word burned like a torch."

## CHAPTER FOUR

1. Harsdörffer was a widely traveled and broadly educated member of the patrician society of the city republic of Nürnberg, which, along with Hamburg, Danzig, and Strassburg, was one of the towns that by skillful and sometimes questionable politics managed to keep from becoming directly involved in the Thirty Years War. Its culture was bourgeois, not absolutistic, and H. was one of its leading lights. Together with Klaj he founded the "Pegnesischer Blumenorden" (sometimes called the "Pegnitz-Schäfer," the Pegnitz being the charming river on which Nürnberg lies). The Blumenorden was one of a number of literary societies which played a highly visible, though poetically speaking fairly peripheral, role in

the Baroque. The most famous and highly respected was the aristo-cratically oriented "Fruchtbringende Gesellschaft," founded in 1617, with the aim of raising the standards of the German language, keeping it "pure," spreading its influence, and encouraging German literature. It was counted a signal honor to be invited to join. Mem-bers were given "significant" sobriquets such as "der Spielende" (Harsdörffer), "der Schmackhafte" (Wilhelm of Weimar), "der Gekrönte" (Opitz, who was admitted only at an insultingly late date), etc. As it came to be dominated more and more by the nobil-ity, the Fruchtbringende Gesellschaft became less and less influen-tial. It ended as an empty ceremonial organization. The Pegnesi-scher Blumenorden had a bourgeois orientation and wore a playful pastoral mask. Its members bore the names of classical shepherds: Harsdörffer was "Strefon," Klaj was "Clajus," Birken "Floridan" and so on. Each had a flower that was "sacred" to him. When H. lost interest in the society, Birken took it over and conducted it in a very businesslike fashion. It exists, at least in name, to this very day and possesses in Nürnberg archives of great value for the cul-tural history of the seventeenth century, a treasure that is only now beginning to be explored systematically.

Harsdörffer was a mediocre poet but a prodigiously productive writer. He is known in German literature more for his manual of poetics than for his poetry, though, together with Klaj, he pro-duced the best pastoral in the language, the *Pegnesisches Schäfer-gedicht in den Berinorgischen Gefilden* (Nürnberg, 1644). His manual of poetics, the famous "Funnel," appeared in three parts between 1647 and 1653. The first part bears the title: *Poetischer Trichter, Die Teutsche Dicht- und Reimkunst, ohne Behuf der lateinischen Sprache, in VI. Stunden* [i.e. lessons] *einzugiessen.* Cultural patriotism is the basic note, the main goal the furtherance of the German language as a literary medium. (This same formula would serve to characterize most of the poetics of the period.)

Johann Klaj was a native of Meissen in Saxony who came to Nürnberg in 1643 or 1644 from Wittenberg where he had been a student of theology and had sat at the feet of August Buchner, who seems to have taken the impecunious but talented Klaj under his special protection. Though Klaj stayed in Wittenberg over eight years, he never took an advanced degree and seems to have spent more time studying the bottom of his glass than his books; he was later reputed to be an alcoholic. His literary success in Nürnberg was almost immediate, though he had to continue to eke out a living by tutoring. His creative period falls almost entirely within the years 1644–50. From 1651 until his death five years later he was pastor in Kitzingen, where he lived in continual strife with his congregation.

Sigmund von Birken (Betulius), was born as the son of a Lutheran pastor in Eger (Sudetenland). Like many Protestants, the family took refuge from the war in neutral Nürnberg. He studied in Jena and was appointed tutor to the young dukes of Brunswick, Anton Ulrich (who became a novelist) and Ferdinand Albrecht, and spent some time in North Germany. From 1648 on Birken was in Nürnberg where he conducted much correspondence and kept an interesting diary. Together with Klaj, he composed a *Fortsetzung der Pegnitz-Schäferey* (1645) and also wrote a number of other pastorals, which show him to be a poet of considerable charm. As director of the Blumenorden and as a theorist of literature—he too produced a manual of poetics—Birken exerted fairly wide influence. His best claim to fame rests, however, on his protection of C. von Greiffenberg and the propagandizing of her works.

Texts: Harsdörffer: selections in A. Schöne, *Das Zeitalter des Barock* and in Cysarz, *Entwicklungsreihen, Reihe Barock, Barocklyrik*, Bd. 2; *Pegnesisches Schäfergedicht* (Harsdörffer and Klaj), ed. Klaus Garber (Tübingen 1966—*Dt. Neudrucke, Reihe Barock* 8).

Klaj: excellent sampling in Cysarz; *Entwicklungsreihen, Reihe Barock, Barockdrama*, Bd. 6, ed. Willi Flemming, contains the complete oratorio *Geburt Jesu Christi*; Schöne contains the complete *Höllen- und Himmelfahrt J. C.*, minus Klaj's notes; *Redeoratorien und "Lobrede der Teutschen Poeterey,"* ed. Conrad Wiedemann (Tübingen, 1965—*Dt. Neudrucke, Reihe Barock* 4); *Friedensdichtungen und kleinere poetische Schriften*, ed. Wiedemann (Tübingen, 1968—*Dt. Neudrucke, Reihe Barock* 10).

Birken: scant selection in Cysarz; Schöne contains a complete pastoral; *Fortsetzung der Pegnitz-Schäferey* in *Dt. Neudrucke, Reihe Barock* 8, cited above; Fischer-Tümpel, *Das deutsche evangelische Kirchenlied des 17. Jahrhunderts.*, Bd. 5, contains 41 selections by Birken, 37 by Harsdörffer and 5 by Klaj.

Secondary literature: Introductions by Flemming and Cysarz in respective volumes of *Entwicklungsreihen*; "Nachworte" by Garber and Wiedemann in editions cited, which also contain further bibliographical information. C. Wiedemann, *Johann Klaj und seine Redeoratorien* (Nürnberg, 1966) is a thorough and highly useful study to which my own remarks are much indebted.

2. We know little about Zesen's life. He was born at Priorau near Dessau in the Duchy of Anhalt, as the son of a Lutheran pastor. He attended gymnasium in Halle, where he studied under Christian Gueintz, a friend and disciple of August Buchner. At the university in Wittenberg he studied under Buchner himself. In 1641 or 1642 Z. moved to Hamburg, where he founded his own patriotic literary-linguistic society called the "Deutschgesinnte Genossenschaft" or German-Minded Fellowship. In 1648 he was admitted to the Fruchtbringende Gesellschaft. Tirelessly active, Z. moved about a great deal, but made his headquarters mainly

in Amsterdam and Hamburg, finally becoming a citizen of Amsterdam. Though he briefly entered the service of the court of Dessau, Z. lived for the most part by his pen, as a free lance writer. He was ennobled in 1653 and married in 1668, at the age of forty-nine. His later years appear to have been spent on the edge of poverty.

Zesen was a many-sided, professional writer. Beside lyrical poetry and novels, he published a number of scholarly treatises (some of them translations) and wrote many religious works designed for use in private worship (*Andachtsbücher*). His most influential book, however, was the *Hoch-Deutscher Helikon*, one of the many baroque manuals of poetics. It is actually almost a specialized treatise on the lyric, notable for its wealth of illustrative material. Widely disseminated, it was the first such manual to go beyond Opitz' *Poeterey* in any essential respects.

With the exception of selections contained in various anthologies and histories of literature and the poems included in the novel *Adriatische Rosemund* (*Neudrucke* no. 160–63), there are no modern reprintings of Z.'s verse. I have had a chance to examine cursorily *Dichterisches Rosen- und Liljenthal* (Hamburg, 1670—Faber du Faur, no. 829) and *Filip Zesens Durch-aus vermehrter und zum viert- und letzten mahl in vier teilen ausgefärtigter Hoch-Deutscher Helikon* . . . (Jena, 1656—Faber du Faur, no. 821) in the Beinecke Library of Yale University.

Important secondary literature: Renate Weber, *Die Lieder Philipp von Zesens* (Diss., Hamburg, 1962); Ulrich F. J. Maché, "Zesens *Hoch-Deutscher Helikon*: Poetik zwischen Opitz und Gottsched" (Diss., Princeton, 1963—microfilm). Rudolf Ibel's dissertation, Würzburg 1922, "Die Lyrik Philipp von Zesens" (typescript), though outdated in its view of the Baroque and unresponsive to Z. as a secular lyricist, contains useful information.

3. How little feeling Z. had for a typical intellectual Renaissance form is shown by his disregard for the "laws" of the sonnet. Cf. J. Minor, *Neuhochdeutsche Metrik*, 2. Aufl. (Strassburg, 1902), 488 f.

4. Goethe was still thoroughly familiar with this line of thought as the following passage from *Faust* II shows. Mephisto has just addressed the griffons in the "Classical Walpurgisnight" as "Greise" instead of "Greife"; they reply:

> *Nicht Greisen! Greifen! Niemand hört es gern,*
> *Dass man ihn Greis nennt. Jedem Worte klingt*
> *Der Ursprung nach, wo es sich her bedingt:*
> *Grau, grämlich, griesgram, greulich, Gräber, grimmig,*
> *Etymologisch gleicherweise stimmig,*
> *Verstimmen uns.* (lines 1793–98)

5. The son of a Lutheran pastor, Schirmer, like Zesen, studied in Halle under Gueintz. In 1641–45 he attended the University of

Leipzig, where he belonged to a lively circle of student poets; in 1645–48 the University of Wittenberg, where he came into contact with A. Buchner, who was instrumental in procuring him the post of "Hofpoet" at the court of Dresden, where Schirmer was placed in charge of the theater, wrote Singspiele, ballets, official congratulatory poems, etc. He was later made court librarian. Schirmer became the forty-first member of Zesen's "Deutschgesinnte Genossenschaft."

Except for selections in anthologies, there is no modern reprint of Schirmer's work. I have used a xeroxed reproduction of *David Schirmers Poetische Rosengepüsche.* . . . (Dresden, 1657—Faber du Faur no. 338). Schirmer has been little studied. The dissertation by Werner Sonnenberg, *Studien zur Lyrik David Schirmers* (Göttingen, 1932), analyzes technical aspects of Schirmer's work and discusses his themes, but fails to give anything like a living picture of the poet, whom Sonnenberg regards mainly as a successful technician.

6. "Give me leave to perform the virtuous act!"

7. Like Opitz and Gryphius, Schirmer accents the stem of verbs with a separable prefix. This is a metrical accommodation only; such verbs were not ordinarily so pronounced in the seventeenth century.

8. Little is known about Stieler's life. He was born in Erfurt, and apparently studied at several universities, including Leipzig and Jena. He was a soldier for three years, then entered the service of various Thuringian princes. He wrote comedies and Singspiele and, above all, grammatical and rhetorical treatises. *Die geharnschte Venus oder Liebes-Lieder im Kriege gedichtet* . . . (Hamburg, 1660—Venus in Arms or lovesongs composed in time of war . . .), the work on which his posthumous fame rests, appeared under the fanciful pseudonym of "Filidor der Dorfferer" and was long attributed to Jacob Schwieger, a minor poet who also called himself "Filidor" ("Dorfferer" equals "Erffhorder," i.e. "Erfurter"). This songbook has long been available in a reprint: *Jacob Schwieger, Geharnschte Venus 1660*, ed. Th. Raehse (Halle, 1888—*Neudrucke dt. Litteraturwerke des 16. u. 17. Jahrhunderts* no. 74 & 75).

9. Cf., e.g., R. Newald, *Vom Späthumanismus zur Empfindsamkeit* (München, 1951), p. 199: "Soldaten- und Feldleben ist Selbstzweck ohne Beziehung zu einer Partei, zur Heimat oder zum Vaterland." And: "Zwölf Jahre nach dem Westfälischen Frieden versucht man, das Soldatenleben wieder in Ehren zu bringen." One wonders what these reflections have to do with the *G. V.*, which Newald is ostensibly discussing.

10. Faber du Faur, *German Baroque Literature* (New Haven, 1958), p. 91, speaks of a *"Zugabe* of insoluble riddles." This is misleading in two respects: (1) the madrigals, not the "Sinnreden," constitute

273

the *Zugabe* proper; (2) the riddles are not insoluble to the impure of mind. I quote one of the most interesting (p. 146):

> *Wir singen. Fillis spielt die Flöten,*
> *den Schall merkt Sie und ich allein.*
> *Lass, Fillis, lass dein Fingern seyn,*
> *Sonst wirstu mich durch Sehn-sucht tödten.*
> *Soll aber ich die Laute schlagen,*
> *so wil ich wol ein Stükkgen wagen.*

11. Even Stieler's admirers seem to have read him only cursorily. H. Cysarz, *Deutsche Barockdichtung*, (Leipzig, 1924), p. 149, calls the first decade "ein Ring von Liebesklagen." So far as I can determine, only one song in this group (no. 8) could be assigned to this category. "Liebesklagen" are found especially in the third decade.

12. Hofmanswaldau was born December 25, 1617, in Breslau, the only child of an influential family. His father, an Imperial Counselor, was ennobled in 1612. We know little about H.'s childhood and youth. He seems to have been a precocious child, early interested in poetry, who "lisp'd in numbers, for the numbers came."

Like other famous Silesians, including Angelus Silesius, H. attended the St. Elisabeth Gymnasium in his native city, where he enjoyed the instruction and protection of its energetic rector, Elias Major, and of the devoted admirer of Opitz, Christoph Köler (Colerus), whom we have had occasion to mention previously. In his "Trauer-Gedicht bey Absterben eines vertrauten Freundes" (1676), the poet recollects the sheltered innocence of his youth, whose charmed circle even the ravages of the plague and the Thirty Years War could not disturb:

> *Es war der Glocken Klang bey etlich tausend Leichen*
> *Uns ein gemeiner Schall, wir dachten, dass die Pest,*
> *Wie grausam sie auch scheint, noch Menschen übrig lasst,*
> *Dass Gluth und Kugel nicht durch iede Häuser streichen ...*

For these boys nurtured in the humanistic tradition, whose daily pabulum was the literature of Greece and Rome, the classical world was real, much more real than the world around them:

> *Es war uns Troja mehr, als Mantua, bekannt,*
> *Und mehr das alte Rom, als Eng- und Niederland,*
> *Es war uns Elb und Rhein ein unbekanntes Wesen.*
> *Was bildeten wir uns nicht von der Tiber ein,*
> *Und was wir von Athen und von Corinth gelesen,*
> *Hiess London und Paris geringe Flecken seyn.*

For two years (1636–38), H. attended the well known Academic Gymnasium in Danzig, which he entered just a month after A. Gryphius had left. Here, according to Lohenstein's funeral oration on his fellow townsman, H. studied philosophy and government ("Weltweissheit und Staats-Wissenschaft") and "begrief die Welsche [Italienische] / Französche und Nieder-Deutsche [Holländische] Sprache gleichsam spielende." Whether he learned these languages "spielende" or not, it is true that H. became an accomplished linguist. In Danzig he made the personal acquaintance of M. Opitz, whom he had long admired.

In the Fall of 1638, following the path of so many upper class Silesians, H. matriculated in Leiden as a student of law. We have already called attention to the importance of Holland in the formation of German baroque literature and, beyond this, in the intellectual life of the seventeenth century in general. Fleming, Gryphius, Scheffler, Kuhlmann, Lohenstein, and many others studied in Leiden. Precisely what courses H. pursued we do not know; there are indications that he was more interested in philology and history than law.

Toward the end of 1639 H. left Leiden in the company of a Prince of Frémonville to begin a grand tour of England and the continent. This was no mere student vacation but a serious educational undertaking. Like Boswell a century later, H. and his friend were intent on meeting and conversing with the great men of their day. England (London, Oxford) was the first stop. H. apparently spent much of his time learning English and gaining some acquaintance with English literature. He later translated a work by the satirist Joseph Hall into German.

By the middle of 1640 we find him in Paris, where he got to know a number of intellectual lights and perhaps also attended gatherings at the famous Hôtel (de Madame) de Rambouillet, the focal point of the *précieux* and *la poésie précieuse*, practised by such poets as Voiture and Benserade (cf. Molière's *Les précieuses ridicules*). The possible influence of the *précieux* on H. needs further investigation. (At least one of his poems—"Auf den mund" —is an imitation of Benserade's "Bouche, merveille . . .")

After six months in Paris, the travelers set out for Rome by way of Lyons, Genoa, Pisa, and Siena, striving never to miss a chance to associate with "hochgelehrte Leute." With Italy, or at any rate with Italian literature, H. seems to have felt a distinct affinity. He later translated Giovanni Battista Guarini's (1538-1612) lyrical pastoral play *Il pastor fido* (The Loyal Shepherd), one of the most popular works of world literature up to the nineteenth century, and greatly admired the work of Giambattista Marino (1569-1625), the famous mannerist and father of Italian baroque literature and probably the most influential poet of his time.

Though H. wanted to continue his journey on to Constantinople, in obedience to his father's wishes he returned in 1641 to Breslau by way of Florence, Bologna, Ferrara, Venice, and Vienna.

He had been abroad for five years. Still an innocent schoolboy when he set out, he returned an accomplished man of the world: learned, urbane, worldly wise, elegant, which is also the surface impression made by his poetry.

In 1643, again in compliance with his father's desire, H. married a noblewoman and had by her four children. In 1647 he entered the service of the city of Breslau, becoming one of its most valued and highly honored officials. He rose quickly to the rank of "Senator," was superintendent of the Breslau school system, undertook diplomatic missions to the imperial court at Vienna, was named "Kaiserlicher Rat" by Emperor Leopold I and died as President ("Praeses") of the city council of Breslau.

Though it is a prime desideratum of German baroque scholarship, no critical edition of H.'s work has yet (1969) appeared, though one is said to be in preparation. All works published during the poet's own lifetime and with his explicit approval are contained in *C.H.V.H. Deutsche Übersetzungen und Getichte* (Breslau, 1679—see Faber du Faur, item 1281, for description of contents). Kürschner's *Dt. Nat.-Lit.*, vol. 36, ed. F. Bobertag, devotes 107 pages to H.; all selections are taken from *D.Ü.u.G.* A separate edition of the *Heldenbriefe*, contained in *D.Ü.u.G.*, has recently appeared: *Herrn Christians von Hofmannswaldau sinnreiche Helden-Briefe verliebter Personen von Stande*, ed. F. Kemp (Frankfurt a. M., 1962).

His most interesting erotica H. refused to give to the printer, though they seem to have been widely circulated in manuscript. In the foreword to *D.Ü.u.G.* he writes: "Die andern Lust-Gedichte, so noch unter meinen Händen liegen, habe ich, zu ungleichem Urtheil nicht anlass zugeben, mit fleiss zu rücke gehalten, massen denn auch viel dergleichen meiner Poetischen Kleinigkeiten allbereit in unterschiedenen Händen seyn." Many of these "Lust-Gedichte" are however contained in a famous serial anthology of the period, popularly known as the "Neukirchsche Sammlung" from its original editor Benjamin Neukirch (1665–1729), himself a member of the Second Silesian School. This anthology appeared in seven parts between 1695 and 1727 under the title *Herrn von Hoffmannswaldau und andrer Deutschen auserlesener and bissher ungedruckter Gedichte*. The first two parts have now been reissued in *Neudrucke dt. Literaturwerke*, Neue Folge 1 and 16, ed. A. G. de Capua and E. A. Philipson, 1961 and 1965. The first volume contains circa seventy poems by H., the second circa forty (the attribution of a number of poems is in dispute). Due to admitted interference by the editor, Neukirch, the text of these poems is not wholly reliable, but the best currently available.

A good representative selection from H.'s whole œuvre is contained in Reclam UB 8889/90, ed. M. Windfuhr (1964); The selection by the poet Helmut Heissenbüttel, Fischer Bücherei 874

(1968—in the series "Poetische Beispiele") concentrates on erotica from the Neukirchsche Sammlung; it is of particular interest because of the foreword. The state of scholarship on H. is reviewed and full bibliographical information provided by Erwin Rotermund, *Christian Hofmann von Hofmannswaldau* (Sammlung Metzler, Stuttgart, 1963), to which I am largely indebted for the foregoing biographical sketch.

13. Our presentation, which attempts above all to characterize the *poets* of the age, neglects to a large degree conventional descriptive categories established by previous literary historians, making quotation marks necessary. "High Baroque" is the final, manneristic phase of the Baroque. It precedes—or introduces—the decline of the dominant manner, its excesses inciting to revolt and reevaluations. Greiffenberg and Kuhlmann are two further examples of poets of the High Baroque. The "Second Silesian School," whose members mostly wrote in the High Baroque manner, derives its name by distinction from the "First Silesian School" (in essence, those whom we have called "Opitzians," not all of whom of course were Silesians). The leading poets of the Second Silesian School were Hofmanswaldau and the dramatist, Daniel Caspar von Lohenstein (1635–83), whose style is ever more "excessive" than Hofmanswaldau's.

14. Of the numerous works on the subject, two outstanding syntheses are: C. S. Lewis, *The Allegory of Love* (Oxford, 1936), and Maurice Valency, *In Praise of Love* (New York, 1958).

15. Cf. C. S. Lewis, p. 15.

16. Cf. Hermann J. Weigand, *Three Chapters on Courtly Love in Arthurian France and Germany* (Chapel Hill, N.C., 1956), pp. 18 ff.

17. Fischer-Tümpel, *Das deutsche evangelische Kirchenlied*, vol. 5, includes three hymns by H., an indication of how acceptable he was to orthodoxy.

18. *H. v. H. Studien zur Erkenntnis deutscher Barockdichtung* (Berlin, 1928).

19. It is not without interest to note that the rhythm and rhyme scheme of this poem closely resemble that of Hofmannsthal's "Lebenslied."

20. Arthur Hübscher, "Barock als Gestaltung antithetischen Lebensgefühls," *Euphorion*, XXIV (1922), p. 519, n. 4, doubts, on the basis of "Schallanalyse," that this poem is by H., but his view seems to have found little acceptance. Regarding Hübscher's theory, A. George de Capua, co-editor of the *Neudruck* edition of Neukirch's anthology, wrote to me under date of January 17, 1967: ". . . it never sold, nor do I care to buy. It seems to me that we might as well accept CHvH's authorship until we get some hard proof to the contrary." Personally, I can only say that if the poem is not by H., it should be.

21. According to the *Encyclopedia of Poetry and Poetics*, the genre

was initiated in 1536 by Clément Marot and was widely cultivated by sixteenth-century French poets. Fleming and H. are its main practitioners among the Germans, another instance of "nachgeholte Renaissance."

22. Cf. Hugo Friedrich, *Epochen der italienischen Lyrik* (Frankfurt, 1964), pp. 623 ff., esp. p. 631.

23. All quotations from Schlegel after René Wellek, *A History of Modern Criticism* (New Haven, Conn., 1955), II, 40 f., 48; emphasis added.

24. *Geschichte des deutschen Verses* (Bern u. München, 1960), p. 39.


CHAPTER FIVE

1. For typical estimates of the progress of German poetry by later seventeenth-century practitioners of the art, see Chr. Hofm. v. Hofmanswaldau, "Vorrede zu *Deutsche Übersetzungen und Getichte*," reprinted in *Poetica*, Bd. 2, Heft 4 (Oct. 1968), pp. 541-52, especially 545 ff.; Benjamin Neukirch, "Vorrede" to the first vol. of his anthology, *Neudrucke dt. Literaturwerke*, Neue Folge, Bd. 1, pp. 6-22, esp. 9 ff.; Joh. Chr. Günther, *Werke*, ed. Krämer, II, 90, lines 37-54; III, 32 f., lines 65-74.

2. The inferior quality of their work is admitted even by Erik Lunding, who sees in the antinomy of courtly and anti-courtly "the central axis of the baroque." Cf. "German Baroque Literature: A Synthetic View," *German Life & Letters*, vol. 3 (Oct. 1949), pp. 1-12. For the sociologist this dichotomy is no doubt of greater interest than for the historian of literature.

3. Joachim Dyck, *Tichtkunst* (Homburg von der Höhe, 1966), p. 113.

4. The story has been told by Erika Vogt, *Die gegenhöfische Strömung in der deutschen Barockliteratur* (Leipzig, 1932). M. Windfuhr, *Die barocke Bildlichkeit*, Teil III, "Die Kritik am barocken Bildstil," pp. 339 ff., offers a lucid discussion of the whole problem of "opposition," to which I am gratefully indebted. Eric A. Blackall, *The Emergence of German as a Literary Language* (Cambridge, 1959), pp. 211 ff., discusses the revolt against the Baroque in the early decades of the eighteenth century.

5. Windfuhr, *Bildlichkeit*, p. 381

6. All quotations from Boileau after F. Vial and L. Denise, *Idées et doctrines litteraires du XVIIe siècle* (Paris 1939), pp. 161 ff.

7. Readily available in *Neudrucke dt. Lit. des 16. & 17. Jahrh.s.* no. 242-45, ed. Max v. Waldberg. For a discussion of Weise's significance, see, besides Waldberg's introduction to the vol. cited, P. Böckmann, *Formgeschichte* (Hamburg, 1949), pp. 488 ff.

8. A selection from Canitz' work is available in Kürschner's *Deutsche National-Litteratur*, Bd. 39, ed. Ludwig Fulda.

9. Cf. Windfuhr, *Bildlichkeit*, p. 412.

10. *Neudrucke dt. Literaturwerke*, Neue Folge, 1 and 16, ed. A. George de Capua and E. A. Philippson (Tübingen, 1961 and 1965 respectively). Date of first editions: 1695 and 1697.

11. Cf. Heinrich Kurz, *Geschichte der deutschen Literatur* (Leipzig, 1888), II, 322.

12. Quoted after Blackall, *Emergence*, p. 225.

13. It is both dismaying and astounding to discover that scholarship on the most important German poet between Gryphius and Klopstock is still inchoate. The standard edition of the works is: *Johann Christian Günthers sämtliche Werke*, ed. Wilhelm Krämer, 6 vols. (Bibliothek des Literarischen Vereins in Stuttgart, 1930–37—reprinted Darmstadt, 1964). Krämer arranges the poems in chronological order and according to subject matter. Each volume is provided with an introduction, but the final volume (no. 7), which was to contain notes and critical apparatus establishing criteria for chronology and choice of texts, never appeared. A sad and irreparable loss, for Krämer probably knew more about G. than anyone before or since. This edition has the further serious shortcoming of not listing entries by title but only first line.

Similar deficiencies plague Krämer's biography of the poet, *Das Leben des schlesischen Dichters Johann Christian Günther, 1695–1723* (Godesberg, 1950—360 pages), from which the foregoing biographical sketch has been abstracted. The volume that was to contain the notes (more than 900!) was never published. There is not even an index. The result is that we are left in the air on hundreds of points; laborious searching is necessary even to find the poems from which Krämer quotes. The book, which is swamped with minute detail alternating with passages of overheated rhetoric, makes difficult reading. As a source of information it is, nonetheless, invaluable.

The second most important work on G. is the monograph by Hans Dahlke, *Johann Christian Günther: Seine dichterische Entwicklung* (Berlin, 1960—*Neue Beiträge zur Literaturwissenschaft*, Bd. 10), in many respects a very useful work, though written in a style one can only call barbarous. Dahlke's interpretive essays on selected poems are crude and unsophisticated, but the information provided is most welcome.

The extensive review of Krämer's edition of the collected works by Hans Pyritz, reprinted in Pyritz' *Schriften zur deutschen Literaturgeschichte* (Köln/Graz, 1962), pp. 129–47, offers a highly informative and stylistically pleasant introduction to G.'s œuvre.

Perceptive and very much in sympathy with its subject is the study by Francesco Delbono, *Umanità e Poesia di Christian Günther* (1959).

A Princeton thesis by Julius S. Winkler, "Johann Christian Günther—A Study in Contrasts and Controversy," 1963, reviews problems of Günther scholarship. Its main value lies in its stress upon the range and depth of Günther's mind and art, his "relatively unknown richness."

14. Here one might point out that the insistence by most poets on the peripheral nature of their art was probably to a considerable degree a protective measure. If society did not take poetry seriously, they could only make fools of themselves by doing so.

15. Since Krämer's edition of G.'s works provides no variants which would have afforded us some insight into the poet's revisionary processes, this must remain largely speculative. I base my judgment mainly on Krämer, *Leben*, pp. 310 f.

16. Cf. Blackall, *Emergence*, pp. 236 ff.

17. The honor of inventing this stanza seems to belong to Christian Friedrich Hunold, who used it in a poem beginning "Immer hin, Falsches Herze, leichter Sinn," published in 1702. It became extremely popular and was used in numerous variations in hymns and folksongs. Wilhelm Hauff's "Reiterlied" ("Morgenrot, Leuchtest mir zum frühen Tod?"—1824) stands at the end of the chain. Cf. Dahlke, *Entwicklung*, p. 50.

18. Again the stanza structure is borrowed, this time from Erdmann Neumeister. See Dahlke, *Entwicklung*, p. 233, n. 21.

19. It is certainly worthy of note, especially when we remember that Ovid was for Günther the very prototype of the poet, that this line is a translation from *Amores* I, 7, 60: "sanguis erat lacrimae quas dabat illa meus" (the tears she shed were my blood), in which, amazingly perhaps for an ancient poet, "the identities of the two lovers are merged in mystic union" (Hermann Fränkel, *Ovid: A Poet between two Worlds*—Berkeley, Calif., 1945—p. 21). Dahlke (p. 61) finds this image "etwas gesucht und lyrisch verbraucht, wie alle ähnlichen Vergleichungen dieses Gedichts *oder des Güntherschen Gesamtwerks überhaupt*." (My emphasis.)

20. The ode to Prince Eugene is discussed at length by K. Viëtor, *Geschichte der deutschen Ode* (München, 1923), pp. 85 ff.

21. Both Winkler, who discusses this poem at length (pp. 146–50), and Delbono (*Umanità*, p. 113) take a different view.

22. Delbono, *Umanità*, p. 145, says with complete justice that the development of Günther's poetry "consisted above all in an enrichment of the poet's humanity, it was not solely a stylistic phenomenon."

23. Günther's birthday was April 8, the poem celebrates the night of April 2.

24. "Günther and Leibniz-Wolff," *Germanic Review*, XXIII (Feb. 1948), pp. 30–39.

25. I cannot agree with Gerald Gillespie in his generally excellent article, "Suffering in Günther's Poetry," *German Quarterly*, XLI (Jan. 1968), 21–38, that the poem is "ultimately metareligious, a sheer cry as in the primeval *planctus*" (p. 36).

# SELECTED BIBLIOGRAPHY

ANGELUS SILESIUS. See Scheffler, Johann.

BAZIN, GERMAIN. *The Baroque: Principles, Styles, Modes, Themes.* New York, 1968.

BEARE, ROBERT L. "Quirinus Kuhlmann: The religious apprenticeship." *PMLA*, LXVII (1953): 828–62.

BLACKALL, ERIC A. *The Emergence of German as a Literary Language.* Cambridge, 1959.

BOCK, CLAUS VICTOR. *Quirinus Kuhlmann als Dichter: Ein Beitrag zur Charakteristik des Estatikers.* Bern, 1957.

BÖCKMANN, PAUL. *Formgeschichte der deutschen Dichtung.* Bd. 1. Hamburg, 1949.

BRAUER, WALTER. "Jakob Regnart, Johann Hermann Schein und die Anfänge der deutschen Barocklyrik." *Deutsche Vierteljahrsschrift für Literaturwissenschaft und Geistesgeschichte* XVII (1939): 371–404.

BROWNING, ROBERT M. "On the Numerical Composition of Friedrich Spee's *Trutznachtigall*." In: *Festschrift für Detlev W. Schumann.* München, 1970, pp. 28–39.

CONRADY, KARL OTTO. *Lateinische Dichtungstradition und die deutsche Lyrik des 17. Jahrhunderts.* Bonn, 1962.

CYSARZ, HERBERT. *Deutsche Barockdichtung.* Leipzig, 1924.

CYSARZ, HERBERT, ed. See *Deutsche Literatur in Entwicklungsreihen.*

DACH, SIMON. *Gedichte*, ed. W. Ziesemer. 4 vols. Halle, 1936–38.

DACH, SIMON. *Gedichte.* Edited by H. Oesterley. Leipzig, 1867. (*Deutsche Dichter des 17. Jahrhunderts*, Bd. 9)

DAHLKE, HANS. *Johann Christian Günther: Seine dichterische Entwicklung.* Berlin, 1960.

281

BIBLIOGRAPHY

DALY, PETER MAURICE. *Die Metaphorik in den "Sonetten" der Catharina Regina von Greiffenberg.* Dissertation, Zürich, 1964.

DELBONO, FRANCESCO. *Umanità e Poesia di Christian Günther.* Società Editrice Internazionale, 1959.

*Deutsche Barockforschung: Dokumentation einer Epoche.* Edited by R. Alewyn. Köln and Berlin, 2 Aufl., 1966.

*Deutsche Literatur in Entwicklungsreihen, Reihe Barock. Barocklyrik*, vols. 1–3. Edited by H. Cysarz. Leipzig, 1937. *Barockdrama*, vol. 6. Edited by W. Flemming. Leipzig, 1933. *Reformation*, vol. 4. Edited by G. Pfannmüller. Leipzig, 1938.

DIETZE, WALTER. *Quirinus Kuhlmann: Ketzer und Poet.* Berlin, 1963.

DYCK, JOACHIM. *Ticht-Kunst: Deutsche Barocklyrik und rhetorische Tradition.* Bad Homburg vor der Höhe, 1966.

ERK, HEINRICH. "Offenbarung und heilige Sprache im 'Kühlpsalter' Quirin Kuhlmanns." Dissertation, Göttingen, 1953 (microfilm).

FABER DU FAUR, CURT VON. *German Baroque Literature: A Catalogue of the Collection in the Yale University Library.* New Haven, 1958.

FISCHER, ALBERT AND W. TUMPEL, *Das deutsche evangelische Kirchenlied des 17. Jahrhunderts.* 6 vols. Gütersloh, 1904–16.

FLEMING, PAUL. *Deutsche Gedichte.* Edited by J. M. Lappenberg. 2 vols. Stuttgart, 1865 (reprint Darmstadt, 1965)

FRANK, HANS-JOACHIM. *Catharina Regina von Greiffenberg: Leben und Welt der barocken Dichterin.* Göttingen, 1967.

FRICKE, GERHARD. *Die Bildlichkeit in der Dichtung des Andreas Gryphius.* Berlin, 1933.

FRIEDRICH, HUGO. *Epochen der italienischen Lyrik.* Frankfurt, 1964.

GEIBEL, HEDWIG. *Der Einfluss Marinos auf Christian Hofman von Hofmanswaldau.* Dissertation, Giessen, 1938.

GILLESPIE, GERALD. "Suffering in Günther's Poetry." *German Quarterly*, XLI (1968): 21–38.

GREIFFENBERG, CATHARINA REGINA VON. *Gedichte*, ausgewählt und mit einem Nachwort herausgegeben von Hubert Gersch. Berlin, 1964.

GREIFFENBERG, CATHARINA REGINA VON. *Geistliche Sonette, Lieder und Gedichte* (1662). Darmstadt, 1967. (Photographic reprint with a *Nachwort* by Heinz-Otto Burger.)

GRYPHIUS, ANDREAS. *Gesamtausgabe der deutschsprachigen Werke.* vols. 1–3. Edited by Marian Szyrocki. Tübingen, 1963–64. (*Neudrucke deutscher Literaturwerke*, Neue Folge, 9 ff.)

GRYPHIUS, ANDREAS. *Lyrische Gedichte.* Edited by Hermann Palm. Tübingen, 1884. (Photomechanical reprint Darmstadt, 1961.)

GÜNTHER, JOHANN CHRISTIAN. *Sämtliche Werke.* Edited by Wilhelm

Krämer. 6 vols. Bibliothek des Literarischen Vereins in Stuttgart, 1930–37. (Reprinted Darmstadt, 1964.)

HANKAMER, PAUL. *Deutsche Gegenreformation und deutsches Barock: Die deutsche Literatur im Zeitraum des 17. Jahrhunderts.* Stuttgart, 1935.

HAUCK, A., ed. *Realencyklopädie für protestantische Theologie und Kirche.* 22 vols. Leipzig, 1897–1909.

HARSDÖRFFER, GEORG PHILIPP; BIRKEN, SIGMUND VON; AND KLAJ, JOHANN. *Pegnesisches Schäfergedicht* (1644–45). Edited by Klaus Garber. Tübingen, 1966. (*Deutsche Neudrucke, Reihe Barock* 8.)

HOFMANNSWALDAU, CHRISTIAN HOFMANN VON. See also Neukirch, Benjamin.

HOFMANNSWALDAU, CHRISTIAN HOFMANN VON. *Gedichte.* Edited by Helmut Heissenbüttel. Fischer Bücherei 874, 1968.

HOFMANNSWALDAU, CHRISTIAN HOFMANN VON. *Gedichte.* Edited by Manfred Windfuhr (Reclams Universalbibliothek no. 8889–90). Stuttgart, 1964.

IBEL, RUDOLF. "Die Lyrik Philipp von Zesens." Dissertation, Würzburg, 1922 (typescript).

IBEL, RUDOLF. *Hofmann von Hofmannswaldau: Studien zur Erkenntnis deutscher Barockdichtung.* Berlin, 1928.

JACOBSEN, ERIC. *Die Metamorphosen der Liebe und Friedrich Spees "Trutznachtigall."* Copenhagen, 1954.

JÖNS, DIETRICH WALTER. *Das "Sinnen-Bild": Studien zur allegorischen Bildlichkeit bei Andreas Gryphius.* Stuttgart, 1966.

JULIAN, JOHN, ed. *A Dictionary of Hymnology.* New York, 1892.

KAYSER, WOLFGANG. *Geschichte des deutschen Verses.* Bern and München, 1960.

KLAJ, JOHANN. *Redeoratorien und "Lobrede der Teutschen Poeterey."* Edited by Conrad Wiedemann. Tübingen, 1965. (*Deutsche Neudrucke, Reihe Barock* 4.)

KRÄMER, WILHELM. *Das Leben des schlesischen Dichters Johann Christian Günther, 1695–1723.* Godesberg, 1950.

KÜRSCHNER, JOSEPH, general ed. *Deutsche National-Litteratur,* vols. 27, 28, 29, 30, 31, 36, 38, 39. (Separate vols. edited by various hands.)

LOGAU, FRIEDRICH VON. *Sinngedichte.* Edited by G. Eitner. Leipzig, 1870. (*Deutsche Dichter des 17. Jahrhunderts,* Bd. 3.)

MACHÉ, ULRICH F. J. "Zesens *Hoch-Deutscher Helikon:* Poetik zwischen Opitz und Gottsched." Dissertation, Princeton, 1963 (microfilm).

MANHEIMER, VICTOR. *Die Lyrik des Andreas Gryphius.* Berlin, 1904.

283

BIBLIOGRAPHY

Mannack, Eberhard. *Andreas Gryphius* (Sammlung Metzler). Stuttgart, 1966.

Markwardt, Bruno. *Geschichte der deutschen Poetik*, Bd. 1. Berlin and Leipzig, 1937.

Merker, Paul and Wolfgang Stammler, eds. *Reallexikon der deutschen Literaturgeschichte.* Berlin, 1925–31. 2. Auflage, Berlin. 1958—.

Minor, Jakob. *Neuhochdeutsche Metrik*, 2d ed. Strassburg, 1902.

Müller, Günther. *Geschichte des deutschen Liedes.* München, 1925. (Reprint, Bad Homburg vor der Höhe, 1959.)

Naumann, Walter. *Traum und Tradition in der deutschen Lyrik.* Stuttgart, 1966.

Neukirch, Benjamin, anthologist. *Herrn von Hoffmannswaldau und andrer Deutschen auserlesener und bissher ungedruckter Gedichte. Erster theil.* Edited by A. G. de Capua and E. A. Philippson. Tübingen, 1961. *Anderer theil.* 1965. (*Neudrucke deutscher Literaturwerke*, Neue Folge, vols. 1 and 16.) ("Benjamin Neukirchs Anthologie")

Newald, Richard. *Geschichte der deutschen Literatur. Vom Späthumanismus zur Empfindsamkeit, 1570–1750.* München, 1961.

Ohly, Friedrich. "Vom geistigen Sinn des Wortes im Mittelalter." *Zeitschrift für deutsches Altertum und deutsche Literatur,* vol. 89, 1958/59, pp. 1 ff.

Opitz, Martin. *Buch von der deutschen Poeterei.* Edited by W. Braune. Halle, 1882. (*Neudrucke deutscher Literaturwerke des 16. und 17. Jahrhunderts,* no. 1.)

Opitz, Martin. *Teutsche Poemata* (1624). Edited by G. Witkowski. Halle, 1902. (*Neudrucke deutscher Literaturwerke des 16. und 17. Jahrhunderts,* no. 189–92.)

Opitz, Martin. *Weltliche Poemata* (1644, 1. Teil). Edited by E. Trunz. Tübingen, 1967. (*Deutsche Neudrucke, Reihe Barock* 2.)

Opitz, Martin. *Weltliche und geistliche Dichtung.* Edited by H. Oesterley. (*Kürschner's Deutsche National-Litteratur,* Bd. 27.)

Pascal Blaise. *Pensées.* Edited by H. F. Stewart (Pantheon Books). New York, 1950.

Pyritz, Hans. *Paul Flemings deutsche Liebeslyrik.* Leipzig, 1932.

Pyritz, Hans. *Schriften zur deutschen Literaturgeschichte.* Köln/ Graz, 1962.

Rist, Johann. *Dichtungen.* Edited by K. Goedeke and E. Goetze. Leipzig, 1885. (*Deutsche Dichter des 17. Jahrhunderts,* Bd. 15).

Rosenfeld, Emmy. *Friedrich Spee von Langenfeld: Ein Stimme in der Wüste.* Berlin, 1958.

284

ROTERMUND, ERWIN. *Christian Hofmann von Hofmannswaldau* (Sammlung Metzler). Stuttgart, 1963.

SAMMONS, JEFFREY L. *Angelus Silesius.* New York, 1967.

SCHEFFLER, JOHANN ("Angelus Silesius"). *Cherubinischer Wandersmann.* Edited by W. E. Peuckert (Sammlung Dietrich, Bd. 64.) Bremen, n.d.

SCHEFFLER, JOHANN ("Angelus Silesius"). *Sämtliche poetische Werke.* 3rd ed. 3 vols. Edited by H. L. Held. München, 1952.

SCHEFFLER, JOHANN ("Angelus Silesius"). *Sämtliche poetische Werke und eine Auswahl aus seinen Streitschriften.* Edited by G. Ellinger. 2 vols. Berlin, 1923.

SCHIRMER, DAVID. *Poetische Rosengepüsche.* Dresden, 1657.

SCHÖFFLER, HERBERT. *Deutscher Osten im deutschen Geist.* Frankfurt am Main, 1949.

SCHÖNE, ALBRECHT, ed. *Das Zeitalter des Barock: Texte und Zeugnisse.* München, 1963.

SCHOOLFIELD, GEORGE C. *The German Lyric of the Baroque in English Translation.* Chapel Hill, 1961.

SONNENBERG, WERNER. *Studien zur Lyrik David Schirmers.* Dissertation, Göttingen, 1932.

SPE(E), FRIEDRICH. *Trutz-Nachtigal.* Edited by Gustav Balke. Leipzig, 1879. (*Deutsche Dichter des 17. Jahrhunderts*, Bd. 13.)

SPEE, FRIEDRICH. *Trutznachtigall.* Edited by Gustave O. Arlt. Halle, 1936. (*Neudrucke deutscher Literaturwerke des 16. und 17. Jahrhunderts*, nos. 292–301.)

STAMM, ISRAEL S. "Günther and Leibniz-Wolff." *Germanic Review*, XXIII (1948): 30–39.

STAMMLER, WOLFGANG, ed. *Deutsche Philologie im Aufriss.* 3 vols. Berlin, 1952–57.

STIELER, KASPAR. *Jacob Schwieger, Geharnschte Venus 1660.* Edited by Th. Raehse. Halle, 1888. (*Neudrucke deutscher Literaturwerke des 16. und 17. Jahrhunderts* no. 74 and 75.)

SZYROCKI, MARIAN. *Andreas Gryphius. Sein Leben und Werk.* Tübingen, 1964.

TRUNZ, ERICH. "Fünf Sonette des Andreas Gryphius." In: *Vom Geist der Dichtung.* (Festschrift R. Petsch) Hamburg, 1949. Pp. 180 ff.

VIËTOR, KARL. *Geschichte der deutschen Ode.* München, 1923.

VOGT, ERIKA. *Die gegenhöfische Strömung in der deutschen Barockliteratur.* Leipzig, 1932.

VORDTRIEDE, WERNER, ed. *Quirinus Kuhlmann: Aus dem Kühlpsalter.* Berlin, 1966.

BIBLIOGRAPHY

WACKERNAGEL, WILHELM. *Geschichte der deutschen Literatur.* 2. Aufl. Basel, 1894.

WARNKE, FRANK J. *European Metaphysical Poetry.* New Haven, 1961.

WEBER, RENATE. *Die Lieder Philipp von Zesens.* Dissertation, Hamburg, 1962.

WECKHERLIN, GEORG RODOLF. *Gedichte.* Edited by H. Fischer. 3 vols. Tübingen, 1894–95.

WEYDT, GÜNTHER. "Sonettenkunst des Barock: Zum Problem der Umarbeitung bei Andreas Grypius." *Jahrbuch der deutschen Schillergesellschaft,* IX (1965): 1–32.

WIEDEMANN, CONRAD. *Johann Klaj und seine Redeoratorien.* Nürnberg, 1966.

WINDFUHR, MANFRED. *Die barocke Bildlichkeit und ihre Kritiker: Stilhaltungen in der deutschen Literatur des 17. und 18. Jahrhunderts.* Stuttgart, 1966.

WINKLER, JULIUS S. "Johann Christian Günther: A Study in Contrasts and Controversy." Dissertation, Princeton, 1963 (typescript).

WOLFF, EUGEN, ed. *Das deutsche Kirchenlied des 16. und 17. Jahrhunderts.* Stuttgart, 1894. (Kürschner's *Deutsche National-Litteratur,* vol. 31.)

ZESEN, PHILIPP VON. *Dichterisches Rosen- und Liljenthal.* Hamburg, 1670.

ZESEN, PHILIPP VON. *Filip Zesens Durch-aus vermehrter und zum viert- und letzten mahl in vier teilen ausgefärtigter Hoch-Deutscher Helikon . . . .* Jena, 1656.

INDEX

The Index lists mainly names. Topics and titles are listed only when of particular importance and when they might not otherwise be easily found.